MIND-SEARCH

opens up exciting new regions of the mind and explores its full range of psychic possibilities ...

"Mind can potentially control the body. With training, especially with the help of biofeedback machines, body processes called 'involuntary' by medical science or beyond conscious control can be influenced at will. Mind can learn to prevent, control and reverse disease. Pioneer research with highly motivated cancer patients is encouraging. Mind can control pain, move objects at a distance through purely mental exertion (psychokinesis) and communicate with other minds telepathically. Mind is beyond the restrictions of our past-present-future clock consciousness, can touch the future and predict what will happen. Meditate properly, and like a battery the mind can be energized. The psyche and the cosmos are intimately interconnected...."

NICHOLAS and JUNE REGUSH
Prologue

ABOUT THE AUTHORS

Nicholas and June Regush have written widely in the consciousness-exploration field and have appeared on more than one hundred television and radio programs stressing the importance of a responsible approach to the mysteries of the mind. They are the editors of PSI: THE OTHER WORLD CATALOGUE and are completing a sequel, PSI II.

Nicholas Regush has taught sociology at New York University and presently teaches in the Humanities Department at Dawson College in Montreal. His most recent book is THE FRONTIERS OF HEALING.

June Regush, who has a degree in visual arts, is a sculptress and has been interested in the methaphysical impulse in art and the creative imagination as expressed in different states of consciousness. Her latest book is DREAM WORLDS: THE COMPLETE GUIDE TO DREAMS AND DREAMING.

NICHOLAS & JUNE REGUSH

MIND-SEARCH

A BERKLEY MEDALLION BOOK
published by
BERKLEY PUBLISHING CORPORATION

Berkley Publishing Corporation
200 Madison Avenue
New York, N. Y. 10016

SBN 425-03544-1

BERKLEY MEDALLION BOOKS are published by
Berkley Publishing Corporation
200 Madison Avenue
New York, N. Y. 10016

BERKLEY MEDALLION BOOK ® TM 757,375

Printed in the United States of America

Berkley Medallion Edition, OCTOBER, 1977

This book is dedicated to the memory of
Anne Gordon
and Dr. Wilder Penfield

Contents

You may control a mad elephant;
You may shut the mouth of the bear and the tiger;
Ride the lion and play with the cobra;
By alchemy you may earn your livelihood;
You may wander through the universe incognito;
Make vassals of the Gods; Be ever youthful;
You may walk on water and live in fire;
But control of the mind is better and more difficult.

—Thayumanavar, a "master" of a
religious shrine in India

PROLOGUE

Cellular Expansion

some, too profound process of life. High human, especially with the help of biofeedback machines bod— processes called "involuntary" by medical science or beyond conscious control can be influenced at will. High can learn to prevent ... before a ... overcome this. A ...

Prologue: Cellular Expansion

We were talking about Mind...

Mind can potentially control the body. With training, especially with the help of biofeedback machines, body processes called "involuntary" by medical science, or beyond conscious control, can be influenced at will. Mind can learn to prevent, control and reverse disease. Pioneer research with highly motivated cancer patients is encouraging. Mind can control pain, move objects at a distance through purely mental exertion (psychokinesis) and communicate with other minds telepathically. Mind is beyond the restrictions of our past-present-future clock consciousness, can touch the future and predict what will happen. Meditate properly, and like a battery, the mind can be energized. The psyche and the cosmos are intimately interconnected....

This was no ordinary discussion and no ordinary meeting. Among those present were: a man famous for his best-selling book on human-plant communication; a woman who is widely sought for her ability to diagnose illness before the body shows signs of it, and who claims to be capable of healing by channeling an energy force through her body to her patient; a scientist who has studied her healing abilities with mice under controlled laboratory conditions; a researcher who had returned from West Germany where he studied ESP; and a woman who teaches her students how to reach another dimension called the astral plane.

We hadn't expected any guests that evening and were planning to get away from our work to see a Mel Brooks movie. Then the phone rang. "I'm in town," announced the plant man.

It rang again. "What are you doing tonight?" asked the healer.

And again and again. It almost seemed orchestrated. The word was out. In about five hours, everyone had converged on our apartment.

It wasn't the first time this had happened. In the seven years we've been investigating mental powers, new and old friends passing through town have gathered to talk about the mind and how it can be used.

The plant man best summed up the atmosphere at some of these occasions: "This meeting reminds me of those secret revolutionary Trotskyist cells. You have to watch to whom you talk about these things."

He's only partly right. People have always talked about powers of the mind, but the "cells" are rapidly multiplying. Times are certainly changing. More people from all walks of life are interested in mind and beginning to suspect they can learn to tap some of their inner resources. We've noticed the change in our travels, by the questions we're asked on talk shows, the coverage in newspapers, magazines and books. Courses teaching techniques to develop more of the mind are sprouting all over. ESP (the idea that we have latent powers beyond our normal five senses) is quickly becoming a household word. People are meditating, exploring their dreams, looking at photographs of mysterious energies being emitted from the fingertips of psychic healers and hearing about people capable of moving objects through mental power. More physicians are seriously considering the role that attitude and emotions may play in the development of disease—that continual negative thinking or a poor self-image may lower resistance.

People are demanding to know more about the "secrets," what they are capable of achieving and how. It's getting more difficult for veterans to see themselves as mind-exploring revolutionaries.

Now that mind has gone public, naturally there's some confusion. Five or six years ago, the veteran could make all sorts of claims for the mind. Personal experiences and testimonies went a long way. Scientists usually dismissed the claims, and the few who poked their heads through the mind barrier didn't have much of an impact on the quiet revolution. Now the closet mind-explorers are out in numbers, joining the pioneers. They are well-armed with scientific tests and theories, and it has made it more difficult for a veteran to prove that he or she has been sending telepathic messages to Aunt Minnie.

You can do telepathy? Great. Let's test you in the lab. You've reached enlightenment? Let's examine your mind-over-body mastery.

This brings up some questions. Who knows what? Who's ripping us off with promises? Who's qualified to teach mind techniques? To explore? So many intangibles.

It's time to reexamine exactly what we mean by mind. We have Eastern and Western views and variations of both. Sometimes they are mixed together.

The point is that the field is wide open!

This book is a mind-search; an extensive search for a better understanding of the range of this mysterious, elusive essence called "mind." It's about some of the mind-explorers and our experiences with them, a critical investigation of some of the training techniques to make better use of the mind, a look at some of the students and teachers and the more intriguing controversies.

MIND-SEARCH presents a cross section of a growing mind revolution—a revolution that is here to stay.

ONE

Some Western
Matters of Mind

Where Is The Mind?

Our friend Stanley says he has a mind. Big deal, you might say. Everybody has a mind! But Stanley insists that his mind and all minds are independent of the brain and can directly communicate with other minds.

Ah, that's a different story. Some, scientists especially, would tell him he's been watching too many science-fiction movies. Like rats in a maze, we're shaped by our genes and environment, they say. We have little control over our destiny, over how we think or act. The mind is only a by-product of the brain, a residue. ESP? Humbug.

But Stanley stands firm. He's convinced his is the side of light, the glowing tip.

First, let's have a look at the brain. Ancient Greek philosopher Aristotle said its main function was to cool the hot blood circulating through the body. Not much more was known until the 19th century, but today just about all of the brain's pinkish gray, three-pound structure has been electrically probed, its regions and their functions tentatively mapped.

The structure of the entire brain shows we basically have three brains. The oldest part—Brain One—is the brain stem which regulates swallowing, coughing, breathing, heart rate and the functioning of some glands and organs. Brain Two, the next in our evolutionary development, is the limbic section at the very center. It regulates smell, taste, our sense of balance, time perception and the autonomic (so-called involuntary) nervous system. The area of major importance here is the hypothalamus which regulates the liver, lungs and body temperature. Brain Three—the cerebral cortex with the wriggly convolutions— is the source of speech, hearing and abstract reasoning. It's also the intriguing focal point of an important discovery:

9

Cal Tech biologist Roger Sperry demonstrated that the
right and left hemispheres of this new brain function
independently of each other and have their own distinct
purposes. The left is the seat of more analytical, logical
thought, and the right, of intuitive, abstract and artistic
reasoning. Sperry says our Western culture tends to be left-
dominant while other cultures, particular Eastern ones, are
more right-dominant. In other words, until we learn to use
more of the right side, we won't be making maximum use of
our intuitive potential.

But where is the mind? Is there a specialized area in the
brain which fully controls how we make decisions, how we
reason or why we pay attention to one thing and not
another?

For centuries, few scientists were even interested in this
question. Voicing the attitude of his time, 17th-century
philosopher René Descartes proposed that since Mind was
an essence of God, the macrocosm, it was inaccessible to
mere mortals. We might, however, come to understand the
universe by studying the microcosm, the body, a material
manifestation of spirit. The physics of Isaac Newton
supported this view. The universe was portrayed as a
massive machine which, once wound up, would run on its
own like an eternal clock.

Better then to study the machine's component parts. So
the body became the laboratory and the mind remained in
the City of God, waiting to be emancipated.

This is a major reason why mind has been left out of
medicine. The patient has become a machine; the physician, a shop mechanic. A little oil here, tighten a bolt there,
and the body-machine will continue to run. Rather than
treat the whole patient, taking into account the role mind
may play in lowering resistance to disease or in refusing to
accept it, the physician has focused on treating parts.
Something not right inside? Pop a pill. Bad heart, kidney,
lung? The motor shop will do a part change. Some
physicians may believe the machine has a mind, but it's too
elusive to deal with. It also gets in the way.

And, of course, there are those scientists who think
they're more sophisticated. They deny the existence of
mind altogether. Having charted the brain, conditioned
rats in mazes, treated damaged bodies with drugs, they've
watched animals and people change their behavior before
their eyes. Mind is nothing but a residue. Tamper with the

brain and we can be turned into two, three and even more very different personalities.

We discussed this with a neurophysiologist friend at Stanford University who is a member of this school of thought. She agreed. She could demonstrate how easily personality can be manipulated. That is, if the law allowed it. "I could make you do anything I wanted by touching areas in your brain," she insisted, with an unsettling glaze in her eyes. "I could make you laugh, I could make you cry, have an orgasm, become an idiot . . ." We quickly left as her voice trailed off. Glancing over our shoulders, we saw her sitting quietly, totally engrossed, her head exploding with the possibilities. She would have given up a few paychecks to work on Stanley.

A Conversation with Wilder Penfield

Few have had the opportunity and the gift to explore the mystery of our "inner space" with as much success as the late Wilder Penfield, a neurosurgeon and scientist of world renown. In 1934, Penfield—together with some of his McGill associates—established the Montreal Neurological Institute which provided access to both excellent research and hospital facilities. There, Penfield directed many scientific and surgical teams toward a greater understanding of the brain's uncharted territories.

In 1975, The Mystery of the Mind *was published. In it, in a language accessible to the serious lay reader, Penfield summarized his scientific writings and evolving views of the mind-brain relationship. In an extraordinary gesture of solidarity with the prophets, poets, mystics and metaphysically-inclined philosophers who through the centuries have stressed the spiritual nature of man, Penfield wrote that the brain's functioning cannot fully explain the human capacity of will, decision-making and feeling attributed to and believed to be exercised by the mind.*

On February 7, 1976, we had our first of two conversations with Penfield at his office at the Montreal Neurological Institute. At the time he appeared to be in good health, but this, we later learned, had not been the case. When he died in April at the age of eighty-five, we felt as though we had lost an old and cherished friend. The news of his death profoundly moved us both. His deep compassion for his patients and his respect for the mind's potential were evident throughout his book and in our conversations with him.

Early in his career, Penfield and his associates discovered that even when it was necessary to surgically

12

remove large sections of the brain's cerebral cortex, consciousness was not eradicated. However, if the higher brain stem had suffered any damage or was surgically interfered with, conscious processes would be suspended. The higher brain stem or "the highest brain mechanism" as Penfield referred to it, has to be active for thought and consciousness to be possible.

But how, we asked, when the functioning of this mechanism is temporarily suspended, does the brain continue to regulate the body? Penfield explained on the basis of the evidence largely gleaned from his surgical treatment of epileptic patients: "The brain functions like a supercomputer while consciousness is suspended. Should an epileptic have an electrical discharge (called a *petit mal* seizure) the body will continue to go through the motions of any action initiated prior to the attack. He or she will, for example, be able to continue walking or driving home, unlock the front door and sit down inside, all the while unconscious of his or her actions. Should someone say hello along the way, however, it won't register. Or traffic lights will be ignored. Only later, when the brain cells have recovered from the electrical storm, will it be realized that an attack had taken place. But there won't be any memory of those activities which transpired during the apparent time lapse.

"You see," he continued, "there is a sensory-motor mechanism in the brain which governs body coordination and continues to function normally when the highest brain mechanism, which is responsible for consciousness, is paralyzed. This suggests that in the absence of consciousness, the brain is capable of operating like a computer, processing the programs previously fed in."

Another discovery provided a further clue to the mind-brain relationship. One of Penfield's former patients, a young South African, had a flashback experience when Penfield's probing electrode touched the "interpretive cortex," which in turn triggered the gray matter of the highest brain mechanism. It was an unusual experience because the man was simultaneously fully aware of being operated on yet mentally reliving a past experience—laughing on a farm with his cousins.

"This double awareness was an indication of his mind demonstrating its independence of the reflex action triggered by the electrode. It seems likely that if the highest brain mechanism created the mind solely through its own action, the patient would have suffered mental confusion as a result of the doubling effect. He did not."

Was he then suggesting that the highest brain mechanism may supply the mind with an as yet unknown form of energy, one not conducted along the circuits of the nervous system?

"Another form of energy—that's exactly the point," he answered. "It has to be different. We've come to the point where we have to ask the physicists, 'What exactly is the nature of this energy of the mind?' Which is there, I think.

"We know—I think we know, from experimental evidence—that it comes from the electrical energy that is within the brain and is formed in brain cells. That's the origin of it, certainly, and I'm sure that the mind gets its energy through the highest mechanism . . .

"In this light," he continued, "the highest brain mechanism which accounts for consciousness can be seen as the 'messenger,' or channel, between the mind and the other special units in the brain which regulate behavior. The mind, in other words, can be seen as the programmer, and the brain as the computer. Mind programs brain. There is no place in the cerebral cortex," he emphasized, "where electrical stimulation will cause a person to believe or to decide."

The implication is that while mind operates through the highest brain mechanism, it is not totally dependent on it.

Are we experiencing a revolution in consciousness? What did Penfield think?

"I might call it 'conscious evolution' just to change that concept a little bit," he chuckled. "It's the mind and brain which have been responsible for social evolution. A thousand years from now, biological evolution will not have significantly changed. But now, how man uses his mind and the computer in his brain is just as important as biological evolution once was for the species."

Would he feel scientifically more comfortable now with the Eastern view that consciousness itself may be the underlying current or root of the material universe?

"The word 'root' may not be sufficient," he qualified. "I think it's clear that there's a plan to the universe, one which generated the extraordinary explosion of the primordial matter which resulted in the evolution of the universe. I believe now that it's a quiet reasonable thought that the whole set of laws were set up and that there was a hope on the part of—I don't dare say some One—but that there was an intention that somewhere in this universe there would be a place where man would develop just as he has, and where the mind and the spirit could dwell.

"Now the mind doesn't appear in the history of the universe for a very long time. And life, as you know, doesn't appear until very late in the day of Creation. Any evidence of awareness, in any animal or organism, appears quite a lot later—after the amoeba and the things swimming in the ocean. It was a long time before we had any evidence of an organism that was aware of itself. Now we have quite a lot of them; the beaver, the dog and the rest of them have some awareness: there certainly is consciousness there. But consciousness comes very late.

"And then, suddenly, man comes and that's a very brief story, as far as biological evolution goes. And suddenly, we have man speaking and recording. Then social evolution starts... and he goes on, with scientific work, to be able to organize and direct his life."

Penfield paused for several moments, allowing us to interject another question. What was his opinion of the viewpoint, expounded by the philosopher Henry Bergson, among others, that the brain is like an "inhibitor," selectively filtering information? That, in other words, we have greater access to information than we would normally expect, given the present and prevalent "materialist" view of the brain.

"Well," he answered, "I think it's quite a simple thing; the truth is always going to be simple: You watch a baby, and in the first weeks of life, you see evidence of purpose. The baby is interested in exploring, and in doing something, no matter whether his diaper is wet or not. The idea is there. There's a purpose, a focusing of attention.

"Now that is the programmer, because all the way through life I find that the brain has never recorded anything to which the individual did not focus his attention. He never learned a skill, never remembered an experience... there's nothing in all our electrical stimulations of the brain to suggest that there has been anything that has touched this computer unless the individual was focusing his mind.

"From the very beginning and, I would imagine, very

soon after birth, the mind—which appears to be acting with energy of its own—is nevertheless not detached from the brain, because it has to get energy. But you see, while the mind *is* there, I have to fill in that gap. What is the mind? It's a mystery. Where is it? I don't know where it is, but it's there: it comes into the world with the infant.

"And from the beginning, there is something that's causing that little rascal to do something on his own. And he's learning. *He's programming his brain.* And if you don't let him do it, and if you don't love him and protect him and make him feel that he's safe, he doesn't do a good job of it!

"But his brain has to learn. His brain has to learn a lot of things that people don't realize: it has to learn to see, and to put things together in the external world. He has to learn to hear. But the brain learns it when the infant tries to see, or is seeing and hearing. And so, the teacher and the mother are not the programmers. They provide the material, which is most important, but we must recognize that *each person programs his own brain. From the very beginning.*

"As far as education is concerned," he added, "It's frightfully important to realize that if you don't catch the student's attention, he doesn't program his brain! But don't go away from the lecture thinking that *you've* programmed anybody's brain, because you haven't! You've provided the raw material—and excited them. Caught their attention. That's marvelous!"

Penfield repeatedly asserted that we need to attend to things before they are recorded. But what exactly was his definition of "attention," we asked.

"Oh gosh! There must be a neurological mechanism of attention that we do not yet understand. If I were beginning at age 30 now, I think I would focus on this question—if I could, if the opportunity was still presented. That is very important, though, and it will be worked out. But we wouldn't be learning anymore about the mind itself. We would learn more about what the mind uses when it decides to pay attention to this instead of that. Aristotle had the same problem. He said the mind was attached to the body. And Hippocrates had a different idea which is perhaps closer to the truth: 'The brain is the messenger of the mind.'"

What advice then, in the light of his extensive research as a "humble pilgrim" of the mysteries of the mind, might

Penfield have for people about optimally living their daily lives?

"Well, you see," he began thoughtfully, "the computer, that is the brain, is amazing. The habitual programmed reactions are all in it. A person can become an automaton and do all sorts of things, like drive a car. I become an automaton every morning when I drive to my office at the Neurological Institute. If I happen to plan to go somewhere else, and become absorbed in thought, I'll end up at the Institute. Well, that's the automaton—my mind, meanwhile, was busy on another trip," he concluded with a laugh.

Then Penfield added, "Life can become the life of a computer and the mind can be used very little—far too little. This is one of the threats of the screen, the radio and the television. They are all very entertaining and we're amused. And we don't do a damned thing to develop our potential."

The message: We have minds. As the programmers of our brain-computers, we can learn to control them and to develop their potential. Our beliefs, attitudes, how we see ourselves—all the programs we have fed in—all can be reshaped and improved upon. If we put our minds to it. Of course, this first requires the will to do so, lots of it. But we are our own programmers.

With Stanley, and the many others who share his convictions, in mind, we were curious about Penfield's opinion of ESP. We felt he might be open to the possibility of one mind directly communicating with another.

It wasn't that simple, however. Penfield was a scientist and understandably reluctant to speculate.

"I think the ESP hypothesis has some evidence in it's favor," he ventured cautiously. One thing he had learned from his famous teacher, Sir Charles Sherrington, Nobel laureate and pioneer researcher of the nervous system at Oxford, he told us, was to keep his options open and not reject any hypothesis until there was sufficient evidence to warrant doing so. It had become a golden rule with Penfield, and perhaps partly for this reason he was able to speak philosophically about an area still largely shunned by scientists.

"If the mind has a source of energy other than that originating solely with the brain, then it may be possible for one mind to communicate with another. Should that be the case, it wouldn't be unreasonable for a person to even hope that after death the mind may awaken to another source of energy." Life after death in some form? Maybe. But science can't talk about it for now.

"I've done my work," Penfield concluded, with a hint of satisfaction and a smile, as we prepared to leave. "Now the physicists can deal with some of the implications."

Mind Over Matter?

Penny Smith, of the Philadelphia-based "Mike Douglas Show," was on the phone. "We want you on, but what can you do?"

"Don't you just want us to talk to Mike about psychic phenomena?" (We had just published PSI: The OTHER WORLD CATALOGUE and were doing a promotional tour.)

Silence. Something didn't click.

More silence and then: "How about bringing someone on the show with you who can demonstrate something?"

"Well, how about Jack Schwarz?"

"Who?"

"Jack can mentally control pain and to prove it, he sticks a needle through his arm."

"It's not a trick, is it?"

"No, he's for real. He's been tested extensively by Elmer Green, director of the Psychophysiology Laboratory at the Menninger Foundation in Topeka, Kansas, for his mind-over-body mastery. He might be willing to be on the show because he wants people to understand that we all have an enormous untapped potential to control our own bodies. Jack's incredibly impressive and comes across with a lot of dignity. He isn't a circus sideshow."

"Okay, we'll fly him in."

We first saw Jack on a film sequence shot at the Menninger Foundation. He's a slim, ascetic-looking man, fortyish with intense brown eyes, medium length straight black hair and silver goatee. Seated in a large, comfortable chair in the lab, he was filmed skewering his left bicep with a sail maker's needle after he'd stomped on it to "sterilize" it.

Wired up to various instruments monitoring his physical reactions, he seemed in total control of his body and emotions. His pulse remained constant as his brain waves registered high amounts of alpha waves, those slower brain waves associated with a state of meditative calm. Green, a psychologist and pioneer in biomedical research (one of the frontier areas of medicine and science), asked him of what practical use it was to be a human pincushion. "I'm not interested in entertaining people," Jack answered impassively. "I want to reeducate people to show them they're capable of far more than they think. I'm using my mental ability to teach others."

If the potential latent in all of us was developed, control over pain, for example, could prove invaluable in an accident. "What I do is mentally detach myself from my own arm and regard it as an object apart from myself," he continued. "I'm not sticking a needle through *my* arm but instead through *an* arm."

Watching Jack do his thing on film, amazing as it is, lacks the total impact of encountering him in person. His appearance on the "Mike Douglas Show" followed our preliminary discussion of the variety of unusual mental abilities. Jack was the living proof. The late comedian, Freddie Prinze, cohost of the show that day, looked incredulous when Jack withdrew the infamous needle from his coat pocket. Probably wondering about the lengths some people are willing to go to, to appear on a national television show, Prinze exclaimed, "Are you serious?"

Jack responded by piercing his own left bicep.

Prinze's jaw dropped. Mike Douglas looked away in anguish. Actress Karen Valentine and choreographer Peter Gennaro forced themselves to look on. For a few moments, everyone's media composure had been shattered. It hurt everyone more than it did Jack.

Jack's demonstration effectively conveys the intended message. When he skewers his arm, contrary to all expectations, he neither bleeds nor panics. Confusion. This is not part of the world we know and should, therefore, trigger a major revision of how we see ourselves. Jack is human, one of us. Humans bleed. They don't react that way. You look again. He's for real, alright, sitting up there in a suit, talking—totally indifferent to the needle, both ends protruding from his bicep. The seed has been planted. If Jack can master pain at will, maybe we can.

Jack wasn't in a hurry to remove the needle, either. It

Jack Schwartz demonstrating his resistance to pain as he drives a sailmaker's needle through his arm. *(Courtesy, The Mike Douglas Show)*

remained grotesquely embedded while he calmly explained how it was possible. With proper training and mental discipline, he says, others can learn. "But I don't want people to try it, especially children," he stressed. "It takes lots of practice."

When he finally removed the needle, there was no blood flow, only two puncture marks on both sides of his bicep. Freddie Prinze was invited to squeeze his arm to induce bleeding. He gingerly reached over. "He isn't bleeding," he testified, visibly shaken.

As for the rusted needle Jack had rubbed underfoot, he matter-of-factly explained that he mentally commands the germs not to grow. Infection is avoidable. The mind can prevent it.

Who is Jack Schwarz? How did he get to be what he is? After the show he explained at a nearby restaurant. At the age of nine, he discovered he had a strange power in his hands to comfort people. Often when his ailing mother was in pain, he found he could relieve it by passing his hands over the afflicted area.

Later, when he worked as a window dresser in a clothing store in Holland, he discovered quite by accident that he could control pain in his own body. One day he was playfully slapped on the chest by a fellow worker and some pins stored in his lapel dug into his flesh. There was no pain and no bleeding. Intrigued, Jack began to experiment. He plunged a large pin into his wrist, two inches through a vein. Again, no "normal" reaction. At the time, he had been reading about the extraordinary feats of Indian yogis. Inspired by his earlier successes, he approached a carpenter and ordered a bed of nails.

With 40 nails set at about seven-eighths of an inch apart, he calculated that his 150-pound body would exert a minimum of thirty-three pounds of pressure on each nail. When the experiment was carried out before a local audience, his body was racked with puncture wounds as deep as three-quarters of an inch, but he neither bled nor felt any pain, and healed almost immediately.

When seventeen and a member of the Dutch resistance, Jack was captured, interrogated and tortured. His persecutor, a Nazi equipped with a cat-o'-nine-tails, sadistically flogged his back for about ten minutes. As he was being whipped, Jack experienced a radical restructuring of his feelings and consciousness. He says he had a vision of Jesus on the cross, surrounded by a jeering crowd, imploring, "My God, my God, why have you deserted me?" The vision, Jack recalled, triggered a revelatory insight: rather than being expressions of God's love, people had fostered hatred.

Opening his eyes, Jack faced his torturer and simply announced, "I love you." Stunned, the Nazi dropped his whip and was further astounded as the wounds began to heal before his eyes. Jack was never again subjected to torture. After the war, Jack lectured throughout Europe on self-healing and mental control, and then moved to the United States. While he supported his family by working in an army surplus store, he waited for an opportunity to demonstrate his abilities. The moment came when Kurt Fantl, a psychologist, was a spectator at one of Jack's nail-bed demonstrations in San Pedro, California. Impressed by the act and its implications, with Jack's permission he promptly arranged performances before the critical eyes of a group of physicians from Los Angeles County. Jack skewered his mouth and cheeks, and held burning coals in his hands. He was meticulously tested before and after the demonstration, and the physicians were satisfied that no deception had been involved. Nor did he have any physical abnormalities such as unusual blood flow, circulation or clotting. Jack's mind had made it possible.

Subsequent scientific experiments with Elmer Green have since firmly established Jack's credentials as a master of his own body. He has had burning ash held against his skin, been burned with cigarettes and, on numerous occasions, has driven the needle into his arm. Physiological monitoring has consistently indicated that he doesn't experience any stress before, during or after the experiments. There isn't any unusual change in his heart rate, breathing and the electrical current in his skin.

Jack has some other abilities. The salmon sandwich he ordered at the restaurant at about 3:30 P.M. was his first meal of the day. "I eat very little," he volunteered. "Sometimes I have only two meals a week, and I never eat more than once a day."

Does he ever feel hunger? "No, not at all. I take in the energy around me, and my body metabolizes it quite normally. In fact, whether I eat or not, I usually have two good bowel movements a day. I always strive to get the very

most out of living. I feel happy all the time, and never allow-
myself to be depressed. I live in accordance with a basic
principle: what you send out to the world around you is
resonated back to you. My nourishment is the happiness I
receive."

Jack claims to dispense with sleep as easily as he does
with food. He only needs three hours. "Prior to my usual
meditation before going to sleep," he explained, "I visualize
and mentally replay everything that has happened to me
during the day. When I feel that there's some mental
garbage to get rid of, I slow down the stream of images and
study them." Jack refers to this technique as *Cosmic
Accounting.* "Negative feelings and thoughts enter our
dreams because they aren't squarely confronted and
conquered during the day. I immediately attend to them so
they won't have the opportunity to remain in my subconscious mind and appear symbolically disguised in my
dreams." The result is a short but deep, undisturbed and
refreshing sleep. "It's like sliding into a glove," he said.

Jack's positive outlook on life, and his demonstrated
mind and body mastery make him a living symbol of
consciousness evolution. He compels a closer look at our
own thought currents. Peering into the inner mirror, we
may get more than a glimmering insight of the way that
entrenched negative attitudes and beliefs could very
possibly influence daily behavior and distort perceptions.

Do we really need them? Do they stand between what we
are now and what we could be without them? As part of a
growing human potential movement, Jack firmly believes
that we can learn to control our own minds, to restructure
our consciousness, self-image and daily life.

Controlling the
Uncontrollable

Sometimes you get chocolates, perfume or shaving lotion for Christmas. Some friends at Thought Technology, a New-Age products firm in Montreal, sent us a curious wooden gadget that emits a steady tone which sounds like a "g" note (think: do, re, me; it's so.) The tag on the parcel said: I'm a Galvanic Skin Response Meter. Use me and welcome to the biofeedback revolution.

Biofeedback is one of the more recent and significant advances in medicine. It's being used to learn how to control an array of disorders such as headaches, high blood pressure and poor circulation. Through the use of instruments which record the body's minute electric signals and feed them back in amplified form through a tone or some visual indicator on the machine, it's possible to be aware of certain changes in internal body processes, to act on them and change the signal.

Example: When we're upset, our muscles stiffen. Our muscle tension is part of a nervous system circuitry related to anxiety. Signals are sent to the brain and we get those gnawing feelings. Through the use of an Electromyograph (EMG) machine, it's possible to reduce muscle tension to zero through willful control.

To do this, a person sits in a comfortable chair with small electrodes pasted on his or her forehead. The EMG tone indicates how relaxed or tense he or she is. High tones indicate considerable tension, lower tones, more relaxation. The aim is to reduce the tone by relaxing. As you listen to the signals and try to relax by giving yourself positive suggestions, you learn to connect the feelings of being relaxed to the corresponding tone. Feeling internal changes as they occur is the key to biofeedback.

Hal's GSR unit might be loosely described as a mini lie

detector. But actually, it's a useful relaxation aid. The accompanying literature claims that by placing two fingers of either hand on its indented brass plates with the tone switched on, you're getting feedback on your level of tension. As with all units with tones, a high tone says you're tense, a low tone denotes relaxation.

How? Because the skin can talk, electrically of course. The skin and the body's internal organs are connected to the autonomic nervous system which indicates our emotional life. The electrical current of the skin carrying the internal emotional message regulates the intensity of the tone.

One way to lower the tone is to focus positively on a suggestion such as "Relax. I am relaxed." Or visualize a calming scene (waves washing up to shore). It works with a bit of practice.

There's a secret to learning how to regulate a biofeedback signal: there are two basic kinds of will power. One is called *active volition*, which is what we use to lug a piano to another room. The other, *passive volition*, is when you confidently tell yourself that you want something to happen and just let it happen. It's necessary to be as emotionally detached as possible from the process. Straining will only increase any existing tension.

That's just what happened to both of us at a biofeedback lab in Washington, D.C. We concentrated on raising the temperature of the right hand, but an ascending tone from the machine indicated the reverse was happening. Hand temperature dropped so much that our hands were freezing. This is what often happens the first time. You strain because you want the tone to go down. When you let it happen and relax, it soon does.

There's a single instrument that demonstrates a similar effect: the common household thermometer. Tape it to a finger and try to raise your hand temperature. Relax. Imagine your hand getting warmer. Don't force it. After about five or six tries, your hand temperature will likely go up a degree or two Fahrenheit.

The Psychophysiology Laboratory of the Menninger Foundation is a major research think tank. Since 1964, Elmer Green has worked closely with his wife Alyce on biofeedback. At the time, both were aware of claims by Yogis that they could control so-called involuntary body

THE "VOICE
OF THE SKIN"

(Courtesy, Thought Technology)

June Regush learning through biofeedback to control muscle tension and hand temperature at the Allan Memorial Institute of Psychiatry in Montreal. *(Courtesy, Hal Myers of Thought Technology)*

functions such as reducing oxygen intake almost one half and controlling heartbeat. Science had generally dismissed these accounts. It wasn't possible. A basic tenet of medicine was that nothing but the skeletal muscles could be consciously controlled.

The Greens wanted to know more. After attending a training program called "Autogenics", which had been developed in Switzerland by Johannes Schultz, at the Menninger Foundation, their interest in voluntary controls accelerated. Schultz's work involved training people to relax their bodies while reducing accumulated stress. Trainees followed a six-part program which began by lying down on a couch, hands at their sides, legs apart, while mentally repeating the phrase "My right arm is heavy" until they were able to feel a great weight on their arms. Next they attempted to dilate their peripheral blood vessels, causing a warm feeling, by repeating "My right arm is warm" over and over. This was followed by an effort to calm their heartbeats, regulate their breathing rhythms, warm their stomachs and cool the surfaces of their foreheads. The Greens decided to use this technique to train thirty-three women to relax and warm their hands, over a period of two weeks. After some encouraging results they added GSR biofeedback to the program to show the women how changes were taking place in their temperature. Those who used GSRs learned conscious control faster than the others. The feedback made the difference.

Since then, their laboratory has become a prestigious stopover for the mind-over-body elite. After Jack Schwarz, the Greens encountered Swami Rama, who demonstrated his amazing control of the major arteries in his wrist by creating a temperature difference of nine degrees Fahrenheit between two spots on the palm of one hand. He also stopped the pumping of blood through his heart for seventeen seconds. Another time, he willed the development of a tumor on his arm in two seconds and dissolved it almost immediately. Then he created it again at Elmer Green's request.

What explanation did the swami have? "All of the body is in the mind, but not all the mind is in the body," he told the Greens. Each cell in the body, says Rama, can potentially be controlled at will because each cell has a counterpart in the unconscious mind. Both the physical cell and the one in the unconscious are part of a mind structure.

Therefore, some of the mind is independent of the physical body. Manipulate the part in the unconscious by expanding your control of the mind structure, and the physical can be changed. This is what he says he does.

Scientists of the brain-can-explain-everything camp think not. It's the genetic patterns, environmental conditioning and, they maintain, unconscious neural activity taking place in the brain's subcortical regions (the brain stem and limbic system) which trigger the "higher" self-awareness functions in our cerebral cortex. The belief that we're in control and have free will, then, is seen as illusory. Because we're not capable of feeling what goes on in subcortical regions, we substitute free will for basic neurological processes.

Elmer Green replies that a person can mentally plant or program the impulse or idea to do something in the cerebral cortex; in turn, the subcortical regions hear about it and the command takes its natural course. He compares this process to a farmer planting seeds:

> There seems to be a correspondence between human physiological responses to volition and the way nature responds in general to human initiative. For instance, a farmer (a) desires a crop, (b) plants the seeds, (c) allows "nature" to take its course and (d) reaps. In a corresponding way, a migraine patient first desires and visualizes a certain kind of physiological behavior. This is a conscious "cortical" process. Next he plants the idea—volitionally—in the unconscious, the "earth" of one's psychological being. Now nature is allowed to take its course. The patient passively allows his psycho-physiological machinery to function, without anxiety or analytically "picking at" what he is trying to do. The farmer does not dig up his seeds to see if they are sprouting. He has "faith" that they will sprout and allows nature to implement the process he has initiated. Finally the migraine "reaps" vascular stability, a completely natural process.

Building on Swami Rama's explanation of mind structure and borrowing a little from the Eastern spiritual master Sri Aurobindo, Green now talks about a "field of

mind theory" which he says can be used as a model to better
understand our mind-over-body programming. This mind
field surrounds our planet as do magnetic and gravitation-
al fields. It's a multidimensional continuum of physical,
emotional, mental and spiritual substance, each associated
with very specific states of consciousness. Aurobindo had
suggested that we think of the entire universe as constructed of matter with physical substance, with form the
densest, and spirit the least dense. Or that form is the
densest level of spirit.

This isn't pie-in-the-sky thinking. The idea that consciousness or some mind force permeates the universe was
best described by astronomer and physicist Sir James
Jeans when he wrote, "The world begins to look more like a
great thought than a great machine." Physicists studying
the structure of matter have found that an electron
sometimes behaves like a grain of matter and at other times
like a wave in a nonmaterial medium. This idea is hard to
grapple with. Basically it means that what looks solid has
another side to it: a shadow world of infinitesimal
structures which when broken down appear to vanish into
nothingness. But nothingness is still something. Some call
it "spirit." Our collective and individual memories, ideas
and experiences have been described as contributing to the
dynamic underlying mind force of life.

The physicist would say that this thought universe is
beyond time and space as we know it in our daily, cause-
effect lives. So there are two sides to us. We're part of the
mind structure—an invisible world—and part of the
physical, which is connected to that thought universe.
Nobel prize neurophysiologist Sir John Eccles suggests
that our material brain may be a sensitive filter for the
world beyond time and space or for physical processes we
still don't understand.

With biofeedback training, Elmer and Alyce Green
believe that we can, to varying degrees, learn to tap parts of
the mind structure and affect the physical body. We can
learn to voluntarily control our unconscious level, reduce
stress, explore inner feelings and move along the path to
greater self-realization.

The Mind and Cancer

A woman with advanced breast cancer arrives at a Fort Worth, Texas, cancer therapy clinic she's been referred to by her family physician. While examining her, the physician casually asks if she has any unusual stress in her life.

Yes, her oldest son was killed two years ago, and her health hasn't been the same since.

Can she confront the idea that this stress may have something to do with her cancer? That her emotions and attitudes may have somehow contributed to her getting cancer?

Yes, she had actually considered that; this is why she came to the clinic.

Would she be willing to probe much deeper into her emotional history, to see whether she can reverse the cancer by emotionally adjusting to her condition and fighting it with her mind as well as receiving radiation treatment?

She is strongly motivated to try. She wants to live.

In 1966, Carl Simonton's work in cancer treatment began with great enthusiasm. He was young and determined to make a significant breakthrough. But a nagging fear of making a mistake prevented his exploring new methods of treatment.

Three years later, he listened to a prominent Portland immunotherapist explain that everyone has cancer several times during a lifetime but that it will only erupt when cancer cells have invaded and overpowered the body's defense system.

This view isn't unusual in immunological circles. Each cancerous cell produces a protein called *antigen* which

31

differs from the body's own protein. It's a crazy cell, feeds on the body's blood supply and gradually devours its host unless the body's immunological system neutralizes it. An *antibody*, also a protein, forms in plasma cells in reaction to the presence of this mad cell in the tissues and normally deactivates it. But some cancers multiply too rapidly, creating too many targets. When this happens, it's likely that the body will lose its control in the early stages of a cancer's development.

The goal of immunological research is to develop powerful ways to stimulate the body's defense system by biochemically inducing defenses to regroup and attack. The strategy goes back to 1796 when Edward Jenner discovered that milkmaids who came into contact with cows suffering from cowpox rarely contracted smallpox. Jenner injected a fluid from a cowpox pustule into an eight-year-old boy and successfully treated him for the disease. The body, it seemed, was capable of identifying the injected disease and mobilizing itself to fight.

In the same manner, the Portland immunotherapist had prepared a solution of abnormal white cells of several of his leukemia patients who had not been helped by routine cancer radiation treatment and applied it to an area of their skin in the hope of triggering a response in the defense system.

At first the results were rewarding. Fifty percent remission, however, decreased to 25 percent, and then to 10 percent as other researchers experimented with this procedure. This curious effect is recurrent in medicine. An experimenter who discovers a new method and is enthusiastic and determined to make it work may find that his results fail to be duplicated.

The implication that an innovator's heightened motivation and interaction with his patients may contribute to their recovery caught Simonton's attention. He was also aware at the time that two to five percent of cancer patients seem to survive against all possible odds and wondered whether the decisive factor was an intense desire to live. Simonton tracked down patients in the Portland area who had battled their cancer and won. He learned from their relatives, friends and physicians that all had been determined to survive. Could this "will to live" be taught to others who had given up hope? If the patient's attitude could be modified and positively restructured, might the body's defense system be rejuvenated to inhibit or reverse the growth of malignancies?

Two important events helped to catalyze his search for a therapeutic procedure. The first was biofeedback training. He had access to some equipment and found it was possible to gain control over his blood pressure, temperature and brain waves. The second was his positive reaction to a mind-training course which taught that visualization techniques were conducive to self-healing and could be used as powerful tools to constructively modify human personality.

His first patient was a sixty-one-year-old man with throat cancer, incapable of swallowing even his own saliva. While using the usual radiation treatment, Simonton gave him a detailed account of what cancer is, how radiation treatment works and how it might be possible to mentally influence the entire treatment process. There were no flurries of unintelligible twenty-letter words to explain the nature of the disease—he explained that through mutual visualization they would attempt to fight the cancer.

Three times daily, his patient relaxed the muscles in his body and vividly visualized healthy white blood cells attacking and dislodging the cancerous ones, flushing them out of the body through the elimination system. To counteract the fact that radiation treatment destroys normal cells along with the cancerous ones, his patient was told to visualize cancerous cells exclusively being destroyed.

The technique appeared to work. Before long there was no further evidence of throat cancer. To cap this off, the patient's other problem—impotency—ended as well.

Simonton wasn't certain of how it happened but was encouraged that mind was the vital factor.

When Simonton was drafted, he was given the opportunity to continue his work as head of radiation therapy at Travis Air Force Base. In a study of fifty patients there, he found there was a strong correlation between negative attitudes about chances for recovery and little or no progress in treatment.

With the approval of the base commander, he launched an extensive program which combined radiation therapy with relaxation and visualization techniques. Patients were thoroughly briefed on all available information about their cancer. Slides of their growths and their X rays were shown and discussed. Photographs revealed how other patients with very visible cancers had successfully responded to the treatment.

In a study of 152 patients at Travis, which measured the success of treatment in relationship to the patient's overall attitude, there was strong evidence that a positive attitude corresponded significantly to a good treatment response. Of the twenty patients who scored the highest responses to treatment, all had been highly motivated. Of those whose condition failed to improve, all had in one way or another decided that it wasn't really worth the effort.

There are over two hundred medical articles related to cancer study that point to the patient's personality as a vital factor in the development and progress of cancer. Carl Simonton, now in private practice in Fort Worth, and his wife Stephanie, a psychotherapist, draw on the literature and their own experiences with patients to suggest that there is a cancer personality.

There are several recurrent traits:

* A poor self-image
* A bottling up of emotions
* A tendency toward self-pity
* A tendency to dwell obsessively upon resentments toward others
* An inability to form and maintain meaningful relationships
* Something significant lost, such as a loved one, a job, etc.

The last trait, the Simontons say, is the most important. It usually happens six to eighteen months before a cancer diagnosis. The cause is not so much the loss itself, but the response to it, particularly that of helplessness and hopelessness. While everyone has some of these traits and none of them can in themselves be specifically associated with the onset of cancer, together, if predominant in the personality, they appear to be emotionally crippling and contribute to the breakdown of the proper functioning of the body's defense system.

"I doubt that we'll ever be able to scientifically document

to our own satisfaction once and for all that the mind causes physical diseases," Stephanie Simonton conceded at the First National Congress On Integrative Health in Tucson, Arizona.* "But I personally believe that if you develop the attitude...that it happened to you for a reason, and that you can benefit from the experience, that you can mobilize many forces within you to influence that condition. It's a far better attitude than assuming you are the victim of something that got you in your sleep over which you have no control."

But that's easier said than done. "Today, some of the patients who come to our clinic," Carl Simonton reported, "are referred by local doctors and specialists. Many of these people come primarily for radiation treatment and balk at any suggestion of psychotherapy. Others are much more open to the total program and indicate they want to take an active role in their own healing process.

"The resistance should be expected," he continued. "We live in a society that reinforces dependency. People believe that physicians are totally responsible for their cure. We've subconsciously been conditioned by advertising to believe that aspirins will cure headaches, cold capsules will eliminate colds and antacids will combat indigestion and so on. No matter what the problem, it seems most of us are convinced that pills or agents external to ourselves will cure us of it."

The Simontons are contacted by hundreds of families of cancer patients every month. Rarely does the patient do so himself. If he or she does, this is seen as a strong indication of motivation to actively participate in the healing process.

They have a package they send out to those who call which consists of written statements of their beliefs and the nature of their therapy and instructions on how to relax and learn to visualize. The potential patient is asked to read the material and practice the techniques three times a day. This is often about as far as it goes. The caller's family rarely contacts them again.

More recently, the Simontons have decided to focus attention on an exceptional group of sixty patients. They're highly educated, the average age is forty, they have read some of the cancer literature and some have already had

* Presented by the Academy of Parapsychology and Medicine, October 8-10, 1975.

psychotherapeutic experience. They are the kind of people, the Simontons say, who are usually considered by physicians as bad patients because they drive their doctors batty with all sorts of questions about their illnesses. They are therefore highly motivated to gradually open up their lives like a can of worms, confront their inner conflicts and pull out what's in there and have a good, honest look. In studying them, the Simontons hope to identify the qualities they could best teach their more typical cancer patients.

The psychotherapeutic part of the program requires that the patient dig deeply into his or her life. They are encouraged to list specific reasons why some part of them wants out of life, and what emotional rewards they feel they are getting for being sick. Sociological studies of behavior during illness show quite convincingly that many people enjoy the "sick role," in part because they feel more appreciated by family and friends.

This is precisely what the Simontons want to crack—the personal code which feeds on the illness. The patients begin to explore other ways they can get the same rewards and a variety of ways to break out of feelings of hopelessness. If someone has lost a job, he or she is motivated to seek out other ways of living and to act out new roles in group sessions. Often in relationships the patients describe as meaningful, the Simontons have found some serious conflict. The patients are encouraged to examine how this conflict may drain their desire to live. Something is being taken away from their lives and they must pinpoint it by honestly confronting and expressing their innermost feelings.

To help them improve visualization techniques used to focus on the cancer, patients describe exactly what and how they visualize. Some of them have difficulty believing they actually have cancer and so have only vague images of it. They are told that the cancer is there; that it's mad, unruly, stupid and confused—but not invincible—and that the immune system can fight it.

Exact visualization can help. One patient said he never had any pain because he imagined a ferocious bulldog chewing it to pieces. The Simontons instructed him to visualize it attacking and wiping out his cancer cells as well, but this didn't seem to work. Perplexed, they asked him to describe exactly what he visualized. He unleashed the bulldog, he said, and it would charge and attack the cancer. Then white blood cells would fall like snowflakes onto the cancer. Stephanie Simonton suggested that he instead visualize the bulldog, or even several, working incessantly at fever pitch, chewing up the cancer.

Another factor to be contended with in treating the cancer patient is the negativism of family members. Cancer kills. No one has a chance. Or so most people are led to believe. Because of this, they harmfully transmit their pessimism to the patient instead of sending hope.

At the Tucson conference, the Simontons told of one patient, a black model whose cancer was quite advanced, having spread to her brain and bones. She became optimistic after her first psychotherapy sessions and almost immediately showed dramatic improvement. She had gotten out of bed at the clinic after the second week and was even walking around. It was one of the best responses the Simontons had ever seen. A month after returning home, she died.

Why? One reason they suggest is that there was excessive tension at home. Once when the husband had visited the clinic, an almost violent argument had erupted between him and his wife right in the office.

For this reason, the Simontons insist on providing psychotherapy to those who are close to the patient as well, emphasizing that any negative attitude, stress creation or reinforcement of fear can potentially overpower the patient's will to live. They are advised to shift their attention to examine the underlying negative traits in their own personalities.

Because the Simontons' approach shows promise, the obvious question is: why aren't more physicians treating cancer patients this way?

One reason, according to Stephanie Simonton, is that "it requires more humanness. I have to rely on my humanness as a person rather than on my professional knowledge. It demands a lot of exposure of me personally. I find that to get them to open up, it seems they do best when I'm willing to share things about myself that I would prefer not to with patients. And if I expect them to believe they are responsible for their cancer, I have to believe the same thing about myself. If I get a cold, I too have to ask myself why I got it. And in their presence you'd better be willing to do it."

This close approach with patients brings up a strategy physicians sometimes attempt called the *placebo effect*. It could be a sugar pill given for pain or a water injection instead of a drug for a disease. Often a patient gets well quickly. Physicians like to wave it off as "suggestion." But what is suggestion?

Carl Simonton is angered about the lack of understanding of how a placebo works. "Much of what we call bedside manner," he stresses, "comes under placebo effect. If you tell Mrs. Jones that she is going to get well and if you show you care, then this may help her enormously. The placebo effect goes into the administration of every form of therapy that we give patients. It has to do with the person's beliefs and those of the physician. If someone gets well when it looked unlikely, then a physician may say it's a case of spontaneous remission."

Carl Simonton feels that if physicians don't genuinely care about their patients, about whether or not they recover, then their medical practice is a lie.

Zapping the Negatives
(Silva Mind Control)

More and more people are "programming." They are attempting to use the mind to zap negative thoughts, to replace them with positives, solve everyday problems, improve memory, get better grades, heal the body and control annoying habits.

The programmer of programmers is José Silva. His mission: to give everyone the opportunity to program changes in their lives. He's come up with a package called Silva Mind Control, guaranteed, he says, to help us do everything better—a package for Professor Harris, clairvoyant Sarah, Uncle Jim the plumber and teenage Debbie—everyone. A man who tested his principles on his own children must have confidence.

Silva was interested in hypnosis and mental powers. If he trained his children using hypnotic induction to screen out mental distractions, would their school performance improve? He says it did, significantly. More training followed. They learned to anticipate some of his questions and demonstrated the ability to fill in details when they were given only basic information about a person or event. They seemed clairvoyant. Silva says he taught them to use their inner consciousness. They were operating at deeper levels of mind with controlled awareness.

He decided to bring these powers to the people. Teaching his techniques throughout Texas, his following grew like wild mushrooms. He taught a four-hour course, often twice daily to meet the demand. People from all walks of life were drawn to Mind Control.

The next stage: train instructors; open centers throughout the country and internationally; package the course into forty-eight hours, twelve hours for four days; get it into grammar schools, high schools, college extension courses; train more instructors.

The result: success. Silva Mind Control is currently second only to TM. Its graduates carrying diplomas and "psi-op" (psychic operator) identity cards have swelled to over half a million. If you don't like the course, you get your money back. If you're a happy graduate and want refreshers, take as many as you like at any Silva Center anytime for free.

More success: only one percent want their money back. Graduates tell their friends and family to take it. Take it and be like me, a better programmer doing and getting things you want. Word of mouth is often better than shopping-bag campaigns.

That's how we learned about it.

We'll remember Jean for a long time. Trained at Silva Headquarters in Laredo, Texas, she said she had mastered all the basic techniques. Effervescent, smiling, very dedicated, she was a former actress who happened on the program and has committed herself to spreading the word and sharing.

"You're here to program your brain and extend your mind," she announced when forty of us were seated in Silva Mind Control, New York, a large room with a rattling air conditioner. "We'll teach you to relax, control your mind, solve practical problems, cultivate a superior intuitive sense by tuning into metals, plants and animals and then ... we'll project our minds into human life to detect and heal people at a distance. You'll be given cases to work on and will see how everyone can learn Mind Control.

"But please, stick with the course sequence. Some things we do may seem a little hokey, but they have been tested. They work. There's a careful logic to everything."

The arch look of scepticism settled on several faces. Jean interrupted our thoughts. "Alright, let's start. Find a comfortable position, close your eyes, visualize a favorite place of relaxation, take a deep breath and while exhaling, mentally repeat and visualize the number "3" three times. Now take another breath, exhale, mentally repeat and visualize the number "2" three times."

When we got to "1," uncoordinated sounds of breathing accelerated and challenged the slow, rhythmic beat of a metronome behind Jean. "You are now at level one. This is the basic plane level that you can use for a purpose, any purpose you desire."

Level one wasn't deep enough. We followed Jean's countdown from ten to one and were to feel ourselves descending deeper. It wasn't easy.

"You are now at a deeper, healthier level of mind, deeper than before. To help you enter an even deeper, healthier level of mind, I am going to direct your attention to different parts of your body." We concentrated our awareness on scalp, forehead, eyelids, belly, thighs, ankles, feet and toes. Meanwhile Jean talked in a slow hypnotic tone, telling us we were geniuses, would never be ill and could project our senses anywhere in the universe.

Our watches indicated twelve minutes had elapsed before we were snapped out by Jean's fingers. Jean said twenty-five. But it seemed more like a five-minute day-dream.

Silva wants this basic relaxation exercise to establish a "point of reference" for us to get the feeling of how our focused attention begins to shift. He says mind is a sensing faculty which exists somewhere outside the brain, a master sense which can transmit and tap energies and thoughts from others. To be aware in Mind Control language means to become more efficient at focusing attention, to become more aware of our flowing feelings and thoughts and learn to use them.

Jean said that experiencing "alpa," a brain wave slower than "beta" (our general preoccupied waking state), would help us to program better. The relaxation conditioning would get us to this deeper level of mind if we practiced.

"Where's there?" someone asked. "How do I know when I'm there? How do I know I'm not deluding myself?" Good questions.

Biofeedback researchers had unwittingly unleashed a magic-maker. Alpha brain waves had been strongly associated with relaxation and the rush was on by opportunists wanting to cash in by selling electroencephalograph (EEG) machines, often poorly constructed, at exhorbitant prices. Small institutes cropped up overnight as soon as the mass media got wind of biofeedback and alpha. Because there was no form of regulation, there was little guarantee for effectiveness.

The biofeedback people felt themselves further invaded by Silva Mind Control and its spin-offs claiming to get you to alpha. Joe Kamiya of the Langley Porter Institute in San

Francisco said, "You would have no way of knowing if your
pleasant feeling was alpha brain waves or just enjoyment
of your lobster thermidor as you digested dinner during the
course." Alpha training without a machine? Impossible.
Where was the feedback? Through proper training a person
could control his or her alpha waves in four to ten hours.
Why be gullible and spend money on any iffy proposition? The alpha cultists were drawing the naive to courses
throwing questionable alpha training into a carefully
calculated package of evangelism and positive thinking.

Jean fought back. "We know that the deeper levels of
mind induced by our conditionings are equivalent to slower
brain waves. Some of us have been tested by biofeedback
equipment and we get down to alpha quickly. Machines
become a crutch. These scientists have their self-interests.
Thousands of people who never spent any time at all
thinking about their lives now have a chance to learn to
control their behavior while definitely at slower brain-
wave levels."

"But what about the conditioning technique, your
instructions and that metronome ticking in the background?" asked an elderly woman with a sad, deflated
voice. "Isn't that similar to hypnosis?"

José Silva had briefed his instructors for this one. Some
people were so suggestible that at the mere mention of
hypnosis, they were "out." So hypnosis is a broad term.
Sure there's a bit of hypnosis in the course, but there's also
hypnosis in meditative techniques, induction techniques to
get people relaxed for biofeedback ("You're getting relaxed.... Your hand is getting warmer...."), so what's so
special about including a mild form of it in this course? The
critics were creating boogies in the dark. There was so
much more to Mind Control than hypnosis.

Jean was glossing. The critics she mentioned included
Elmer and Alyce Green. We had chanced upon their
impassioned article condemning alpha training courses
prior to enrolling. They described the countdown procedure
used to get to "level one" and "deeper levels of mind" as
classic hypnotic induction. They fear it can trigger bizarre
experiences in some people who may be psychologically
unstable. A century of psychical research has accumulated
evidence that certain states of mental dissociation such as
hypnosis can activate latent psychic abilities.

Because hypnosis is generally believed to be the most easily induced and manipulated state of consciousness, the Greens aren't happy about the extent to which mind-training programs fail to maintain responsible checks on their coast-to-coast operations. Psychic transference can take place between instructor and student, and if the student is highly suggestible, the motives of the instructor had better be clean. What if you get a Svengali at the helm?

José Silva maintains there's a difference between the hypnosis the Greens are talking about and what is used in Mind Control. A form of hypnosis (called heterohypnosis) exists, he says, when the subject is under the unquestioned control of the hypnotist. He explains that while hypnotized, a subject's self-control decreases the deeper he is taken. Whether or not he is told he is in perfect control, it is highly improbable that he will, in fact, be capable of asking any questions. But Silva insists, "In Mind Control, it does not matter how deep you go; your mind functions inductively and deductively. You're always told in the conditionings that you are in complete control. You answer and ask questions, and the deeper you go, the more controls you have and the more you remember."

All Silva exercises use the basic three-two-one count-down method to get you to your "level." The first "how-to" was guaranteed to cure insomnia. An incredible claim. Over thirty million people in North America suffer the "I-can't-fall-asleep" syndrome. They count sheep, beer bottles, take sleeping pills, potions, warm milk, exercise, have snacks, even try acupuncture treatment (two needles are inserted, one on the heel, another just above the elbow). After brief relief, they're usually back where they started or worse off: sleepless, frustrated, heavier, physically tolerant of (and often immune to) sleeping pills and suspicious of any new therapy. The insomniacs in the class had their ears wide open.

"All right, get down to your level," Jean directed. "Visualize a blackboard, and imagine holding a piece of chalk in one hand and an eraser in the other. Mentally draw a large circle on the board and a big "X" in its center. To the upper right of the circle, write the word 'deeper.'"

The rest is similar to counting sheep: write the number "100" in the middle of the circle. Erase it. Go over the word "deeper" at the right of the circle with your imaginary chalk. The same for 99, 98, 97...until your mind gets so bored, you fall asleep.

"Sounds like the old counting sheep routine," came a voice from the back. Jean smiled triumphantly. "The key is the visualization combined with the deeper levels of mind you're working at. Programming is better at these levels, so remember, first count yourself down."

What Jean didn't mention is that insomnia is no longer considered to be only a psychological problem which mental programming might gradually bring under control. Researchers are now pointing to the possible neurological disorders of some insomniacs. At modern sleep laboratories such as the Sleep Disorders Clinic at Stanford University's School of Medicine, they have the equipment to measure a sleeping subject's breathing, body reflexes, the amounts of oxygen and carbon dioxide in the blood, muscle-fiber activity and brain waves. Disorders relating to these body functions are known to cause or to aggravate sleeping problems.

Jean: "Practice and programming. That's what counts. We can do anything we want if we try hard enough."

The next exercise taught us how to become our own alarm clocks. Something of value for those who need three or four radio blasts and irritating rings to finally wrench themselves from a cool, comfortable pillow. Getting shot from a cannon is not the way to greet a new day. We felt Jean was talking to us.

The method is simple enough:

* Get to your level before sleep.
* Visualize a clock with its hands adjusted at the desired time.
* Mentally repeat: "I will awaken at the desired time and be wide awake, feeling fine and in perfect health."

To stay awake, you tell yourself while at your level that you are sleepy and don't want to be. Count up from one to five, and at two or three tell yourself five will see you wide awake.

Before we could catch our breath, we were already programming for headache control. "Mind Control at no time desires to replace traditional medical practice," Jean whispered. "Anything learned here should not be seen as a substitute to visiting your doctor. We recommend headache control for tension headaches and migraines."

Headaches are as recurrent as smog these days. If there really is a quick, efficient way to control the temple-throbbing, then José Silva bottled a powerful product. It's a simple recipe: needed are your level, a firm resolve to get rid of the headache, mentally repeating that you don't want the headache and presto, the headache is gone. For migraines recycle all of the above three times.

Does it work? Well, that depends largely on whether you're really relaxed or just think you are. A study by biofeedback researchers Thomas Budzynski and Johann Stoyva indicates that tension headaches could be significantly reduced in about 65 percent of people by teaching them to relax forehead muscles. So if a Silva graduate can really slip into a relaxed state at will, the recipe may sometimes work.

From the simple recipes we were on our way to what Jean described as the "hokier stuff." "Give them a chance. These techniques really work. They are ways to reinforce and activate your own Mind Control."

Their names were strange to say the least. The first was the ominous-sounding three-finger technique. Here it is: bring the tips of your thumb, index and middle finger together while going to your level. It's a triggering device to bring you to your level quickly and strengthen programming. Jean matter-of-factly announced that in doing so, important information could be recalled at will.

Some of the graduates in class taking refreshers swore by it. One spidery looking man claimed he used the technique on a quiz show and won $500 .... Three fingers together, down to your level, the answer is waiting, instant and easy once you get the hang of it.

The glass-of-water technique made us aware of how thirsty we were. (The air conditioner had short-circuited with a hiss). The technique involves drinking a half glass of water with a squirt of lemon in it before climbing into bed. While drinking, the trick is to roll your eyes slightly upward ("Because brain waves begin to slow down"), mentally repeating the phrase, "This is all I need to do to find a solution to the problem I have in mind." The glass is left within reach of the bed, the remaining half to be ingested when waking. The same phrase is repeated.

"I know, I know," Jean repeated, "it sounds crazy, but believe me, it isn't. You see, during the day or in the content of a dream a flash of insight often surfaces with the solution to your problem, usually within seventy-two hours after programming for it. Why don't you try it and see? How can you criticize until you try?"

Actually, it does make a bit of sense. People have been using these induction techniques for centuries, particularly to program for answers to problems in dreams. Ancient Egyptians reinforced their regular prayers and expectations with elaborate rituals prior to sleeping. One scenario called for a clean linen bag on which the name of five appropriate deities were written. The bag was folded, saturated with oil and then transformed into a lampwick. It was then set afire as the petitioner repeated a formula seven times before finally collapsing into bed. The Ultimate Eclectic, José Silva, had picked a glass of water to act as a focus and augment expectations.

Moving right along, Jean announced: "Now we're going to learn how to heal ourselves." The technique was glove anesthesia, designed to combat sudden emergencies such as bleeding and severe pain:

* Seated comfortably in a chair, drop your hands to your sides.

* Visualize a hot bucket of water beneath your stronger hand. If you are able to think of a lemon and mentally taste its sourness, this shouldn't be too difficult.

* Drop your hand into the bucket.

* Imagine the sensation of steaming water on your hand.

* Feel a tingling sensation or numbness—anything really but it must feel different from the other hand.

* Transfer the feeling of the stronger hand to parts of the body.

* This is called "anesthesia." When in an accident,

use this technique and say, "Gone, gone, gone," and the pain, hopefully, will stop.

Silva graduates say it works. One claimed that when he was in a car accident and suffered a deep gash on his left arm, he automatically invoked "gone, gone, gone," applied the "anesthesia" and immediately stopped his bleeding and pain.

Well, we had heard of this claim before enrolling and visited pain specialist Ronald Melzack at McGill University's psychology department for his theories.

His "gate-control" theory of pain claims there is a mechanism in the body's pain-signaling system consisting of fibers which can be opened or closed. Under certain conditions, pain signals can be blocked from reaching the brain. The older view held that there were simple pathways from tissues to the brain.

Melzack says that psychological factors act on the pain-signaling system by either opening or closing the "gate" in various parts of the nervous system. If pain is expected, the "gate" will open wide. The stimulus runs through. Some people, he says, who have learned to control their levels of anxiety, can learn to manipulate the on-off switches (like Jack Schwarz).

Melzack uses alpha biofeedback training with arthritic subjects and others who experience chronic pain. After eight weeks of training, they can, with varying success, control the pain at will without resorting to biofeedback machines. Relaxed, the gates don't open as wide. Some diminish the pain by forty to fifty percent; others as much as eighty.

He says that ego-strengthening techniques (such as positive thinking) and relaxation without biofeedback can influence chronic pain, but the evidence is not highly significant. Can someone stop severe bleeding and pain during an accident? Melzack is not very convinced. Maybe certain highly exceptional people. Headaches, maybe.

Jean disagreed when we brought it up. "Never say never," she insisted.

Thoughts are energy.

Experiences are thoughts crystallized on the physical level.

To change your life you must be aware of your thoughts and how to use them.

Positive thoughts have positive energy.

Negative thoughts, negative.

A formula from José Silva for "mirror of the mind" exercises.

"The mirror of the mind technique," Jean explained, "involves the creation of a mental screen. Close your eyes. I want you to project onto this screen a full-length mirror with a black frame. Whenever a personal problem has to be solved, mentally project an image of it onto the black-framed mirror. Study the problem. The next step is to project what you think the solution might be onto a mirror with a white frame. Undesirable habits like nail-biting, compulsive eating and chain-smoking are not irreversible."

Have a smoking problem and want to quit? Silva suggests you project the cigarette, your yellowed fingers and smoke onto the black-framed mirror. Admit you're hooked to smoking. Believe it! Then imagine yourself on the white-framed mirror doing things without a cigarette in hand. Silva advises against extreme action. Instead, visualize yourself progressively reducing your smoking by maybe one cigarette each hour until no cigarettes at all are reflected on the white-framed mirror. Take thirty days.

For weight control, resisting the glorious hot-fudge ice cream sundae, the cheesecake covered with juicy fresh strawberries or bright red cherries—you name it—can be projected onto the black-framed mirror. Mentally desecrate them with a big red "X." Nonfattening foods are then visualized on the white-framed mirror with a very slim You beaming beside them.

When the urge hits, program.

And so on. Got a problem? Use the mirror technique. Silva graduates have flooded centers with success stories. Jean had a handful to read. One woman had been an insomniac for forty years. She's sleeping well. Another who improvised with weight reduction programming lost twenty-six pounds in four months:

I visualized a dark frame and saw a table loaded with ice cream and cake. I drew a large "X" through the table and saw myself in a mirror which made me look very wide (the kind you find in a carnival fun house). Next, I visualized a scene surrounded by a golden light: a table on which all the high-protein foods rested—tuna, eggs, lean meat. I placed a large golden check mark on this scene and saw myself in a mirror looking very tall and thin. Mentally I told myself that I craved only the foods on the protein-laden table. I also heard my friends telling me how fantastic I looked and saw all this happening on a specific date.

"People use the mirror of the mind for virtually everything," Jean said, adding, "One amputee is even growing a new leg."

We grimaced. A classroom sceptic groaned.

"Cancel-cancel. Cancel-cancel." You hear it in the hallway during a coffee break. In the bathroom. During lunch hour. It can drive you to distraction. If you should dare tell anyone you can't do something, "cancel-cancel" comes at you like a karate shot to the chops. It's the Silva graduates on the prowl, looking for negatives.

"Anything bothering you can be conquered," Jean echoed. "Program for anything you want. Do it at your level. You can be anything. You can do anything. Forget what other people tell you. If it's a negative, say 'cancel-cancel.' Zap it."

Mind Travel

Neutralizing negatives in daily life is only the first phase of Silva Mind Control. The rest is more offbeat, some might say kinky. It involves mind travel. Through walls, into plants, metals, other bodies and minds. Silva calls it "effective sensory projection."

Getting back to our "levels" again, Jean pointed to a large philodendron at the front of the room. It was a trifle small for forty of us but she wanted us to imagine our consciousness traveling through its leaves and stem. "Think of how silky it feels," she intoned. "Feel yourself mentally traveling."

Who knew what to expect? Maybe some people talk to their plants, but who claims to travel inside them? And what if the plant didn't like the idea? Someone volunteered he felt a sensation of splashing through water while examining the main stem of the plant. To be honest we didn't feel anything.

"Now try it with the metals I've given you to touch, and then feel yourself traveling through someone's pet." Again, complete blanks. Maybe we didn't really want to invade our own dog. He usually sleeps on his favorite couch and gets cranky when disturbed.

A woman reported a feeling of weightlessness while gliding through her cat's circulatory system. Her husband shook his head, rolled his eyes and muttered something about going fishing inside a giant whale. Others appeared to be confused. This was way out.

Jean was harking to greater things. "This is only a preparation," she asserted. "We want to learn how to mind-travel through someone's body but first we need some help."

What she had in mind was the mental creation of our own laboratory. It could be anything, a scientific workshop, a hut on the beach, any shape, place or size. We had to equip it with basic tools which would help us to solve problems. A desk, chair, clock, file cabinets with vital information, chemicals, medication. We also need counselors or guides, wise men or women who would share their storehouse with us when we needed certain information.

A three-two-one conditioning got us to our level. We were to imagine an elevator descending to the main floor of our lab with the counselors (at least two) inside. When the door opened, they would identify themselves.

Could we get anyone we wanted? No. Whoever came. We would be surprised.

"Hey, I got Saint Thomas Aquinas and Pope John," gasped a woman in a pink dress. A man wanted Raquel Welch and got Bob Hope.

One of us got Germaine Greer and Sarah Bernhardt and the other a committee, no less, comprised of Sigmund Freud, Carl Jung, Wilhelm Reich and Albert Einstein.

Had Silva concluded that we lack confidence in our own resources? That this might be bypassed by certain imaginary guides? Would the counselors, as collaborators, serve to override our fears of failure when the big test came? It was a subtle but highly controversial mental trick to get around snags—one which hadn't eluded Silva-watchers.

Several, including Elmer and Alyce Green, warn that creating imaginary counselors may be dangerous. Cases have been reported, they say, in which the counselors, when ordered to vacate a person's consciousness, became hostile and refused to do so. They're not simply figments of the imagination, the Greens charge, but mind-constructed realities who may linger as psychically real at other levels of consciousness.

The Greens also say that people enrolling in these courses can be psychically catapulted into realms in which they are unable to protect themselves from dangers arising from either their own unconscious or from psychic manipulation by other persons or "entities" existing at other planes of existence. Alyce Green had mentioned to us that they knew of reports of people suffering severe emotional traumas as a result of psychic manipulation. If someone's mentally unstable, there could be identity problems after mentally connecting to these guides.

To our knowledge, beyond a brief questionnaire which had been handed out on the first day, no actual screening of

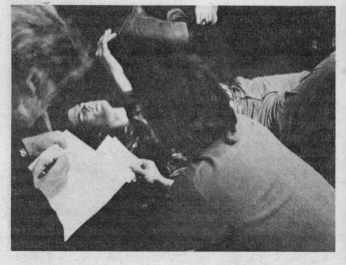

A Silva Mind Control student attempts to pick up information psychically about someone who may be hundreds of miles away. *(Courtesy, Joanne Howell of Silva Mind Control)*

New England Director Christian Jensen teaches a course in Silva Mind Control. A brain wave chart is used as a study guide. *(Courtesy, Joanne Howell of Silva Mind Control)*

students had taken place. Who is about to list a known mental problem on a questionnaire, anyway?

Jean: "In Mind Control, you're always in control. Your counselors can come and go as you desire. Use them when you need them."

Tension was building. Feet shuffled. No one was smiling.

"Your aim is to mentally project yourself into a human body and scan it for disease," Jean said. But what if the mind could detach itself in this manner and travel anywhere it desired? Wasn't it unethical to invade someone without permission?

Jean dodged. No harm could be done if the intention was honorable. We weren't satisfied, but decided to press on with the rest.

We were divided into teams of three. Each person filled out three cards citing the name, age, height, weight and area of residence of friends or family members; on the flip side, what physical or mental problems they had.

One team member was to act as "psychic." He or she would do the traveling and scanning and use his or her counselors to help detect illness (Not "diagnose," Jean stressed, to avoid possible confrontations with the medical profession). Another played guide, or "orientologist," and was required to encourage and keep the psychic talking. The third was the scribe whose card the psychic had drawn. If the psychic correctly said, "I see a tumor in the stomach," the scribe would verify. If the psychic hit on something unknown to the scribe, "I do not have that information" was the appropriate response. After each case was worked, roles would be rotated.

The instructions were simple enough but who knew how to "travel" through a body? We had been given beautifully illustrated physiology manuals that would have made medical students envious, but it all seemed senseless. Who was about to memorize the body structure at a glance?

Jean: "Don't worry about a thing. Start anywhere in the body, but remember if you spot a blood clot, a tumor or a condition of ill health anywhere, mentally picture it perfect. You have to work at it. Your mind knows more than you think. Just say what comes into your mind."

To everyone's surprise, even ours, we all did remarkably well. Or so it seemed. We scored hits after consulting our counselors each time. Once, when a vague feeling was registered that there was something wrong with a case's midsection, nothing else came through.

"Try asking your counselors," the orientologist prompted. The disgruntled committee at the conference table revealed nothing. Finally, Freud broke the silence, reluctantly volunteering, "Aaghhh, it's the bladder." It happened the woman was diabetic and had bladder problems. The Greer-Bernhardt team cooperated and gave exact information on the appearance and health problems of a woman in her thirties. She was visualized with blonde hair, about five feet four inches and wearing checkered pants. An impression of stiffness in her legs was picked up. The scribe in the group was her father and was impressed. She had had a leg operation.

Were these lucky guesses? Or examples of clairvoyant perception triggered by the cumulative exercises, positive suggestions and expectations?

Mental travel was at best awkward. Few people seemed to know the difference between the location of, say, the pancreas or the liver. When the "psychic" projected, he or she would say things like, "Oh yes, I see some blockage in the midsection" or "I feel something is wrong with the intestine." No one seemed to have a clear vision of any of the internal organs but only instant dartlike impressions.

There was also a lot of prompting going on. The orientologist, aware of the case's specific problem, would say, "Do you see anything wrong in the skull area?" This would direct the "psychic's" attention there. To what degree this influenced imagery is difficult to say.

Could this be explained as telepathy?

Jean: "Even if it is, isn't that really something? Telepathy in forty-eight hours?"

Silva critics aren't impressed. They generally view the promise of creating clairvoyants as fraudulent. In one oft-cited study conducted by psychologists Robert Brier and Gertrude Schmeidler with the help of a physician, five cases were supplied to each of five Mind Control graduates. Only chance results were obtained. In a repeated test, only one subject who aspired to become a Silva instructor produced a marginally significant better score.

Silva advocates reject these results. The experimental procedure, they say, is hostile and heavily biased against the graduates. They will conduct their own research.

And so it goes.

Hypnotic Boat Rides

We're on an imaginary boat ride, confidently secure in the darkness surrounding us as we float along an underground river, winding our way through a long tunnel. At the tunnel's end is a light—brilliant, friendly, radiating hope. It intensifies as we approach. Patiently we wait; there's no rush, we're getting there, drifting closer to the answer.

We've taken this underground search through the labyrinths of the mind to solve a problem, to get the answer that's eluded us in our preoccupied, clouded waking lives.

"Wait for the solution .... Take your time.... You have enough time.... Wait.... Wait...for your ESP experience," the omniscient soothing voice tells us.

Now we're in a balloon. The voice guides us: "You imagine and feel you are being carried by a balloon, higher, higher toward the light, toward the light, toward the sun, listening only to my voice and feeling this pleasant, elated feeling of being high above the earth, high in the air...flying high in the air, carried by the balloon."

We're enjoying the flight, waiting for impressions, the solution to a problem. The wind pushes us on.

"Your balloon is now entering a cloud ... such a big cloud of a dense mist...a big, vast cloud ....There is light everywhere around you...a lot of sunshine outside the cloud, but you are now inside, and all around you there is this dense, heavy, opaque mist.... You are looking into that dense mist.... You are looking around through the mist.... All the time you are curious about what you will see, how soon you will see it clearly.... Your vivid vision will come by itself.... Allow my voice to help you and bring you the desired vision...."

The voice on the cassette recording belongs to Milan Ryzl, a psychical researcher and expert in hypnotic induction. His aim is to induce the proper state of mind conducive to ESP experiences. The exercises are part of a home-study package we received from him via the mail. A program designed to help a person relax and gain control of latent psychic abilities.

It's possible to use hypnosis to train people to develop psychic abilities and bring experiences of this nature under conscious control. That's Ryzl's strong conviction and preoccupation. In his native Czechoslovakia, Ryzl had attempted to train about five hundred subjects and claims about fifty were more or less successful. One of them, Pavel Stepanek, who had not previously been involved in any psychic probing, became a willing subject for any researcher who wanted to test his remarkable acquired ability to correctly guess ESP cards.

The Czech secret police were impressed, thinking of the espionage potential. In 1967 Ryzl defected to the United States in order to protect his work.

Ryzl's interest in hypnosis began as a lark during his student days in Prague when he casually hypnotized his sixteen-year-old niece. He asked her to describe what his father was doing in another room and was stunned by her response. He was reading a newspaper, she reported, and correctly described the page headlines.

Years later when Ryzl became professionally interested in ESP, it occurred to him that the highly erratic abilities of psychics could be improved through hypnosis. Hardly an unprecedented view.

The sudden meeting with unusual powers of mind that often occurs when someone is hypnotized was readily evidenced in the mid-18th century by the investigations of Anton Mesmer, generally regarded as a pioneer in the study and practice of hypnosis. In many of his experiments he often found that "mesmerized" people exhibited paranormal behavior. Some hypnotized subjects appeared capable of mentally projecting their consciousness to distant places, accurately describing events taking place. One of his volunteers even demonstrated a talent for clairvoyantly diagnosing disease.

In the 19th century, the relationship between hypnosis and ESP was explored under the auspices of the Society for Psychical Research in London. A society founder, Sir William Barrett, claimed he could induce mental travel in his subjects as had Mesmer and his followers.

More recent psychical research shows that hypnotized subjects score better in ESP tests, though not by a wide margin. Some researchers believe the answer may lie in the fact that in various altered states of consciousness, including the hypnotic state, receptivity to information barred by normal sensory limitations is enhanced.

Ryzl adds two important qualifiers. He says that the person must believe (have confidence) in his or her ability and be in the proper mood. One classic ESP study bears this out. Psychologist Gertrude Schmeidler of New York's City College asked students to guess what ESP card was in a number of opaque envelopes. After the first calculations were in, she separated her subjects into two groups based on whether or not they believed in ESP. It turned out that the believers scored better than what was expected by chance; the disbelievers scored *below* chance. The implication: the disbelievers showed ESP ability in the wrong statistical direction. Their results indicated they might have strongly believed they would do poorly. They failed with such success that their scores were poorer than that expected by chance.

Ryzl adds further to these implications, saying that each of us continually makes use of psychic abilities, only it usually eludes our conscious perception. He says that extensive questioning in looking for answers to problems produces a potential ESP effect. Our subconscious projects the question as an energy form (thought is energy) to a universal information bank. The information, he says, is retrieved and processed through the brain. But if the mind is burdened with a maze of complex imagery and competing stimuli, it's unlikely that the answer will surface to conscious awareness.

The mind, therefore, must be trained to become as blank and receptive as possible at will, expectantly receptive to the answer. Hypnotic induction can be used to intensify the questioning process and facilitate reception of the ESP response. Ryzl says during hypnosis the subject can enter a state of mind which inhibits the intrusion of kaleidoscopic mental imagery and thought currents. At the same time an alert state can be maintained. The hypnotist can help the person focus on a specific task, be receptive to signals which are normally blocked out and learn to discriminate between poor and high quality psychic imagery.

Most people can be hypnotized, but those who tend to be compulsive, hyperactive and find it difficult to relax are usually poor subjects. This is the conclusion based on a study by Stanford University psychologists Ernest and Josephine Hilgard. They compare the state of mind of a person who is easily hypnotized to the experiences of a long-distance runner who, in the course of a race, becomes trancelike, oblivious to extraneous stimuli. A good subject, then, has the capacity to willingly suspend patterns of waking consciousness to become receptive to and accept the reality patterns introduced by the hypnotist.

Ryzl is well aware of how long it can take someone to learn to work with the state of consciousness produced by hypnosis. It's a borderline state of mind somewhere between sleep and waking; maintaining the right balance is essential to the use of latent ESP abilities. With this in mind, he designed a five-part system which injects the essential ingredients of security, guidance and reinforcement. Patience and motivation are vital keys to success.

Ryzl first interviews his student to establish a rapport and bolster his or her confidence. People sometimes begin with fears of failing which, if unchecked, could effectively undermine any progress. Ryzl's discussion aims to neutralize these fears. Stage Two involves hypnosis. He tells the student to fixate on a glittering object while he softly intones relaxation suggestions. When the student is relaxed, he tests for suggestibility by trying to hypnotically inhibit some physical movement. Your arm can't rise, your feet can't move.... This is followed by inducing visual hallucinations until the student's images become steady and vivid—the basic requirements for ESP.

At Stage Three, the ESP work begins. Ryzl might ask the student to tell him what ESP cards are in opaque envelopes. Or to imagine flying around a room to scan for a concealed object. The next stage involves perfecting the reception of these impressions. Ryzl says that once his student gets good at it, the floodgates may open wide, and ESP abilities become more consistent.

This isn't as easy as it sounds. It can take months, one reason why some of his former subjects who were aware of "instant" ESP courses got discouraged by the pace and quit, thinking they were wasting their time. To learn to visualize well takes practice. Correctly interpreting incoming signals is another matter. There can be many sources of error. Here's a summary of some Ryzl has listed. They reveal how difficult it can be to consistently demonstrate ESP:

* The hypnotized student is very suggestible and the hypnotist may influence impressions.
* The student can be influenced by personal wishes and apprehensions.
* Appearing impressions are often hazy. Details can be overlooked. Fragmentary impressions may be incorrectly combined, resulting in a false overall picture.
* If the student is tired, inattentive or doesn't like the experiment, the ESP ability may be lost.
* The student may have a correct (i.e. "psychic") vision but be incapable of accurately expressing it (perhaps in the form of a drawing). The experimenter may misunderstand his or her conclusions.
* The student may incorrectly evaluate time intervals or have difficulty in following impressions in chronological order.
* The experimenter may hurry the subject, forcing hasty evaluation of impressions.

Difficulties may seem insurmountable, but Ryzl says it works for some. He then tries to induce the ability to use what has been learned in conjunction with the student's five basic senses. For example, when the student has psychically located an object, he's instructed to mentally touch it.

The final stage of the program is to help channel the student's abilities into daily life so that hypnosis is no longer necessary. "The hypnotist," Ryzl says, "may help the subject achieve the final objective by giving him posthypnotic suggestions about bringing himself into the proper state of mind."

Does the student indefinitely retain his abilities? Ryzl explains that since ESP is an extremely dynamic faculty, it should be improved and reinforced, or some aspects of it will be lost.

Ryzl's psychical research colleagues are intrigued by his work but not convinced. Psychologists Charles Honorton and Stanley Krippner have surveyed research attempts to replicate Ryzl's technique and have found little to confirm his results. But they also mention that other researchers have not utilized all the features of Ryzl's extensive program—partly because he hasn't adequately specified the scientific criteria necessary for comprehensive testing. Ryzl might have devised a method to test some of his students before they trained to measure how it compared with their performance through various stages of the program. Nevertheless, few would question that his program is a challenging route for potentially developing conscious ESP control.

After brief research stints with Joseph Rhine at the Foundation for Research on the Nature of Man at Durham, North Carolina, and at Silva Mind Control, Ryzl incorporated his basic ESP principles and hypnotic techniques into a home-study program complete with cassette tapes and workbook.

He sees exercises, such as the boat ride and balloon flight, as forms of meditation or self-hypnosis. The label matters little to him because he believes that "trances of mediums, the religious ecstatic state and all forms of meditation are merely variations of self-hypnosis."

There is hardly any feature of hypnosis, he says, which can't be found in our daily waking state. We're continually bombarded by a wide range of messages from the environment. Any practice which ultimately leads to any narrow focusing of attention may be identified as a form of hypnotic state. Ryzl feels that it's important to counterbalance some of the manipulative, hypnoticlike aspects of commercial image making, in particular the influences of all forms of advertising.

Hypnosis, then, is very different from what we have been led to believe, according to Ryzl. It can happen in some form at any time. When someone captures our undivided attention during a lecture, or while we are absorbedly watching television, that's hypnosis. When we have our own undivided attention, we're giving ourselves hypnotic suggestions. Ryzl claims that those who use his program are given the chance to gain greater control over their everyday thoughts as well as develop ESP abilities.

To Ryzl's credit, his instructions do not fan illusions of becoming an instant mental marvel and encourage exploration of other methods of increasing self-awareness.

"Whatever method you use," he instructs, "don't become its slave. The method is for you; it should serve your needs."

He also advises against setting up a rigid schedule for self-development. Practice when you can. If you're tired or emotionally upset, forget it. Try again later. "Don't expect miracles," he says. "ESP doesn't come as a gift. You must persist in trying."

How does this mail-order program compare to actually sitting in a class? For one thing, it's less expensive. Also the tapes can be used whenever desired, and the program followed at a preferred pace.

Shortcomings? A qualified instructor can't check up on you to see if you're doing it right. But individual attention is hardly given in many mind-training classes, especially when there are between 40 and 250 in a large room. Also, some people need to be around others to reinforce and sustain motivation. Those who work better alone, then, would best benefit by a home-study program.

Winsights Into Hyper-Learning

Remember the old cliché, "When I'm with so and so, I can smell the wood burning?" That accurately conveys our first impression of Win Wenger, who describes himself as an educator, researcher, lecturer, author, ideasmith, social theorist, interdisciplinarian, systems theorist and specialist in hyper-learning. Translation: as an educational psychologist with considerable teaching experience, he's completely immersed in developing learning programs aimed to develop and utilize human potential.

"There's a great misconception about what we're capable of achieving," he told us. "There's a tendency to believe that the limits of our intelligence potential are determined at birth. According to this view, it's unrealistic to expect to extend beyond a certain level of excellence. This is a limiting belief, and as such, real only insofar as we resign ourselves to accept it. I believe, however, that each of us can learn to develop and expand our intelligence—continually. But for intelligence to grow, it must be nourished."

How? The vital clues, he says, are in our childhood development. "As children, we gradually assimilate new things in our environment with past experiences, and then accommodate new views. The way we are stimulated to do this is highly important."

Psychologists such as Jean Piaget and Jerome Bruner speak of stages of development which involve acquiring specific skills before maturation can properly continue. In Piaget's system, there are four stages. During the first (from birth to eighteen months), the child is unable to think of an object unless he or she can see it at the same time. This gradually gives way to the ability to use words to describe objects. But until he or she is about seven years old, it's difficult for the child to take another person's point of view into account. From the age of seven to about eleven, the child becomes aware of the relative qualities of objects. Things are bigger, smaller, lighter or darker. But abstract reasoning doesn't emerge until around eleven or twelve.

Piaget's conclusion about the growth process is that a child must have sufficient experience in one stage before proceeding effectively to the next. Otherwise, he or she might be handicapped.

"Now Jerome Bruner at Harvard altered Piaget's four-stage sequence of child development in one important way," Wenger explained. "He reduced it to three stages which more or less correspond in developmental terms, but Bruner maintains that all stages of development remain active throughout adult life. So while heredity is an important consideration in evaluating intelligence, we can see how environmental handicaps can prevent maximal development of our-day-to-day intelligence."

In short, a lack of stimulation from the environment, such as encouragement from parents and game playing, in our youth contributes to a limited use of brain cells. Wenger does some interesting calculating. "We use perhaps 5 percent of our ten billion brain cells," he says, "which are matured beyond the preinfantile condition at which they began. Of those paltry few cells which are developed to any extent, most have only a few hundred, or even a few dozen, circuit connections with other cells. Yet some of these developed brain cells have been found to have up to twenty thousand connections."

The implication: think of what it might mean to develop the potential of our brain circuitry. "Our real development as compared to our potential," Wenger says, "is like a grain of sand compared to a gigantic beach. On the beach of potential, there are plenty of grains of sand to go after."

This is exactly what Wenger has been doing. He's convinced that 99 percent of our experiences are driven into our brain cells below the level of conscious awareness. As children, we were much more open to and aware of this flow. Maturation in a well-focused educational system, however, trains us to become very selective about what information input from the total environment will be allowed to filter into conscious awareness. But what eludes our consciousness, Wenger insists, can be retrieved and actively used.

One example of this retrieval ability comes to us from

Vladimir Raikov, a Russian psychiatrist and master of hypnosis. He claims to have hypnotized people and given them suggestions to act out the roles of famous people from the past. So, for example, when they painted, they did so as a Vincent Van Gogh or a Henri Matisse. Through a schedule of hypnotic reinforcement, their acquired skills became stable, and gradually they developed their own styles. Raikov's explanation? The students, while impersonating these masters, stimulated a great deal of previously dormant brain cells. Their potential, or intelligence reserve, was activated.

Wenger became preoccupied in trying to understand what methods could be devised to get at this extraordinary reserve. "I saw that the old heredity-versus-environment argument was far too simplistic."

While working for a frontiers-of-science organization in Washington, D.C., Wenger became aware of a new system of education called *suggestopedia*, developed by Bulgarian scientist Georgi Lozonov, and began to investigate.

To maximize learning, Lozonov argues, we must rid ourselves of the negative, limiting belief that we can only remember or learn so much. He believes that this negativism is generated and continually reinforced on a societal level. Not realizing the flexible nature of our belief systems, consensus reality is mistakenly seen as absolute, and we hesitate to venture beyond.

In a typical suggestopedia class to teach a foreign language (say French), twelve students sit comfortably in reclining chairs in a loungelike room with subdued lighting for approximately four hours. The teaching process includes presenting students with material in the context of real-life dialogues. Sometimes skits are acted out. Students assume identities other than their own to break down their own inhibitions. So if you're John, you become Jean-Claude for the duration of the forty-five day course. Each day begins with a review of material taught the previous day in the form of dialogues among the students and with the teacher.

The next phase of the suggestopedic procedure requires that the specially trained teacher twice repeat the new material to the students. The first presentation is done in an exact rhythm with varying intonations. This closely resembles the teaching procedure in a regular classroom, only the manner of delivery differs considerably. In the second presentation, the teacher repeats the information against a background of calm, soothing music. The student is instructed to become absorbed with the music and not concentrate on what is being said. At the same time, the student is encouraged to breath rhythmically.

The breathing exercise derives from yoga. The belief is that concentration is difficult if the body is tense or tired and respiration disorganized. Proper breathing, proper attention. Rhythmic breathing, according to yoga precepts, will reduce ego interference and enhance telepathic receptivity. In this relaxed, passive state of mind, more information can be internalized.

With the body relaxed and the alpha brain wave rhythm predominant, Lozonov claims information is absorbed as if the brain were a giant sponge. Memory, he says, is a boundless enterprise. A reverielike state induces the ability to retain the information; interfering inhibitions are swept away.

The early claims from Bulgaria in 1970 were awesome. Students in language training were learning over a hundred words a day. Lozonov once attempted to hit two thousand and was successful. The amount of learning, he argues, is largely a matter of what amount of information is expected to be learned and retained. However, the norm seems to be about eighty to one hundred words a day.

The idea of rapid or hyper-learning generally has been viewed as a mixed blessing by educators. Speed or immersion courses do produce retention, but only for a short period of time. In fact, the general rule has been that the more quickly a person learns, the more quickly information is forgotten. The rationale became: well, it's not a total waste; the next time around with the same information, more will be retained.

The amazing feature of Lozonov's system is that, quite to the contrary, students recall more and more of the information directed at them each day. Gradually, retention of all information comes close to 95 percent over several years. The term for this is *negative forgetting*.

"The real key to Lozonov's methods," Wenger explained, "is the altered state of consciousness induced by relaxation, rhythmic breathing and music. The semi-trance state, of course, occurs quite spontaneously from time to time, and I suspect many of the detailed minutiae or memory vignettes we retain of our past experiences are strongly absorbed during these times and remembered. In effect, what Lozonov is doing is attempting to sustain this mental state for long periods of time."

Wenger points out that this basic learning principle is quite natural during childhood. "The preverbal, spontaneously learning child is free to vary his levels of consciousness. You know the way children seem to be totally absorbed in some activity and fail to pay attention to a parent or teacher. Learning is going on while they are in this trancelike state. But as the child progresses through the conventional educational system, he or she is increasingly obliged to attend to information in a dominant waking state of consciousness and, in the process, neglects the rest of his or her brain."

Here's Wenger's understanding of the key element involved: different areas of the brain are the primary recipients of information at different levels of consciousness. Get the same information into different areas of the brain, and there will be stronger learning. This is why Lozonov has his instructors repeat information, and why the induced state of relaxation combined with rhythmic breathing and music reinforces what has already been pounded in.

"Conventional recall," Wenger continued, "appears to be governed by what gets sorted and cross-indexed by the part or parts of the brain receiving information and is then transmitted to the rest of the brain for long-term storage at accessible levels. Transmission from the part of the brain getting the information appears to be essentially one-way and a portion of that information is lost. But if several different parts of the brain receive the same initial information, their retransmissions will not be one-way but to each other. Information is gained rather than lost. What one part of the brain misses, the other parts receive, relay and retain."

"But how does this explain negative forgetting?" we asked.

"Putting information into the brain from as many levels of consciousness as possible establishes very durable recall patterns. A certain amount of integration takes place making the information more readily accessible."

Wenger is now interested in restructuring the Lozonov method to suit basic everyday learning needs. "One problem with the valid Lozonov method, despite its obvious improvements over what passes as education in the schools today, is that it requires a carefully trained instructor who's capable of delivering the correct speech rhythms, and who also has to be authoritative enough to render the students almost childlike for greater receptivity."

Another problem is politics—how to get the original Lozonov system into the schools. And last, but definitely not least, Wenger is aware of the brainwashing potential of the system. "It can actually be seen as a prototype system for total suggestion, a doorway to a brave new world where information of a desired kind is effectively pumped into the brain."

His aim, therefore, has been to use the whole-brain learning aspects of Lozonov's methods and modify them so that any person working alone or with others can begin to learn better, regardless of the institutional teaching techniques to which they have been or are exposed.

The result: a system of learning called "Psychegenics," which provides a wide variety of techniques and which can be creatively extended by the student.

Psychegenics is more than just a twenty-hour workshop in the development of human potential. Presently given in the Washington, D.C., area, it's a quickly expanding system based on "Winsights" and practical applications of the newest concepts in learning theory.

While participating in a basic psychegenic workshop is valuable, says Wenger, the exercises can be beneficially practiced in the comfort of your own home. That's because at least three-quarters of the workshop training involves students training each other. So all you really need is a partner. Once the basic instructions are understood and practiced, they can be condensed to suit personal needs and be taught to others.

"I'm not interested in holding back or hoarding knowledge," Wenger emphasized. "There's no reason why people shouldn't transmit the basic psychegenic techniques to others. The purpose is to further learning."

Wenger is now condensing key sections of the basic course into learning packages, available for 35 cents, which he encourages to be reproduced in any manner (tape, photocopy, etc.), providing that the integrity of the exercises is maintained, and that Psychegenics is mentioned as the copyright holder.

Noise-Removal Breathing as a Way of Life

The psychegenics manual we received in the mail was chock full of easy-to-follow techniques.* The first phase of instructions deals with relaxation, an essential preliminary to any form of self-development. The body must first be cleared of "noise," as Wenger puts it, to clear away stresses and anxieties which obstruct the ability to be receptive and clearheaded. Once we're relaxed, the mind can be put to good use.

All the exercises can be practiced with another person. It's not absolutely essential—you can tape them and be guided by your own instructions—but Wenger says working with someone provides valuable feedback and motivation: he refers to this interaction as a coprompter system.

The basic exercise we went through designed to get rid of "noise" was called "Breathing as a Way of Life." Here's the essence of it, which Wenger says prepares you for stronger learning experiences:

Read the following instructions to your partner in a slow and soothing voice:

1. Stretch.
2. Take a good deep stretch, all through your body.
3. Slide down into the afterglow of that stretch into a relaxed position. Hold that afterglow feeling.
4. Holding that afterglow feeling, reflect back on how it feels to be relaxed, as if you were in bed at night on the edges of sleep (though this time you stay awake and don't miss the fun). If you are already trained in some form of meditation, reflect back on one of your best experiences of meditation and on how that felt. If you are religious, reflect back on how it feels to listen in prayer.
5. Whichever experience you reflect back on, remember it more and more completely. Remember more and more clearly what it feels like, what elements in the

---

* Due to the extensive number of exercises in psychegenics and their interchangeable nature, in this chapter we present what we feel is a representative sample of the rationale of the entire program. We've also edited the exercises when necessary.

experience go along with that feeling. (Pause fifteen seconds.)

6. What things were there for you in that experience, which went along with the feeling you remember from that experience? (Pause fifteen seconds.)

7. Remembering an experience recreates the mental and physical bases of that experience, and this is why you are already virtually back in the quality of this experience you are remembering, this experience you are remembering more about, more and more clearly. (Pause fifteen to thirty seconds.)

8. While remembering the feeling and quality of this experience, now slowly breathe in deeply and breathe out deeply, three to five times, then just let your muscles go a little more, and relax more deeply. (Allow whatever time is needed, around forty to sixty seconds.)

9. Become more aware of what you are feeling and experiencing within you, and become more aware of your surroundings. It's surprising how much of a mental picture you can build up of your surroundings just from what you can hear.

10. Taking about six seconds to do so, let's breathe in slowly and very deeply.

11. Let's exhale as slowly and very deeply; with your lungs empty try to blow out an imaginary candle a foot in front of your face. That's how deeply you should exhale.

12. Let's go on inhaling and exhaling as deeply as you can, very slowly, six seconds or longer each way.

13. Go on inhaling and exhaling, deeply, slowly. By doing so, you are already sending strong, clear signals to the autonomic nervous system which runs your body and the automatic, unconscious processes of your body. By this inhaling and exhaling, deeply, slowly, you are beginning to change what's going on in your body, in ways similar to what you are about to picture in your imagination. The things I'm going to ask you to picture in your imagination will send still stronger, clearer signals through your body and makes these effects stronger. Go on inhaling and exhaling deeply, slowly.

14. In inhaling, let's help the process along by imagining you have a nose in your feet. Imagine having a nostril in the bottom of each foot, between mid-arch and the sole of each foot.

15. Imagine as you breathe in deeply that you are pulling in air up through your feet.

16. Feel as if each breath comes in through your feet, pulling up through the spaces and interstices of your legs and body. Breathe in against the pull of your breath having to work through your tissues and cells. Feel each breath coming up through your normal nose or your mouth.

17. Feel as if each breath coming in through your feet and pulling up through your legs and body is swirling up through the tensions, toxins, tiredness and other noise that has been cluttering the tissues and cells of that part of your body. Feel your breath swirling up through and carrying away all that unwanted stuff. Feel your exhaled breath carrying that noise out of your body, carrying away anything that doesn't belong.

18. Feel your exhaled breath to be laden with that stuff you are pulling up and carrying out of your system. Especially that extra warmth and richness is felt near the end of your exhaled breath, so really push that noise out of your system by exhaling very deeply.

19. Once such noise is out of your body and into the light and air, it just becomes good clean life energy which you or anyone else can later tap and put to good use. Like any other form of pollution, those tensions, toxins, tirednesses and other forms of noise in your system were just energy in the wrong form in the wrong place. As you pull noise up from your body and push it out with your exhaled breathing, you are not only cleaning up your system but doing a good thing by creating a lot of new life energy.

20. You may begin to feel lighter as your burdens of whatever didn't belong are lifted up and away by your breathing. Continue this noise-removal breathing, deeply and slowly.

21. When you get this noise-removal breathing going at its most powerful, you will feel more than just the extra heat and richness of your exhaled breath. You will begin feeling extra heat in your throat and upper chest from all that is concentrated in your breath near the end of each exhalation.

22. Keep noise-removal breathing very deeply, pulling noise up and loose with your breath, and especially

23. breathe out very deeply, and sooner or later your noise-removal process will get into really high gear.

23. Experimentally, noise-removal breathe in through different parts of your body. Feel a real pull as your breath comes in through those different areas, swirling up and carrying away the noise you are pushing out with your exhaled warm rich breath. (Encourage for one to two minutes.)

24. Now that you've established this experience of noise-removal breathing, you can turn this process on at any time, in any level of consciousness.

25. To become extraordinarily more productive, do this noise-removal breathing for ten to fifteen minutes before any major task or before any creative work, then go straight from this breathing meditation into the work itself. Each time you do your work this way, it gets better. If you ever run into problems or difficulties, use your breath to draw up and away impatience, frustration or disappointment aroused by that snag which could have stood in the way of clear, effective solution and response to that situation.

Images for Deepening Relaxation

Psychegenics stresses that the ability to remember a pleasant experience can be used to induce deep relaxation. "Once a profoundly deep meditative state has been created by any means whatever," Wenger said confidently, "you will be able to remember how to return to that state with increasing ease. The importance of getting into this state has been consistently observed in just about every discipline teaching some form of meditation."

The following are psychegenic images for activating deep relaxation. Actually, they're only examples of scenarios anyone can invent and use in time of need. Begin by having a coprompter read them to you or simply put them on tape and listen:

1. Spaghetti

I am thinking of my arms and legs and body as

resembling dry sticks of spaghetti. I'm cooking the spaghetti in water and it's beginning to soften…soften….The spaghetti is becoming limp….The spaghetti is completely limp and relaxed; now my arms and legs and body are utterly limp strands of spaghetti just lying there….I put on my favorite sauce to cover the spaghetti….

2. Snowflake

Feeling very light, I am a soft, feathery snowflake drifting very high among the clouds; the wind is carrying me higher and higher and further in an immense world among the clouds and I feel lighter and freer and more at peace as the wind carries me higher and higher among the sky clouds.

3. Sun Glitter

I feel myself, my awareness, like the glitter of sunlight on a pond riffled by breezes, consciousness dancing around….Now the pond's surface is stilling, my sungleam consciousness steadier, more coherent, my sungleam consciousness becomes brighter, more intense, as the pond's surface becomes mirror-smooth….

Get the idea? Any fantasy will do as long as it's a scenario which can be remembered for its pleasant experiences, and which you wouldn't mind turning on to feel more relaxed.

The Circulation Flush

"The brain is physical," Wenger reminded, "so it can be altered through physical processes."

One method for doing so, he believes, is to improve the brain's circulation system. The carotid arteries provide the brain with oxygenated blood. Whenever there is an increase in carbon dioxide in the bloodstream, the carotid valves open wider to let more blood flow past. The valves, he's convinced, can be trained to be permanently opened wide, allowing more blood through to the brain.

The training technique is called "masking." You rebreathe your own breath from a bag (medium-size grocery bag) for a half minute every one-half hour and continue this practice for about two to three weeks. Do it during a lazy vacation, he suggests. And have someone with you at all times. For further safety, insert a small tube or straw through a hole in the bag.

Another psychegenic technique is called the "circulation flush," a process of producing strong flushes of circulation in any part of the body. These flushes can then be applied to the brain. Wenger says that information stimuli and blood circulation are the two principal factors controlling the extent to which the brain is able to develop and function. Past the age of thirty, the average person loses more than one hundred thousand brain cells per day due to the diminishing power of the cerebral circulatory system, a contributing factor to the reduction of learning potential. Producing this flush, according to the psychegenic system, drastically reduces this process, stimulating previously underdeveloped brain cells to develop and function.

Here is one technique we tried and a way to reinforce it:

Remembering a Circumstance with Feelings Attached to It.

1. First, you must be relaxed.
2. Remember clearly when you previously experienced a flush of increasing circulation to some part of the body, with capillaries opening wider—either that prickly tingle you've experienced with returning feeling and circulation to a numbed limb or that warmth, even heat, you've experienced with a very cold hand being returned to normal temperature.

Or

1. Create a new experience of tingling such as holding one hand in cold water for a few minutes and capture the feelings you have as it warms up. (Remember you can create any scenario you want that will help.)
2. Move the hand to various parts of the body, especially to the head.
3. Practice daily to become able to create the flush

experience instantly, at will.

4. Attempt to create the flush experience instantly without the in-between steps.

To Heighten the Circulation Flush

A tape could be set up in the following way or another person (coprompter) could present the material while you relax:

I've become aware of a nice tingling sensation in my writing hand. It's very warm and comfortable. This tingling is becoming more definite and almost tangible, very pleasant and very deep, like an inner massage .... It's a good feeling, this tingling which results from capillaries opening up, my enhanced circulation carrying more and more oxygen, food energy, nutrition and purification to the tissues of my hand, to the very cells themselves, refreshening, restoring, reviving, reenergizing, rejuvenating these cells and tissues in my hand as it tingles pleasantly....

I feel the tingling more and more definitely, more strongly now .... I perceive a four-inch ball of bright, tingling energy centered in my hand....

I wonder how my other hand would feel if it were experiencing this tingling energy .... The more I think of it, the more it seems my other hand can feel it, too .... I find the tingling energy to have diminished in my writing hand but getting quite definite now in my other hand....I discover the bright ball of tingly energy has also been moving over to my other hand .... I feel that energy more and more strongly in my other hand until it is far stronger than I felt it in my writing hand; the pass made the energy far stronger....

Now as I pass the bright warm tingle back to my writing hand, that tingle is even more definite than it was in my other hand .... Building the flush and building experience with the flush, I can pass the tingle back and forth between my hands, each pass making that feeling more definite and tangible.

Attempts to Improve Learning

The following two exercises involve more direct attempts to improve learning ability. The aim, Wenger asserts, is to free the mind, allowing it to roam as freely as possible. Practicing the preceding exercises and becoming accustomed to doing them in a flash, he says, will serve to prepare you for creative and exciting learning experiences.

Predict, Project, Recognize

Whenever you face a new task which seems difficult because of its novelty, or whenever you must study material which is either difficult or very unfamiliar to you:

1. Enter a state of deep relaxation by whatever preferred method. Use noise-removal breathing to get rid of interfering feelings, tensions or anxieties. Then mull over what you already know about the subject.
2. Return to beta (normal waking consciousness) and jot down some of the things you know. Then skim the material and note trivia, topic headlines, descriptions of illustrations used, whatever else catches your eye. Then return to deep relaxation, and mull over both these trivia and what you had jotted down before.
3. In deep relaxation, tell yourself the precise task you are about to undertake or the subject of the material you are about to study. Then in your imagination write a paper or give a talk on that subject. Picture the act of presenting that subject or task—then do noise-removal breathing until you have a very clear experience of writing a paper or giving a talk on that topic. Then reminisce on what you've done, locating key points or ideas and getting them organized.
4. Return to beta and attack the task or study the material, checking to see where it agrees with your imagined presentation and where it differs. You will find yourself recognizing clearly most of what you are studying, without it being difficult or unfamiliar at all—in fact, your presentation may even, sometimes, prove superior to that of the author.

Psychegenic Problem Solving

Work this exercise with a partner. Choose any problem you want to work on: job-related, domestic, intellectual, etc. Then relax, and, with your partner, take a moment to

visualize yourself happy with the result of the exercise.
Your partner guides you this way:

1. Let's picture now what it's like to walk through a
   beautiful woods in early summer.
2. Look around you and see tall shade trees. Deep mossy
   forest floor. A few beautiful wild flowers here and there.
   Notice different kinds of trees. Notice how the pattern of
   bark on each tree is different.
3. Notice the breeze sighing and rustling through the
   canopy of leaves overhead. Notice how good the air feels.
   Perhaps you can hear birds singing in the distance.
   Between branches overhead you can catch glimpses of
   deep blue sky with an occasional small white cloud
   moving through it.
4. In a while, in walking through this woods, you will come
   to a space among the trees, a small clearing, a kind of
   natural cathedral of trees. There you will find displayed
   for you the somewhat surprising solution to your
   problem—either directly or symbolically displayed. But
   for now we will walk through this woods for sheer
   pleasure, for its beauty. When you come upon the natural
   forest cathedral it will happen of its own accord, giving
   your inner mind the opportunity to surprise you with
   what it comes up with. Let's walk through this beautiful
   woods now for pleasure.
5. Feel the deep, cool, soft moss carpeting the forest floor.
   Do you hear the sound of a brook anywhere?
6. Find that you can answer me in this state of deep
   relaxation, that the deliberate act of answering me will
   deepen your state of deep relaxation . . . that describing
   what you are experiencing will make the experiences
   come clearer, in better detail. The more you can tell me,
   the more will happen. Moving deeper, tell me what you
   are experiencing.

Fish more details from your partner by such questions as:

> * What are you hearing now?
> * What are you seeing now in front of you?
> * Can you describe colors in what you are looking
>   at?
> * What do you see to your left?

* What do you see to your right?
* What's overhead?
* Describe the surface you are on.
* What's behind you?
* In what ways is this experience changing as you
  look at it?

The structure and content of psychegenics gives the impression that a very busy mind has diligently combed through a vast cross section of relaxation, visualization techniques and research on the human brain. It's an ongoing creative system with no end in sight. "It's always improving, never static," Wenger proudly announced. "We're not interested in smugly resting on the laurels of past successes. Concepts in learning must always progress, and those who choose to participate in and experience our system have the opportunity to build on their own experiences and needs."

TWO

From Ego to Being

Trips to the Garden

A decade ago, most Westerners were mystified by the swami who sat cross-legged meditating in front of his Himalayan cave. (Does a Kalahari Bushman know what a polar bear is?) Now we're more sophisticated. Meditation has become a byword of the seventies. Now we can better understand that the swami has taken a trip to a mental oasis where everything is peaceful, serene and where he won't be assaulted by noise, stress and a tyrannizing ego which enslaves us to an endless cycle of rarely satisfying materialistic pursuits.

Many still wonder whether the swami's been given a phoney ticket. No, he would say, he's traveling to a huge universal garden of life where trees, flowers, animals, rocks, minerals and all of humanity are units of a flowing life force called Being. The trip from Point Ego to Being can be a long one. His goal is to discover the kernel of life within him or the nature of his authentic Self. Only then will he gain entrance to the garden of enlightenment. That's why he's devoted his life to the trip. Anything less is a weekend vacation.

He would probably politely suggest that many of us would find it difficult to accept the same ticket, because having grown roots at Point Ego, it is difficult for us to believe this garden exists.

Well, we're not as grounded as he may think. We have been more willing to listen to descriptions about the garden lately. The problem is, he's not the only one traveling. Others who believe in the reality of the garden might say that he's only traveling second or third class. Almost everyone claims to be selling first-class tickets and the best routes.

Do all roads lead to the same place? Or are some too cluttered with detours?

Flowing and Growing

Wingate Paine was once a world-famous fashion photographer. Now he doesn't even own a camera. He threw that and his Connecticut blue-blood past away to become a convert to the spiritual growth movement.

Over dinner he told us why. "I still scratch my head at times wondering how it happened. I think I simply came to a point in my life when I realized that, despite the good times, something vital was missing."

Wingate is sixty-one but doesn't look it. Maybe forty-five, you would say if you met him. He attributes his good health to a change in lifestyle.

"One important event spurred me on my way," he continued. "One day I found myself in an antique shop operated by a disciple of Swami Nityananda. He had spent years in India and returned to New York himself a swami. Something clicked between me and this rather unattractive, fat, bald-headed man from Brooklyn who called himself Rudrananda (Rudi). I soon was meditating with him on a regular basis and finding myself more and more detached from worldly possessions and the old ways."

Rudrananda once wrote: "We are all detached, like the seed of an onion, in layer upon layer of tensions which separate us from the flow of higher creative energy and binds us to the earth. The purpose of spiritual work is to take in enough nourishment to free us from our tensions and consciously reunite our energy with the flow of higher creative energy from which we came." This is Wingate's philosophy in a nutshell.

Rudi recently died in a plane crash. His death was philosophically received as a sign to Wingate and Rudi's other disciples that you can't live in the shadow of a master forever. You have to go it alone to improve yourself. Sometimes a master can make it seem impossible for you to reach his level. Here was the opportunity to confront this challenge.

Now Wingate continues the "work" as director of a Growth Center in New York. "The center, as I see it," he explained, "is really a place for anyone who wants to continually 'till the soul.' We have morning meditations where we work at energizing the life force within us, and once a month I give the Growth Course, which reflects more or less where I'm at in my own development. It's a weekend workshop in growing consciousness and is designed to promote and strongly reinforce the idea that we're living in a New Age, one in which more and more people are learning about and wanting to tap a higher state of consciousness. Let's face it, the Age of Technology has had its chance and has failed. It has left us a legacy of world-wide crises and alienation. The new direction will be inward, into the magnificent dimensions of consciousness, an inner life that we can reclaim and make whole again. What I try to do is provide some of the tools for growth."

Would we attend his next Growth Course, he asked.

A tiny greenhouse is nestled on the roof of an East 39th Street building. The penthouse, formerly Wingate's photography studio, leads up to it. A plant-filled split-level suite with a tree-lined terrace, it has a calm atmosphere conducive to meditation. Scattered Eastern spiritual drawings and the huge patch of sky visible through the full-length window upstairs where classes are held make it a center of calm in the hub of Manhattan.

Wingate stood shuffling through his notes at the podium and smiled when he saw us arrive. When the thirty people were finally seated, he began in a warm but calculated manner. "The aim of the course is to till the soul, to cultivate it and to become friends with it. Instead of fighting life or just giving up on problems, we're going to learn how to flow and grow with it. Flowing and growing. I kind of like the sound of that. Don't you?"

Wingate believes that a better world is nothing but a dream without better people to live in it. Working on the Self through meditation is, he says, a prerequisite for any kind of widespread social change." A definition of a New-Age man and woman," he offered, "is that they are people who believe that by controlling the kind of thoughts they have, they can do a great deal to determine the kind of

THE GROWTH CENTER

Nicholas Regush

has successfully completed the Advanced Growth Course
in New Age Gardening Techniques and is hereby certified a

TILLER OF THE SOUL

with all the rights and responsibilities this entails.

February 23, 1975
New York, N.Y.

Director

world they live in. They think less in terms of good and bad
and more in terms of every experience serving their growth.
They don't dwell on the past as much or worry about the
future. They're more in the here and now."

Questions pop up. Wingate encourages them.

Isn't it untimely to conceive of the priority of personal
growth in the midst of widespread human despair? "I don't
have the answers," he concedes. "While it's important to
keep this issue in mind, this problem can best be
approached individually from the standpoint of the inner
self. We have to learn to talk to this essence and feed it with
the special energy foods it needs for growth."

This brings up how we should see ourselves in the total
scheme of things. "Look at it this way," he suggested.
"Look at your ego as representing your personality. If we're
too caught up with it, it can limit our awareness of being
intimately connected to other things in the universe. Most
of us are trapped by thinking that all we are is a mixture of
flesh and blood. There is another 'ego' with a capital 'E,'
which you might think of as an expression of a universal
life-force or all-pervading spirit, and then, finally, 'EGO,'
which is the universal essence itself.

"This EGO, or being gives birth to individual egos,

sustains them and draws them back into itself. So if we want to experience our Self as united with being, the goal is to seek enlightenment through meditation. Looking at it this way: your feeling of being separate is really an illusion and a barrier to personal growth.

"Therefore, when a person asks whether he's the master of his fate or has free will, the question comes up about which 'I' he is talking about. Is it the I of our ego, or a force far greater? To be free and enlightened, we have to consider the need to break away from the ego and aspire to a state of cosmic consciousness."

This brought up the issue of reincarnation. It's a generally accepted Hindu view that when the physical body dies, the spirit or psychic component of the person survives and later becomes associated with another physical body. Through each incarnation, this spirit is seen as taking care of its "karma," or the sum total of all behavior in past lives, which has to be worked on and overcome in the new incarnation. What you do in this life accounts for what you'll have to experience in the next, and so on. Wingate suggests that karma and ego are aspects of the same life process. To have karma would be the same thing as having an ego. By ridding oneself of ego, the law of retribution could be bypassed as a person moves toward a state of enlightenment. Each person then adds to his growth as all his actions become motivated to produce positive results.

The basic idea of the New-Age fits right into this. It's a revolutionary period in human history and a preparation for the continuing evolution of a collective consciousness to which each growing person contributes. It's a steady movement toward an awareness of a universal Being based on the power of positive action and love. In sum, it's an expression of body consciously invested with spirit on a universal scale.

You can't just wish yourself to the garden; you have to work at it. First some basics. "Most of us don't know how to breathe correctly," Wingate chided. "In the tradition of Yoga, life is in the breath. A life-force called *prana* is an ocean we all swim in. We need nourishment from this ocean of energy to charge ourselves like batteries. Improper breathing prevents this."

Judging from the staccatolike breathing in the room, we were all disasters. "No, not like that," he said. "Begin

Meditation room at the Growth Center in New York. *(Courtesy, Wingate Paine)*

breathing slowly. Draw the air into your solar plexus. Slowly, slowly, don't rush, don't strain your lungs. Be aware of its rise and fall. Belly breathe. Don't worry, nothing will happen to you. This is a basic meditation. You'll need it to do other things, so practice."

Many breaths later, we moved on to step two. "Forget about the past, forget about the future, I want you to experience the here and now." Each person was given a flower. "Look at it and don't analyze it," Wingate instructed. "Don't compare it with other flowers. Feel yourself becoming at one with it. It's a beautiful flower and you want to touch all of it with your entire mind and body."

Simple? Hardly. Concentrating on anything is difficult if you haven't practiced. Your nose may twitch, you might get a cramp in your leg or the bill you forgot to pay may suddenly wipe out the flower. "When you practice this at home, use any object. When you're washing the dishes, blend with the act itself, when you're making love, don't worry about the time. Concentrate. Enjoy."

It was time for the "growth book." To practice meditation and sustain interest, people need to make a commitment to it; otherwise the effort will go the way of the hula hoop. While some people keep diaries or journals recording events, these aren't personal progress books. "You can begin to chart your spiritual growth today," said Wingate. Everyone received a brown loose-leaf binder, pencil and written instructions. Each book had a number, and, if it was ever lost, the Growth Center would pay a modest reward to whomever returned it.

"I want to get you committed," he continued. "Whenever you meditate, write up your experiences. If something pops up in your mind, especially something that's bothering you, you may learn from the experience. This is active meditation. You're to use your time to clear your egos of all the confusions and debris which prevent you from seeing more of the world around you."

The book could be structured into projects. If you want to stop smoking, he said, a dated record can be kept of the steady progress and flashes of insight you get about this problem while meditating.

But wouldn't this commitment interfere with meditation, asked a young woman.

"Not at all," Wingate insisted. "It shouldn't take you long to get your eyes closed and your body relaxed again. You'll develop a rhythm in doing this, and before long it'll be second nature. The book will take on a life of its own, and you'll have a record of your inner life."

Wingate didn't feel meditation should tyrannize a person. "Flow with it," he said. "Use it for a purpose."

Our growth books were started. We knew more about our breathing and had experienced the reality of a flower. The final step was an introduction to Kundalini Yoga, often called the yoga of Being-Energy. Ancient Indian and Tibetan books say that our nervous system is a hierarchical structure; energy and consciousness are one, and there are seven major energy centers, called *chakras*, located in a channel of the human body, which begins in the interior of the spinal column. Each chakra represents a consciousness potential. In ascending order, they're described as located at the base of the spine, at the genitals, below the solar plexus, in the heart region, in the throat below the larynx, between the eyebrows and at the crown of the head.

At the very base of the spine is an energy force described as a white coiled serpent called Kundalini which can slowly rise to each succeeding chakra. To get it to move upward requires discipline, certain physical exercises (a variety of yoga postures), meditation and proper breathing.

If the coiled Being-Energy remains inactive, the books say, the energy will lie dormant. The person will tend to be materialistic or egocentric, and thus totally oblivious to his or her inner nature and spiritual potential. Release of this energy propels a person to greater self-realization.

If Kundalini has moved upward to the level of the second chakra and remains there, a person will experience a great surge of sexual energy and will have to learn to conquer it; at the third chakra, one must deal with power needs and even violence; at the fourth, a change begins to take place with love and compassion for others becoming more central to the personality; the fifth represents the beginnings of spiritual fulfillment; the sixth, a degree of mystical illumination and, finally, at the seventh, enlightenment.

To most Western psychologists this entire schema is an unsubstantiated pipe dream. Demanding proof that Kundalini exists, they argue that people are confusing metaphor with scientific fact. They say the term "energy" is a much-abused and little understood term bantered around by meditators and "New-Agers."

Gopi Krishna, a yogi adept and authority on Kundalini, replies that there is sufficient literature and personal testimony to generate scientific interest to study it. He believes our bodies are infused with prana which directly fuels the reproductive system. This system serves a sexual function but can also stimulate the evolution of consciousness. The goal is to get the evolutionary part of the system working properly so that when prana streams into the body, it can be propelled upward through the chakras, leading to an explosion in consciousness as energy floods into the brain.

Wingate wasn't promising the explosion. He was offering some basic steps to begin working on the prana and taste what it was like working with a teacher.

"What does a teacher have to do with activating Kundalini?" someone asked.

"Throughout the exercises I want you to focus attention on me," he continued. "I'll attempt to consciously send some of my prana to each of you, one at a time. It may help you to get untracked a little." It's believed that someone who has reached enlightenment can help awaken the Being-Energy of others by simply touching them. Wingate wasn't "there" yet but says that in learning to draw prana from the atmosphere through correct rhythmic breathing, it is possible to transmit vitality to others.

It wasn't easy. The exercise required careful coordination of breath and visualization. But Kundalini's movement remained intangible for both of us. Maybe it had moved, maybe not. Wingate directed his attention to us and concentrated on sending his prana. Returning the concentration seemed to activate our tear ducts. Still, there was a definite feeling of intensity, some sort of magnetic interchange.

Here's the exercise: Step one is to begin breathing rhythmically. The idea is to draw your breath (prana) to the heart chakra (you have to visualize it in the heart region). Hold it there for about ten seconds, slowly releasing a small amount of breath. Step two is to repeat the first exercise but to continue to draw breath from the heart region down to the solar plexus. This can be repeated any number of times. Should an energy sensation or series of vibrations be felt either in that area or around the genitals (the next lowest chakra), then focus attention on the base of the spine. Rocking slowly from side to side on the base of the spine, you attempt to release the tension there, and Kundalini may suddenly activate.

Some people claim to eventually experience a vibrating feeling and a rush of energy as the serpent begins to uncoil. Another result can be a quick snapping of the neck as the energy reaches the throat chakra. If and when this occurs, Wingate says no attempt should be made to inhibit its movement. Flow with it.

Had he considered the widespread criticism of many yogis that Kundalini wasn't for everyone? That its practice should be restricted to the holistic yogic context of body purification and spiritual aims? That it was dangerous, especially for those who might have "blocks" in some chakras which would obstruct the energy flow up the spine? These people, critics say, may find themselves with a surplus of energy at one of the chakras and be incapable of dealing with the psychological ramifications. Too much at the solar plexus, a great hunger for power; at the genitals, sexual preoccupation, and so on.

"Sure there's some danger," he said. "There's also some danger in crossing a New York street. There are potential risks involved in any attempt at personal growth, something which should be understood by anyone desiring to directly explore and experience New-Age principles. A lot of information we're working with cannot as yet be verified scientifically pro or con. So if we want to personally test it out by following certain ancient systems for inner growth and expansion, we may open ourselves to potential problems. But I've only given you a brief introduction, a taste. None of this will be of value to you if it's not seen as only one part of a total life commitment to heighten your consciousness.

"This is where a good teacher comes in. He can watch your development closely and help you grow more quickly. His own example can be followed and tested. But if his teaching doesn't feel right to you, then you shouldn't follow. It's your choice, no one else's."

For those who wanted to do further Kundalini work with Wingate, meditation sessions were offered daily at the Growth Center.

The TM Caravan*

Transcendental Meditation (TM) has sold more seats than any other caravan to the garden of enlightenment. Books, records, television ads, celebrities like Merv Griffin, Joe Namath and some politicians—all have contributed to its promotion and the departure of about two million. The fee: $150 for single adults. If you have a student card, there's a discount.

At the very first meeting of my charter group, the TM lecturer made some promises. Very early in the trip, body stress would reduce significantly; metabolic rate would decrease, mental activity would be refined and subtle states of thought experienced. All that was required was to learn the proper technique of simply sitting with eyes closed for fifteen to twenty minutes each day before morning and evening meals, mentally repeating a sound, or *mantra*, which had been specifically chosen for each of us.

TM is a seven-step system, involving two free introductory meetings, the actual initiation and then follow-up group discussions, so the lecturer had been careful to withhold the specific meditation procedure. Instead he had enticed us with the potential benefits by referring to several analogies designed to convey the aims involved.

"The mind can be compared to an ocean," he said, drawing a diagram on the board. In this schema, a wavy line at the top represents the conscious mind; circles of decreasing sizes descend in a column to a base line. This is the source of thought. During meditation, attention withdraws from the active surface level of the mind to the very source of thought where our thoughts originate and mental activity decreases. With each "dive" while meditating, the mind emerges energized by its contact with pure

* This is June Regush's TM experience

Being, leading to clarity of mind, stamina, greater productivity and enjoyment of life. Obviously it isn't that simple. Being is at the very end of the trip, and no one will get there without refueling.

Therefore, the dyed-cloth analogy: each "dive" is compared to a dyeing process. A cloth dipped into a vat of yellow dye and placed on a line to dry is soon faded by the combined action of sun and air. After repeated dippings, it is permanently yellow. To get to Being requires repeated meditation. When the dye becomes permanent, we're there.

"It's all so simple, so effortless, so beneficial, everyone must learn to do it," the lecturer enthused with a glowing smile.

The caravan leader is Maharishi Mahesh Yogi. It is claimed he spent his spiritual apprenticeship in the Himalayas studying the *Vedas* (Hindu sacred writings) and meditating with Swami Brahmananda (or Guru Dev, meaning "divine teacher"). In the mid-1950s, as a monk aiming to spread the teachings of his guru, Maharishi visited a temple in southern India, where a man approached him.

Would he impart some of the wisdom of the Himalayas to others? No he wouldn't. The man reportedly persisted, eventually persuading Maharishi to give a series of lectures. They were so successful that more were arranged, bringing his teaching to many parts of India. And at a 1958 gathering in Madras for his late guru's birthday, he announced that the spiritual regeneration of all mankind was under way, an announcement so well received that the Spiritual Regeneration Movement (SRM) was founded.

Then came the slow impact on the great American frontier. It started with his arrival from Hawaii to the United States mainland in 1959. An SRM base was established in Los Angeles, but Maharishi had to be patient; the appearance of yet another guru on the American scene didn't impress too many people. Only after he had attracted the attention of the Beatles and other celebrities did the public begin to take notice. The proof of this was the standing-room-only flower-power rally at Madison Square Garden's Felt Forum in New York in 1967 and his appearances on major television network shows. But soon the Beatles came to see him as a superstar mired in a growing "establishment," so they dropped him, leaving the Beach Boys to tour the continent with him.

Destiny, however, neglected Maharishi until the early seventies, when the time was ripe to capitalize on the growing public interest in meditation and inaugurate the World Plan. His present dream is to improve society by having one in every hundred citizens practicing TM daily. To reach this goal requires one TM teacher per thousand population. While still far from his goal of the necessary 3.6 million teachers, there are already close to ten thousand and counting—a leap from only one in 1965, and enough to make any corporate president tremble at the inadequacy of his own company's growth rate.

How can you talk about paradise if you haven't been there? Or to quote one TM advocate: how can you describe a strawberry if you haven't eaten one? So there I was at the doorstep of the TM terminal in Montreal ready to be initiated and receive a mantra. I arrived armed with the required fee, plus six fresh flowers, three sweet fruits and a new white handkerchief to be used in the initiation ceremony.

I was immediately directed to an oblong room furnished with about forty wooden chairs. An elderly woman busily arranging papers and placing ceremonial flowers in baskets handed me a form to fill out and notified my appointed instructor, Brenda, of my arrival.

Questions on the form included: Have you ever used any form of meditation or other program for self-development? What is your present state of health? Do you sleep well? What books have you read about meditation? What courses have you taken? What is your present state of mind? And, at the bottom of the questionnaire, an injunction demanding that the TM technique and my mantra be kept secret. No one was going to take the trip without paying, I thought.

Soon Brenda appeared. A medium-height brunette with curly hair and large brown eyes, she led me, form in hand, to a room upstairs. Skimming my answers, she stopped at the various books and courses I had listed and remarked with some surprise, "Oh, you've really been searching—but that's fine, that's okay." Many people, she said, had tried other programs before sticking with TM.

Finally, the moment of initiation arrived. I removed my shoes at the doorway to the altar room, whiffed the burning incense and followed Brenda inside. Candles flickered on

the altar table, which held some brass items and a framed
picture of Maharishi's teacher. Standing at Brenda's left, I
silently observed the ceremony which, according to the
introductory lectures, is a "guarantee" that the TM method
is rooted in an ancient tradition going back to the Vedas. It
also allows the instructor to pay his or her respects to the
tradition. In a pronounced British accent, Brenda chanted
Sanskrit phrases, made some candle passes in front of the
picture, dipped my flowers in a small brass basin of water
and shed the drops on some rice in another brass dish.
Kneeling, she motioned with her hands for me to follow
suit.

Closing her eyes, she concentrated. Then slowly turning
to me, she said, "Ima," with a mildly stoned look in her
eyes. "Is that my mantra?" I asked. A solemn nod
confirmed it. I next followed her instructions to repeat the
mantra verbally several times and then mentally for
several minutes with my eyes shut. Still whispering,
Brenda stressed that the mantra would have greater power
if kept private. "Wouldn't you agree?" she asked.

I was then led to another room to practice mentally
intoning "Ima." Then another questionnaire was filled out.
Did the mantra fade while I meditated on it? Did noises
distract me? Did thoughts disturb me? Aside from a general
feeling of calm, my mouth seemed parched. Was something
wrong? "No, it's fine," Brenda later assured me. "Different
people have different experiences."

The next day I was to practice for twenty minutes before
breakfast and dinner. Two days later when I returned to the
TM terminal, a young blonde woman, about twenty-five,
and a man about twenty were the leaders of a group
question-and-answer session.

"How do I know I'm meditating?" an elderly woman
asked. "I seem to have thoughts interfering with the
mantra. Is this really meditation?" (She was probably
wondering whether she had the right ticket.) Standard
questions, standard answers. Scientific studies showed
that the brain waves of those practicing TM indicated a
state of "alert relaxation," while there was no noticeable
difference in the nonmeditators. Therefore, all of us were
meditating. Interfering thoughts reflected the natural
releasing of stress and were not to be resisted. "When the
mind wanders," the blonde woman advised, "gently draw
your attention back to the mantra."

I wanted to know more about the mantra. How was it selected for me? What guarantee did I have that Brenda was qualified to make the right choice?

The blonde woman flashed a smile (barely concealing a hint of irritation). "Yes, those are good questions. The mantra is arrived at on the basis of certain specific scientific criteria. We look at the answers to our question-naires and observe your personality. It's arrived at very scientifically. Instructors go through an intensive six-month* training period and learn how to choose the mantra, but we're not allowed to divulge the exact method."

That was it? I persisted. "You're throwing the word 'science' around a lot but not answering my question."

Enter the young man. "By 'science,' we mean that the benefits derived from practicing the mantra have been substantiated by research. Let's focus on the benefits derived from practicing the mantra, rather than on its selection."

Impasse. People in the room were getting restless. They were paying for the trip. Who was I to spoil it for them? I relented, resolving to pick the matter up with Brenda the next day. Not surprisingly, she offered little more. "We never choose a wrong mantra," she asserted. As for the secrecy of the method of selection, she defended Maharish-i's insistence on maintaining the "purity" of the procedure. Were they to divulge the method which she said was really very simple, others might become self-appointed imitators and distort the tradition. "Why worry about how; just do it," she concluded.

Many Imas later, I was having trouble at Point Ego. I felt dizzy, depressed and tired after each twenty-minute session. Stranger still, far from energized, I would often have a strong urge to sleep for about an hour.

Was this only a passing phase? The next weeks proved not. I had bought my ticket to the garden, but I wasn't going anywhere. Could it be that something was wrong with the mantra?

Thousands of travelers had sent their friends I-wish-you-were-here cards, but I couldn't help but wonder how many were wishing they had taken out cancellation insurance.

---

* The training period was recently extended from three to six months.

Can the TM Trip
be Hazardous

Are the facts really facts? Can TM be everything for everybody?

The first thing to understand about science is that nothing is ever proven in a final sense. There is evidence to support or question a given hypothesis based on the scientist's interpretation of his or her experimental results.

A common saboteur of objective research is experimenter bias. This simply means that a researcher can unwittingly interfere with the results of an experiment; to prove a certain point, he or she may set up controls and selectively interpret the results, ignoring or overlooking conflicting elements. Since an airtight, foolproof method to eliminate this subjective interference remains to be devised, it's a factor with which scientists will have to live. And that's why they're always suspicious of any "proof" claiming to be conclusive (we all know how cyclamates, monosodium glutamate, red dye #2 and thalidomide were pronounced harmless). Little wonder that research going on investigating TM claims in over one hundred scientific laboratories throughout the world (most are in the United States) suggests that the caravan to Being may have some as yet unresolved engine problems, or that other trips may be just as comfortable, relaxing and efficient.

TM-backed studies have been questioned for focusing exclusively on those meditators who choose to stick with the caravan, often to become instructors. Which is to say, no attempts have been made to study the TM dropouts, how they differ from those who continue and why this particular ride to the Garden may not be suitable for them. Might there be very different personality types with very different needs?

Research conducted outside of TM auspices has been revealing. When TMers chosen from the general population (from a randomly selected group of travelers) were tested for improved self-esteem in a study by psychologist Leon Otis at Stanford Research Institute (SRI), there were no significant signs of improvement in those who continued the experiment for a year. Otis also questions the TM assertion that each stop on the way to Being (supposedly as the dye becomes more permanent) brings improvements to body and mind. In testing whether psychosomatic problems such as headaches, insomnia and fatigue decline along the way, he found that good results had more to do with the motivation for leaving Point Ego than from reinforcements at each refueling. Otis says the desire to get launched helps the traveler in the same way that a sugar pill will act when someone is given an expectation of success.

This view is supported by psychologist Jonathan Smith at Roosevelt University in Chicago who found that while TM appeared psychotherapeutic for highly anxious people, a control group instructed to sit down twice daily with their eyes closed equally benefited.

This introduces the question of whether TM has, as it claims, the monopoly on first-class seats. Harvard cardiologist Herbert Benson, whose early work with psychologist Robert Wallace (now president of Maharishi University in Fairfield, Iowa) showed TM reduced stress, now has his own version of the TM trip. The meditator is instructed to sit in a relaxed posture with eyes closed and proceed to progressively relax his muscles, starting with his feet and working up to his face. While exhaling, he focuses his attention in a relaxed manner on mentally repeating the word "one." Intruding thoughts are to be accepted, not condemned, while reverting to the mantra (as in TM). This is practiced twice daily for ten to twenty minutes, and Benson claims this "relaxation response" has more or less the same benefits as TM.

Have TM proselytizers overlooked some vital issues? Definitely so, according to Otis at SRI. One factor is psychological desensitization. This refers to how some people who tend to habitually suppress their emotions, fears and feelings may find that shortly after their trip has begun and they've relaxed, the sudden release of accumulated tensions may be too overwhelming to cope with. Certain psychosomatic ailments previously under control, such as stomach ailments and allergies, could consequently resurface as major problems. This can be likened to the warnings often given by heart specialists to highly active people to not suddenly stop their routinized behavior but to allow the body time to adjust to a different schedule.

While the scientists continue to battle it out, the TM trip has been criticized from another perspective, that of spiritual development. To many who are committed to developing their mental and spiritual potential via various "maps" to inner growth, TM has been dismissed as "spiritual kindergarten." TM is hardly a ticket to Being, they contend, but rather more of a weekend vacation. According to consciousness researcher John White, the TM trip has all the markings of a blind devotion or first love. Nothing can persuade the infatuated to open their eyes to the various shortcomings of their beloved. The suggestions that a more mature level of love may lie ahead elicit ear-plugging reactions. They don't want to hear about it.

And how moral is the trip? The swami in the Himalayas believes that spiritual maturity is a necessary prerequisite to reaching the Garden.

Critics of TM charge that it's amoral; that the general message, particularly in introductory meetings, is that *everyone* can join the caravan regardless of the nature of envisioned personal benefits. This open promise has led some writers to wonder whether, for example, the more mercenary executive might anticipate improved overall exploitive abilities; the hunter, greater killing power; and so on.

What of greater creativity? TM describes itself as the "Science of Creative Intelligence." Psychotherapist Rollo May agrees that TM may help someone to understand there is more to life than growing roots at Point Ego, but that "the aspects of struggle, of tension, of constructive stress are forgotten." May refers to the work of psychologist Frank Baron at the University of California at Santa Cruz which questions the TM claim of increasing creativity. Baron found that when assigned the task of allowing taste preference to dictate selection of various patterned cards, groups of TMers demonstrated a preference for symmetrical forms, the exact opposite of his results with creative people.

While May believes TM can serve as a form of relaxation, he says any trip requires the ability to face unexpected problems and to have the necessary tools to actively deal with them. We can better understand this point by thinking of fixing a car. If you've forgotten your basic tool kit, you'll have to sit there and wait for help. If you forget about the nature of your beliefs or attitudes and don't understand the need to continually evaluate them, the problems may build up, and no amount of relaxation will solve them. Harvard psychologist Gary Schwartz says that creative ideas often emerge in drowsy states of consciousness, but that to use these ideas the meditator needs activity and a great deal of rational thought. Drowsy forms of meditation or too much meditation may inhibit rational action.

Gopi Krishna suggests travelers to Being are often confused about what's needed to get there. Passivity is fine to some extent, but the transformations of mind and body that the journey requires cannot occur unless a person actively uses his or her mind to gauge what each turn in the road means and brings. Letting the mind "effortlessly" meander, as TM requires, is akin to sleeping in a car and not seeing the changing landscape. Furthermore, you only know you're there when someone announces it. The swami who keeps his eyes open would frown on such a blind approach.

What about the effects of the mantra? TM initiators stress the vital role it plays as a vehicle to Being. This sound is supposedly selected to suit the unique characteristics of each traveler. An inappropriate mantra, TM claims, can be dangerous. Harold Bloomfield and his coauthors of the best-selling TM travel guide; *TM: Discovering Inner Energy and Overcoming Stress*, are very emphatic about this.

> The danger of using a mantra of unknown effect is dramatized by numerous ... reports from people who have used nonsense syllables, euphonious sounds, or words with pleasing meanings. In every case, meditation with these mantras was less favorable than the correct practice of TM. *In several cases the aftereffects were negative or unsettling, and included headaches, disrupted attention span and anxiety.* It is unfortunate, with the increasing popularity of TM that some self-styled "experts" of relaxation or other meditative techniques have been indiscriminately advocat-

ing their own makeshift mantras, unaware that
severely deleterious effects can be experienced by
their unsuspecting practitioners. [our italics]

"Because individuals differ in the quality of the
vibrations which constitute their individual personalities,"
Maharishi writes, "the right selection of a thought for a
particular person is of vital importance." Ancient yoga and
modern physics both assert that everything in the
universe, whether solid or not, vibrates, and can be
influenced by other vibrations. Sound waves have very
specific effects on objects. If sound can shatter glass, what
can it do to skin, bone and nerves?

But the TM mantra is mentally repeated! How can it
have the same effects as vocal sound?

Psychologist Bernard Glueck of the Hartford Institute of
Living, cited by Bloomfield and colleagues as supportive of
TM claims, suggests why. He says the resonance (or
vibratory rate) of the mantra influences the emotional
center of the brain (limbic system) through the sub-vocal
mechanism in the brain's speech center. This means that
when a mantra is mentally repeated, a specialized unit in
the brain decodes the resonance that is produced. The
nervous system then treats it as if it were a spoken sound.
This has the effect, according to Glueck, of reducing the
effect of stress on the brain's emotional center. Since the
limbic system is largely responsible for regulating many
so-called involuntary processes such as heart rate, respiration and blood pressure, mantra meditation has the effect
of slowing down all these activities, and body tension is,
therefore, reduced.

The important question then, is: if a mantra may have
such an effect on the body—apparently in just a matter of
seconds—why is the TM mantra system believed to be
better than any other? Why is Benson's "one," "Om,"
"Rhim," or "Rhom" dismissed as inappropriate?

The best-selling TM travel guides and the initiators all
maintain that the TM procedure and the "purity" of the
ceremony guarantee that the initiate is given the correct
mantra and is being properly instructed in an ancient,
time-proven technique. If a person wants to get to Being,
it's important that the take-off and vehicle be absolutely
foolproof. An astronaut wouldn't knowingly climb into a
faulty space capsule.

According to TM literature, the tradition of mantra selection has ancient roots going as far back as 3000, B.C., or even earlier, to the origins of the Vedas, the oldest recorded spiritual teachings. An examination of these roots reveals that the earliest writings on Indian musical science are to be found in the Sama Veda as expressions of the understanding of the ancient *rishis*, or priests, of the relationship among sound, the individual and the cosmos. They believed that a primal or original sound set the wheels of Creation into motion.

Their spiritual objective was to rediscover this sound so that they could understand the nature of all things. The mantras evolved in the course of this search, each being a composition of sounds whose vibratory power was believed capable of controlling natural phenomena. Everything in the universe had its unique sound. Everything was part of the underlying primal sound.

While there are many different mantras, they can be placed into two general categories. The *bhija* mantra, or "seed sound," refers to the basic notes or vibrations, such as Om, Rham and Rhim, which have been used for thousands of years in India and other Asian countries. They were first the province of the rishis but gradually were more widely used by the masses. A *siddha* mantra, as it is sometimes called, is, on the other hand, a sound discovered by a person believed to have arrived at a realization of Being. The mantra was supposedly passed on to a disciple through the teacher's direct contact with his vibrations and an understanding of what sound was appropriate to him or her. Through correct repetition of the mantra, it was believed to speed up the initiate's vibrations, elevating him or her to an advanced state of consciousness. These mantras were assigned within the context of a ritual or ceremony in order to create a feeling of devotion or proper receptivity. Once transmitted, the recipient was to practice it privately, personally energizing it.

TM initiators, says Maharishi, greatly enjoy the ceremony because it puts them in the right frame of mind. He claims that they cannot select a wrong mantra due to the purity of the ceremonial tradition. The implication—it's never stated as such—is that the initiator presents the prepared traveler with a siddha mantra, one appropriate to his or her particular vibrations.

This is an extraordinary claim. It assumes that the

initiator, after six months of concentrated instruction, has traveled sufficiently far from Point Ego to have acquired the power to psychically read each student's unique vibrations. It's far more likely that TM mantras are various bhijas, suitable for anyone's use. Even so, viewed as something special by the buyer and as a signal that meditation is about to begin, the mantra can be seen as a powerful vehicle to reinforce the motivational basis for the trip.

The ritualistic mystique of the ceremony which invokes Hindu deities, however, clouds a basic issue. Just how far can a person travel with his or her mantra?

We're dealing here with an ancient cosmology which stresses that the journey to Being cannot take place without adequate preparations; that the initiate must be receptive and inwardly prepared for the imparted sound.

Before the use of mantras became widespread and used often as spells for countless trivial purposes which had little to do with attaining higher states of consciousness, the rishis had attempted to hear the universal sound, or, as the ancient Greek mathematician Pythagoras described it, "the music of the spheres." To hear it, the traveler had to be spiritually open to it, meaning physically and psychologically well integrated.

In our culture, we're unceremoniously bombarded by sound. To what extent has the power of the "word" and our receptivity and attunement to its subtlety diminished? Indian civilization has greatly stressed the power of listening, while the West has been generally preoccupied with vision.

Is the mantra, then, as a key element in departing from Point Ego, as effective a tool as it once may have been in our civilization? Might the repetition of a sound—either mentally or vocally—and its impact on mind and body be a far more complex traveling aid than presently believed by the TM trip organizers?

Alfred Tomatis, research director of Association Internationale, D'audio Psycho-Phonologie (a large complex of language and sound research centers and clinics in France and Spain), believes that most of us are neither psychologically nor physiologically prepared to use mantras. A physician and medical scientist, Tomatis studies how people develop speech and hearing difficulties and the effects of sound from the environment on the body.

Tomatis was due to arrive from Paris at the University of Ottawa Child Study Center, a new two-million-dollar research training facility where his work is being applied to treat children with learning disabilities. So we made arrangements to meet with him in the hope that he might shed some light on why June had a negative reaction to TM.

Tall and physically trim, Tomatis, now in his late fifties, exudes a sense of well-being and vitality.

He believes his extensive clinical investigations of the effects of sound on the body are sufficient to warrant stopping the TM caravan in its tracks. Mantra meditation, he says, can be highly dangerous and can adversely affect our health. People who assign mantras—any mantras— are unfortunately ignorant of their true effects. A bold claim, to say the least, at a time when great numbers of people are beginning mantra meditation.

"The mental or vocal repetition of a mantra," he explained, "cannot benefit a person unless the subject can both hear and pronounce it correctly. Each time a sound is repeated, the entire body is affected, so that when a sound is incorrectly intoned, it is not properly embodied and can have the effect of wearing us down."

Then can a mantra be effective? "Yes," he said. "But it must not affect bodily organs. It must directly energize the brain. If, in improperly repeating a mantra, the vibrations descend to the abdominal or visceral region—as I'm sure they would for most people who have not developed a high degree of body control and well-coordinated hearing and speech—it will only irritate any problems we have there. If, for example you tend to overeat, you may find yourself increasing your food intake; if you have stomach disorders, problems with the colon or sexual problems, these will probably be further irritated."

Tomatis is seriously questioning whether most of us are sufficiently prepared at Point Ego to take the trip to Being. He's talking about a neurological preparation; whether our nervous system is working with optimal efficiency as it should for a mantra to be effective.

But surely many people claim to have benefited from mantra meditation! Should those of us who are not perfectly attuned forget the whole thing?

Let's look more closely at Tomatis's position. His work

shows that most of us are born with a normal hearing range. This means we have the potential to hear a range of low-, medium- and high-frequency sounds. As we mature, this range undergoes distortion, and consequently our ears become blocked to, or filter out, certain frequencies. He says psychological and physical factors develop which prevent a normal integration of sound, and our ability to be maximally energized by the bath of sound surrounding us is reduced.

One way to determine a person's hearing curve is an audiogram test. This involves playing low, middle and high tones and having the subject respond "yes" or "no" to whether they are heard. Tomatis's major claim is that an inability to hear certain sounds is often largely rooted in psychological factors stemming from early childhood and even prenatal life.

The extensive animal research conducted by well-known ethologist Konrad Lorenz revealed to him that an unborn duck or bird could recognize his mother's voice, and Tomatis wondered whether the same is true for a human being. He is now convinced that the fetus is capable of hearing the sounds of the mother's respiration, heartbeat and language. His theoretical framework goes like this: At birth the child's attraction to the mother's sounds continues to grow as he or she begins to pattern speech—his or her own range of sounds—after hers. To do this effectively the child must be psycholgically motivated through love and encouragement to hear and tune in to the personalities in his or her immediate environment, especially the mother. Unless the motivation to do so exists, the hearing circuits centralized in the auditory center of the brain's left cerebral hemisphere will not develop normally, resulting in distortions in the range of the hearing curve. Tomatis, when treating such children, has found a recurrent trait in their childhoods: they were often rejected by their mothers.

There's another important element in our ability to speak and listen which is important to understand to appreciate Tomatis's theoretical background for his views on mantras. He says his clinical research with thousands of subjects indicates that hearing properly with the right ear is vital to speaking well and developing a correct listening attitude. Sound travels from the right ear to the left hemisphere of the brain, he explains, and orderly functions of communication occurs. But if a person is left-eared, that is, if he or she listens more with the left ear than with the right, the communication circuit is at a disadvantage because the sound must first travel to the brain's right hemisphere and then be circuited back to the left. Tomatis says this produces a delay in one's ability to organize thought. In other words, the hearing, thinking and speech relay system of a left-eared person will be slower than those of someone who's right-eared, and not as well coordinated.

There's another important system operating which influences speech and hearing. Tomatis stresses that sound travels along yet another pathway. The right vagus nerve extending from the tympanum of the right ear energizes the abdominal region and acts as a feedback circuit to the brain, carrying our emotional feelings. This right-eared vagus circuitry is shorter than the left vagus pathway and provides a quicker neurological processing of emotions which Tomatis says, influences underlying attitudes to hearing and speech.

The implication is that a left-eared person will have a general inability to listen to and integrate all sounds including those of his or her own voice. Some of us, then, will not be able to correctly pronounce a mantra because those sounds filtered out from our hearing curve due to a left-eared dominance (largely rooted in psychological factors) will not be present in our voice. Vital frequencies will be lacking.

Every thought and spoken word registers in our nervous system, says Tomatis. How we speak and think influences what parts of the nervous system will be stimulated. For example, the auditory nerve, which is couched in the deepest part of the ear, is connected to all our motor nerves and serves to recharge the cerebral cortex with energy. The vagus nerve plays an important role in our emotional life by triggering activity in the larynx. Remember that occasional lump in the throat or the cutting off of the breath? The vagus also touches the heart, lungs, penetrates the abdomen, the stomach, the solar plexus, the intestine, kidneys, spleen, pancreas, liver, bladder and genitals. Each time we excite our inner communication network with sound and thought, we can touch this nerve. Our voice—our inner voice as well—can be used to induce calm or anxiety depending on how we affect ourselves internally. Tomatis says his electronic and clinical equipment shows that mentally repeating a mantra has the exact same effect as vocally repeating it.

The ancient purpose of using mantras, Tomatis asserts, was to try to recharge the brain to raise levels of consciousness. This required a high degree of psycho-physical integration and hence excellent hearing so that the resonance of the sound would go directly to the brain rather than trigger visceral reactions via the vagus. He questions the validity of the current TM mantra initiation ceremony as it is practiced, pointing out that the instruction is of a purely mechanical nature. It doesn't consider the possible distortions of the initiate's hearing curve and therefore whether the initiate is really capable of reprodu-cing the sounds of the mantra with his or her own voice. He or she is simply given a mantra and told to repeat it. Then, too, the initiator must have the perfect voice for presenting the mantra.

"We are all constantly bombarded by all kinds of sounds," Tomatis said, "but if we don't know how to properly listen to them, we don't know how to analyze them and therefore reproduce them correctly. A mantra could potentially be an excellent tonic for us if we knew how to use it. But were a spiritual master to say, 'Do this like me,' you would not be able to. Caruso, the famous opera singer, might have said, 'Sing like me,' but who could? A person who wants to teach you a mantra would have to know how to listen to your voice and fully understand how you are integrating the universal flow of sound.

"TM people have wanted to see me because TM is becoming interested in my electronic equipment," he continued, "but I haven't had the time for them. I do know that the Maharishi has an exceptional voice, but don't think for a moment that he can teach you to use your voice in the same way. If you were to get a mantra from him, unless you can hear as he does, you would probably repeat it incorrectly. Of course, once in a while, people will hit it properly due to their correct listening ability, but this is like playing cosmic roulette. I'm not surprised at all that more and more devotees of masters, including those in Mahari-shi's movement, are coming to me with hearing disabili-ties as well as with visceral ailments. You can destroy your body with your own production of resonance by continually repeating the same sound."

Tomatis believes that, before repeating mantras, people must find out how capable they are of integrating elements of the sound universe, how they are neurologically connected to relate to that universe and how they may gradually build up these connections to be more involved biologically and psychologically with the life-force. This calls for an active building up of Self—of mind and body—not withdrawal from life. This is why he and his colleagues do not use any form of meditation in the clinics in France and Spain. Body and mind must be well integrated before we are capable of ridding ourselves of ego involvements.

Could his view possibly explain why the TM mantra "Ima" had seemed debilitating for June? "Any mantra you might use," he replied, "whether you repeat it mentally or vocally, would prove to be damaging. There are two important aspects to each voice: the semantic value of what's being said and the quality of the voice which should recharge your brain if all the frequencies are incorporated. It's obvious to me, after years of clinical experience, that you, like so many others, don't have enough sound quality [timbre] in your voice. Your voice lacks higher frequencies because you have difficulty in hearing them and therefore in reproducing them. Should you talk for a long time or mentally repeat any particular sound over and over for a length of time, you will become tired because your brain is not being sufficiently recharged. Instead, the sounds you are producing inside you, which would be largely of lower frequencies, will serve to discharge your electrical potential. Your brain has to work harder to get the right nourishment.

"In properly examining you for this deficiency at one of our clinics, I would first want to take a series of listening tests to determine exactly how you listen. A painter could have a good eye, but if he doesn't learn to use it well, then his paintings will suffer. The same is true for the ear. Because you have no idea of how your nervous system operates, whether you are left- or right-eared, or what psychological blocks you may have developed which prevent the necessary motivation to hear certain sounds, the claim—any claim—that a mantra will bring you benefits is an absolute lie. The task of transcendence is not quite as simple as people are being led to believe."

If Tomatis's clinical investigations are on the right track, many of us may have a lot of trouble reaching the Garden. In fact, we'll have trouble leaving Point Ego.

Maharishi has said many times (once on the "Merv

Griffin Show") that further research on the benefits of TM is unnecessary; that it should be immediately applied everywhere. Of course, it's his trip. He's the organizer and has his interests at heart. Ours too, he claims, but while the road to Being may not be rocky for him, it may be for others.

Tomatis is basically concerned with how our psychological inabilities to hear certain sounds prevent our being mentally and physically better coordinated. Until we get ourselves better coordinated, he claims, the trip to Being is a mirage. While further research must obviously be conducted by other researchers before we begin to jump to any conclusions about Tomatis's jarring perspective, he has given us sufficient food for thought about what may be a prerequisite for correctly using mantras.

There are, however, other problems, aside from the psychological factor, in distorting our hearing curve.

Westerners are suffering from extensive noise pollution. The United States Environmental Protection Agency estimates that at least 16 million people have suffered hearing damage as a result of environmental overkill. According to the National Institute for Occupational Safety and Health, a two- or three-year daily exposure to ninety decibels of sound is sufficient to cause deafness. Background noise in a city like New York comes close to seventy decibels. Those who are frequently exposed to loud rock music and noisy machines like snowmobiles or construction drills are assaulted by as much as one hundred decibles or more, enough to burst cells of the inner ear. The high-frequency cells, which, according to Tomatis, are highly involved in sending energy to the cortex, are the very first to be destroyed.

Clearly, we know too little about the sound bath we live in and how sound affects us inside. Those who are trustingly gathered at Point Ego for the trip ought to know more.

The Tomatis Treatment

The average person is trapped in a self-created mental prison.

Is this a Western or Eastern view?

It's both. But the escape routes differ.

The Easterner says the world, as perceived by the ego's limiting belief systems and filtered through the senses, is an illusion. It reveals only a distorted fraction of the total environment or Cosmos; it prevents our experiencing the unity and interconnectedness of all life.

Therefore, we must learn to transcend the ego by dissolving our individuality into the universal sea of Cosmic Being.

The Westerner says ego serves a function. I have it for a reason. Rather than renounce it as a creator of illusion, I can perfect it. By systematically integrating and clarifying all aspects of consciousness, I can gradually become more fully conscious and ultimately unite with the God within. By learning to master myself, I will transcend the illusory shadows and fears which plague me and function better in all areas of life.

Psychoanalysis is an example of ego integration and polishing. It involves exposing and critically examining the contents of the unconscious mind; the inner conflicts, the hidden emotions and destructive tendencies. Having made this constraining inner world conscious, one comes to terms with it, and the personality is integrated and liberated from mind-created barriers, or complexes. One can then proceed to discover and develop the multifaceted aspects of human potential.

During the dissecting process of analysis, deeply entrenched, limiting attitudes and fantasies rise to the surface. Through the careful guidance of the analyst, *consciousness* itself is actively used to become aware of the roots of behavior and beliefs, and personal vision is expanded. As the expanding sea of information becomes increasingly manageable, inhibitions are met head-on, their true illusory nature revealed. They are supplanted by a more open, life-embracing perspective.

The result (at least the potential) is a rebirth or re-structuring of Self. The psyche can be dissected, analyzed and constructively restructured into a new unity.

As long as conflict continues to go unchecked, conscious-ness will be muddy, insight obscured, behavior will be automatonlike and compulsive. In this state of dishar-mony, consciousness is narrow, and the ego's potential contracted. Hence the mental prison.

One problem with psychoanalysis is that it often takes a very long time. Fantasies have to be dragged up from the unconscious. The patient must then consciously work them out.

Enter Alfred Tomatis.

His contribution has been to provide psychoanalysis with a medical counterpart called psycho-phonology, and perhaps a shot of rejuvenation as well.

"We are antennas of consciousness," he told us. "We must build up the ego, our connection to Being, through integration and then illumination. It's possible to free ourselves of the automatisms of daily life (escape the mental prison) and continually transcend the here-on-earth as refined vehicles or instruments of Universal Consciousness. That can be done by tuning the body, which is the instrument through which Being functions—molding it biologically and psychologically to allow the life-force to flow through without constraints."

The key to Tomatis's entire system of polishing is sound therapy, or, as he calls it, psycho-phonology. Unlike psychoanalysis, which attempts to free deeply ingrained fantasies through the therapist-patient relationship, Tomatis claims his treatment, which is electronic in nature, works directly on the structure of the entire nervous system. A person, he says, must become capable of integrating the cosmic sound bath of which he or she is a part. Only then will the ego be able to function without physiological and psychological constraints.

The task of self-development, Tomatis asserts, is to direct one's Self (or ego energy) outward, to connect with external and cosmic reality. When relatively unimpeded by stress, anxieties and psychological blockages, a motivated person can become increasingly conscious of his or her higher Self and transcend limiting cultural beliefs and impositions. This brings the person into closer contact with Being, the higher Self within.

Tomatis believes most of us have internalized a lengthy, complex, subconscious "tape" of experiences which play a determining (restrictive) role in the Self's maturation. Like some psychoanalysts, he looks upon birth itself as a traumatic experience, as the beginning of our anxieties. He especially sees prenatal life as the first stage in the communication process. The fetus, he says, responds to the mother's sounds (especially her voice), and these sounds become part of the child's memory circuits. Birth is a symbol of becoming free, but because the child finds itself threatened by an unknown world, it remains intimately tied to the mother, through her voice, which brings back the prenatal memories.

How the mother responds to the newborn will strongly influence the extent to which he or she will be motivated to discover and explore relationships to the environment, and with the Cosmos itself. If rejected by the mother, the child will retreat from communication, withdraw into itself and become preoccupied with infantile pleasure-seeking. If the mother encourages the infant's dependence on her, this introversion is prolonged. The child then fails to make the necessary connections with the environment.

Becoming a person (an individual) in the fullest sense, says Tomatis, requires a careful unfolding of communication with the outside world, a projection of Self into objective realities. Through this process, a constructive self-identity emerges.

The Child Study Center of the University of Ottawa was designed with a love of children in mind. The brainchild of director Agatha Sidlauskas (a psychologist and educational specialist), the center motivates and inspires. Its colorful rooms, open classrooms, playrooms, gymnasium, cafeteria and bedrooms reflect for its resident children the underlying philosophy that human personality needs nourishment from the environment to grow and mature.

The children, who either live at the center or attend on a daily basis, have learning or emotional problems; some

can't read, some stutter badly, others are totally withdrawn
from the outside world.

All of them are involved in a program based on the
Tomatis treatment. Tomatis's apparatus is called an
"Electronic Ear." It consists of microphone, earphones,
speakers, filters, amplifiers and magnetic tapes. Its
purpose is to regulate the input of the various frequencies of
sound and provide the children with different ways of
listening to themselves and to external sources. The idea is
to use sound to awaken in the whole organism a desire to
respond to the total environment. By educating the right
ear, the language centers in the left hemisphere of the brain
are stimulated, compelling cortical differentiation. These
children have had difficulty developing the correct neurological connections due to an inner lack of motivation.
They have become psychologically blocked, and Tomatis
argues that the right ear has not neurologically opened
sufficiently to correctly accommodate sounds.

For example, researchers who have worked with
dyslexic children, who have reading and writing difficulties, find that their voices are unusually low, flat and
lacking in timbre. These children, Tomatis says, almost
always favor their left ear. Their inability to recognize
certain sounds of the frequency range interferes with
organization of thought. Reading difficulties stem from the
inability to correctly translate a letter into a sound (words
are sound symbols). With his listening focus off the mark,
the child is then unable to analyze and translate the words
he reads. He or she is further handicapped in that the
neuronal system is unable to adequately integrate sound
impressions from the outside world. When spoken to, the
child's inability to sufficiently integrate information and
then respond makes it more difficult to communicate.

The extreme dyslexics, Tomatis discovered, were in
many cases rejected by the mother and have withdrawn
almost entirely from communication. In treating over
twelve thousand dyslexic children, Tomatis says the
psycho-phonology treatment has refined their right ear
and sense of tonality. With improved self-listening (the
ability to hear themselves), a more acute body awareness
develops which quickly leads to improved reading, a
greater regulation of voice intensity and improved speech
rhythm—all within a few days. The child is suddenly

aware of the universe's sound bath to which he must connect.

This is how the therapy unfolds: A child wears the "Ear" and listens to a recording of his own mother's voice as she reads children's stories. Her voice is then rerecorded, and the child listens to its higher frequencies. The purpose of filtering the voice in this way is to regress the child to early memories of how the mother's voice, as filtered through the aquatic environment of the womb, sounded to the fetus. Tomatis says this reawakens a desire to reestablish this primitive relationship with the mother and calms the child, enabling him or her to forget the traumas experienced during and immediately after birth. This launches the treatment.

From this point on, the therapy will attempt to generate a rebirth by guiding the child through a process of generating a desire to communicate with the outside world. From the twenty-first session, the mother's highly filtered voice is listened to for thirty minutes, and gradually the entire spectrum of her voice is introduced to the child. This brings about what Tomatis calls a "sonic birth," liberating the child from any overattachment to the mother. If the child has difficulty in recognizing the mother's voice, six tapes are then presented; each provides the child with a wider range of the mother's voice spectrum. Eventually the voice is recognized and then the mother's nonfiltered voice is listened to for four sessions.

Following this, the next twenty-four sessions (sometimes more, if necessary) provide the child with filtered classical music rich in high frequencies (primarily Mozart) interspersed with a filtered voice presenting a vocabulary also rich in higher frequencies. Tomatis says this stimulates the child's cortex and activates the cells of the inner ear that process higher frequencies of sound.

The child listens and relaxes, or can try his or her hand at a jigsaw puzzle. In the next session, he or she is asked to repeat words on the tape, again those rich in high frequencies. Gradually the words on the tape become barely audible and the child is forced to become consciously attentive in order to repeat the words. Posture quickly improves. The implication here is that the child begins to learn to monitor the entire body and regulate sound output.

The next phase in treatment is to introduce the lower

frequencies of the father's voice. Tomatis says that in the maturation process, the father is the major stimulant which motivates the child to deal with the world of thought, or the world of the "other." This is due to the need of the young child to, in effect, learn a new language, since the first communication process is entirely with the mother.

Treatment ends as the child, now motivated to be actively involved in the sound world, learns to sing Gregorian chants which are very rich in high frequencies and are literally full of sound.

Unlike psychoanalysis, then, the Tomatis treatment reeducates the organism to respond without constraints to the outside world without involving the patient in the lengthy process of confronting and decoding infantile fears and fantasies. The therapy is direct, as the rebirth of the ego involves erasing psychological blockages from the unconscious. Now more physiologically coordinated, the body is on its way to becoming more in tune with the environment. Life and more life is the aim. The ego can now gain greater control of life's changing conditions, having reached a higher stage of integration. The task remains to continue to transcend psychological limitations.

"We can bring most patients to this stage," Tomatis told us. "It's a liberating experience, as one feels that the crippling programmed behaviors have died, yet one lives, and feels a greater attunement with the Cosmos and one's innermost Being."

The important point about the widespread applicability of the Tomatis treatment is that anyone can be seen as dyslexic to some degree. The definition can be broadened to include any difficulty one has in relating to one's own cultural group, that is, in responding as effectively as humanly possible.

The molecular structure of the human organism contains approximately eighty percent water; the rest is mineral. We can "polish and shine this bit of matter," Tomatis muses, "enabling it to be like a polished crystal reflecting the universe itself."

Yoga Camp Diary

Thursday

Brief Notes on Yoga (The Night Before)

The union of the individual with universal reality is the ultimate aim of yoga and India's primary route to the Garden of Enlightenment. The word itself comes from the Sanskrit root *"yuj,"* meaning "bind," "join," or "unite." The human spirit is to be resurrected and the ego crucified. Only then will the true transcendental Self emerge to freely and creatively participate with the universe's underlying spiritual essence.

Yoga involves the attempt to purify the body through the practice of *asanas* or physical postures, the control of vital breath (and the releasing of the Serpent Power at the base of the spine) and the control of the mind through meditation. In sum, both mind and body are to be strengthened and their limitations transcended. Teachers of yoga, however, differ in their approaches. We have been given the opportunity to observe how Swami Vishnu-Devananda has packaged his trip to the Garden.

Friday

A Flashback

It's foggy, cold and raining. Hardly the way to begin a July 4th weekend. But having lived in the Laurentians for over two years and endured the perenially soggy climate, we have learned to be philosophical about gloomy weather conditions and to inwardly rejoice whenever the sun does manage to break through.

We remember our sole visit, five years ago, to the Sivananda Ashram-Yoga Camp near the tiny village of Val Morin, forty-five miles north of Montreal. Stories about a swami who had flown to the Middle East on a peace and love mission in a plane psychedelically artscaped by the then fashionable designer Peter Max had filtered through to us from Laurentian gossip. The swami, we learned, had flower-bombed Cairo.

The swami had not been at the camp when, propelled by curiosity, we had visited one afternoon in the middle of the winter of 1971. He had already flown to his Paradise Island retreat, in the more temperate Bahamas, entrusting to his devotees the management of his sixty-acre camp. A few quick glances around the grounds reveal a snow-covered swimming pool, adjoining Finnish sauna, administration building, yoga hall, geodesic Krishna temple and a scattering of cottages; this had been the extent of our introduction to the yogic way of life.

As it happens, we have been invited as guests of the swami for a Yoga and Psychic Festival and will have the opportunity for a closer look at a North American yoga community—and at Swami Vishnu and what he represents in the highly competitive mind marketplace.

Orientation

We observe a basic camp rule as we kick off our shoes, muddied by the trek from the parking area, before entering the administration building. Not a bad habit to permanently adopt, Indian custom aside.

The standard camp brochure that accompanied our invitation had requested that participants come equipped with blankets, sheets, plastic dishes and towels, a hint that Hilton Hotel standards do not exist at the camp. But as guests, we learn, everything has been taken care of for us. Our room on the third floor further challenges the oft-repeated contention of the cynics that all Hindu swamis operating in the West are rolling in money. The door swings open, revealing two tiny cots, one wooden chair topped with a bowl of fruit and a small vase of wild flowers. And water pressure in the shower outside and down the hall, we soon discover, is down to an irregular trickle. A bit jarring at first, but simplicity has a way of inviting reflection upon the anxieties and preoccupations that materialistic obsession usually elicit. The competing thought, of course, is that two nights do not make a lifetime.

Simple environments, however, do not preclude the posting of rules and regulations. Prominently tacked on the wall above one of the cots is a yellowed sheet enumerating twenty dos and don'ts. The first series of injunctions reveal the swami's sound business sense: personal checks are not accepted. Cash remains the passport of the New Age—full payment upon arrival. Deposits are to be made for blankets borrowed at the front desk and such. Check-out time follows a Howard Johnson's regimen. No later than 10 A.M. Please notify the desk if you desire to stay on. Other instructions are fairly routine: keep the place clean; a laundromat is available in the neighboring village; a boutique downstairs is supplied with yoga-oriented books, records and Indian imports.

Item 18 proscribes the smuggling of meat, fish, eggs, onion, garlic and pets onto the campgrounds. Smoking is prohibited. We had fortunately, in the weeks previous, been experimenting with vegetarianism—a convenient coincidence which would spare us the usual symptoms of sudden withdrawal. But as we mentally braced ourselves for the austere regimen of two meals a day, our eyes fell upon item 20. Visitors are welcome to frequent the camp's Vegetarian Health Hut. Meatless pizza made from wholewheat dough, fresh fruit juices, fruit, sandwiches, raisins, nuts, etc. We smile at the welcome opportunity to violate the two-meal schedule, and prospects for the weekend brighten. So much for self-denial, willpower and yogic asceticism; if our inner resolve crumbles, we can always indulge. Amazing how much small compromises are appreciated.

We Raise An Obvious Question

As expected, the Health Hut is jam-packed, but the pizza has yet to be made. We settle for apple juice and a pizza sandwich. Back at the lounge in our building, we mill with friends and others invited as the swami's guests. One has studied yoga with him for about seven years, and the talk centers on the Swami's organizational skills. President and founder of the Sivananda Yoga Vedanta Centre Corporation, North America's largest yoga organization, boasting forty thousand students, the swami has been described by some as a shrewd student of corporate logistics and investments. The camp is an example. Bought for $25,000 twelve years ago, it is now valued at close to a half-million dollars. The rest of the corporation's real estate includes a fifty-acre ranch near Woodburne, New York, in the Catskills; a forty-acre farm in the Sierras, in Grass Valley, California; the Paradise Island retreat; and another recently acquired forty-acres in northern Spain which the swami intends to convert into a yoga resort. In addition, there are forty Sivananda Vedanta Centers around the world.

"The swami, you see, must be an excellent administrator," we are told.

"But how spiritual a man is he?"

"He doesn't crave devotion as some of the other gurus do, and openly admits that he is not fully self-realized. But I've noticed a discernible change in him over the last twelve years. He has been growing spiritually."

Might Vishnu Devananda's open humility explain why he fails to make headlines, much less attract the interest of the spiritual movement press? We instead regularly hear of Satchidananda, Maharishi, Maharaj Ji, Jr., Sri Chinmoy and others. Is his self-effacing posture hindering his public image at a time when so many gurus either claim to be avatars or to, at the very least, have reached the Garden?

The Swami: First Encounter

A magazine published by the Ashram provides a few details on the swami. Born Kuttan Nair, he was raised in a well-to-do Indian family. One day, while rummaging through a wastebasket, he found a pamphlet written by Swami Sivananda, a yogi and prolific author whose ashram in Rishikesh in the Himalayas and Divine Life Society attracted many seekers. Swami Vishnu was captivated and immediately recognized that this famous saint would have much to offer him. Shortly thereafter, he entered an apprenticeship at the Sivananda Ashram and, at the age of 18, took his vows of celibacy and renunciation as a swami.

Ten years later, Swami Sivananda pointed to the west as the path for Vishnu, where he was to spread the word about yoga. Arriving in 1958, it took him only one year to

Spiritual Self-Discipline

We wanted to talk with someone who is in contact with a spirit world, a medium who has spirit guides. We found one in Eve Weir, a petite, vibrant woman who says she communicates regularly with spirits, or "teachers," from another dimension. She has a personal "teacher" (or spirit guide) who is both an advisor and go-between for other spirits, especially those who are specialists in the arts and sciences.

"Never strike a happy medium," she said to us over dinner. That's one of her mottos and it shows. Eve is a positive-plus to be around, an essential quality for mediumship we learned, as she unraveled her role as a medium.

She became aware of her psychic ability at the age of seven. "My parents didn't discourage me at all," she said. "Children are natural psychics, but they get programmed by their parents to ignore their so-called imaginary playmates." Her grandmother helped out in a big way, taking her to Spiritualist churches to get the feel of what mediumship was all about. But Eve's not a Spiritualist in the sense that she is a member of that worldwide organization; nor does she give readings to people for a fee as is the current practice amongst many mediums working under the Spiritualist umbrella.

For the first twenty years that she had mediumistic abilities, she very rarely gave out any spirit information. "I served as a secretary for a very fine medium and learned from her. It was an important apprenticeship which taught me the laws of mediumship that must be respected."

Eve gets knots in her stomach when she hears about courses promising instant psychism. It's largely an ego thing, she says. "Those who place their ego above everything else severely compromise their abilities. I think

151

that any overnight psychic has to be questioned, and there are far too many of them giving readings today."

What then is required for mediumistic development? Eve says a medium has to study her profession as a physician must study his. "There are rules of conduct which are essential. The next plane of existence is a thought dimension, and, in order to channel through this thought, a medium's mental processes must be refined. This requires a strict meditation regimen, a time to learn to still the mind and clear it of excess baggage." Eve says a person must be mentally stable, live a balanced life, both mental and physical, and fully integrate any psychic abilities with everyday life. Without this, unexpected personal problems and the inability to neutralize them obstructs opening a clear channel between the two dimensions.

During dinner our conversation was periodically interrupted. Eve was getting sensations of gentle pressure around the back of her neck and shoulders and a tingling through her body; then she saw spirit forms around us. Those who cared for us were those spirits who wanted to help us in our work and were therefore clamoring to be heard.

"But what about malevolent spirits?" we asked. "Don't they come into the picture at all?"

"Sure they do, but I refuse to let them through. I demand quality. I always have. The law of attraction in mediumship says that if you ask for sensationalism you'll get it. I've demanded quality all my life as a medium and have gotten it. I've never had any problems with any spirit guide."

For these reasons Eve is strongly opposed to experimenting with a Ouija board. The Ouija board is comprised of large letters of the alphabet which are distributed in two rows. In the upper left corner of the board the word "yes" appears, and on the upper right the word "no." The planchette which rests on the board is a triangular, three-legged, mini-table which the two players hold with both hands. As the planchette moves over the board, directed by the subconscious muscular activity of the players, it spells out answers to questions posed.

One interpretation of the results is that the person's subconscious opens itself to messages from "spirits" existing at another dimension; another, more generally accepted, is that the messages issue from liberated aspects or fragments of the player's personality. English psychical researcher F.W.H. Myers once referred to possession as extreme motor automatism. For this reason, many mediums, including Eve, believe that emotionally unstable people, in resorting to the Ouija, risk the possibility of unleashing a flood of emotional disorders. *Psychic News*, a popular newspaper covering the mediumistic and psychic scene in England, even campaigned in 1968 against the sale of the Ouija, basing its argument on the widespread irresponsibility of many of the board's users, and the resulting emotional damage.

On the other hand, there are those who feel that the Ouija is a quick and efficient means to draw latent psychic abilities to the surface. They suggest that with responsible use, no harm can be done. They caution that should negative messages begin to come through, the questioning should be terminated immediately, and that, if there is frivolous intent, it is best not to use it at all.

Eve says a person who doesn't understand the power of psychic channeling shouldn't tamper. "If by ignorance we expose our minds to anything or anyone in the next dimension via the board, then we have to expect trouble. How can you have a quality control with this kind of method?"

"But aren't there some novices who claim to have had pleasant and even extraordinary experiences with the Ouija, who have become very psychic and learned to sustain it?" we asked.

"They're exceptional people," she said, "and probably emotionally balanced and ready for the experience. Because of this, they will attract spirits of a similar harmonious temperament. They can be compared to people who seem to be naturally successful in life without knowing how they do it. People of a habitually negative nature or of uneven disposition can attract unpleasant experiences."

Eve feels her mediumship has been progressively integrated with her total way of living. She has lectured extensively on psychic matters and has been working on a number of audiovisual programs designed to generate new ways of educating people and to tune in to their inner selves. "I live my philosophy," she said. "And I only give information to people if I feel they will use it constructively."

Eve's mediumship developed gradually. She never took a course but rather learned from another medium and through her own stream of experiences. But courses are available, especially in England, which probably has more mediums per capita than anywhere else.

We had heard of the College of Psychic Studies in London, that it provides students with classes in relaxation and mediumistic development, has lectures, a large library and the kind of emotional support necessary to cross into the spirit dimension. So when we were in London, we decided to visit.

Paul Beard, its elderly president, has a reputation for approaching the training of mediums in a hard-nosed, no-nonsense manner. He's a Spiritualist (one of many in the college's membership) and prefers the hypothesis (as he calls it) that a truly objective spiritual dimension exists which can be tapped through a clear mediumistic channel.

The college, originally formed as the London Spiritualist Alliance in 1884, has maintained the working hypothesis that this channeling is possible. But no member, Beard emphasized, is required to believe in it. The college, he said, is a community of people engaged in a study of common interest—the psychical world—however varied its aspects.

Beard is acutely aware of the fraudulent practices of some mediums. Some of them have even used expensive electronic gadgets to fabricate images of dead people to placate bereaved clients. So naturally he abhors any mediumistic training program conducted in a flash. "There are many mediums of the instant variety in this country," he said bitterly. "It isn't long before they're advertising in the magazines. Many of them really believe that they have the ability, but can't distinguish between an open psychic channel and their distorted imaginations."

Beard asserts that a medium must be sincerely motivated to help people. A strong mind and self-discipline are also vital. Some people, he finds, may discover that they have certain abilities but are unable to improve the quality of mediumship due to unresolved personal problems which obstruct the clear channeling of information. Personality integration is an essential first step to systematically confronting and transcending all negative personality traits.

One common problem is the inability to sustain an open channel. When the flow of genuine spirit communication stops, Beard believes some mediums resort to "filler" to satisfy the client rather than rescheduling the appointment and squarely indicating that they are having an off day. Financial considerations—pure economic survival—account for these dishonest situations.

"A good medium," Beard explained, "is someone who can penetrate his or her mental barriers, provide detailed evidence of the identity of the spirit entity which appears and keep this channel operating for a long time, even for thirty minutes or more. As you might expect, there are not that many good mediums in England today who would meet all these requirements."

Beard says they do their best at the college to train people, but the statistics aren't as impressive as they would like them to be. Training takes a long time and is demanding. "Opening up the psychic channel," he said, "reveals an entirely new world to the student. New ideas and new knowledge must be assimilated. You can't expect someone to integrate all this new information overnight into his or her way of thinking and living. Important adjustments are essential, and for some people this can take a very long time. The personality must emerge strongly balanced."

A pamphlet written by Helen MacGregor and Margaret Underhill and distributed by the college reinforces Beard's concern, adding that "the forces which are contacted by the psychic are just as real as electricity, but as yet we are ignorant of many of the laws by which they are governed." In sum, there are no shortcuts. Preparation for opening up the psychic channel is equivalent to the training undergone by the qualified scientist, musician or artist.

If someone wants to enroll in the course, he or she is interviewed. Beard wants to know why they want to become mediums. The course itself usually lasts for only ten to twelve weeks. The student must attend one evening a week. Beard isn't too satisfied with this and hopes it can be extended, but he says, "At least the course is measured out and the student working in a small group with the instructor has the opportunity to receive personal attention and a lot of personal corrective feedback and reinforcement."

We looked at a brochure advertising a course.

Many people are "natural" psychics and have experienced heightened perception. That this latent capacity can be developed and put to the

service of mankind is well established, but psychic
unfoldment should not be embarked upon without
considering the inherent responsibilities. The
objective is a blending of the psychic faculty and
the spiritual potential, as only in this way can
mediumship fulfill its true function.

"The courses at the college usually begin with exercises
in meditation," Beard explained. "A teacher may then
want to assess which students seem to have a natural
ability to pick up information while focusing on an object."
Teachers at the college appear to feel they can weed people
out very quickly who simply don't have what it's going to
take. Those who finish the course who haven't at least
shown promise, says Beard, learn about the idea of proper
spiritual development and develop a greater compassion
and love for humankind. Those who have responded to the
teacher's reinforcement may demonstrate considerable
skill in letting images flow across their mental screens
when they begin to tune in to objects or people.

Beard says an attempt is made to help a student perfect
his or her own unique mode of receiving information. Fewer
and fewer mediums work from a trance state, as the earlier
mediums did in the United States, but instead receive
visual impressions (clairvoyance), impressions of hearing
things (clairaudience) or get impressions of feeling (clair-
sentience) while in a relaxed, meditative state. While all
three gifts are closely related, the student is encouraged to
develop the method most natural to him or her.

The underlying rule throughout all of the training is that
the medium must always be the master. The impressions
must not be allowed to take over the personality unless they
are "invited" to do so.

Beard says that if a student shows the proper signs, that
is, sustained channeling, an exam is set up to determine
how well he or she might perform in a real situation. No
diplomas are given out at the college. The reward is the
official recognition of the student by the college, and the
student's name is entered in the referral file.

"I wish I could be more optimistic," Beard conceded,
"but we have not had the greatest results. Occasionally
someone goes through the entire program and emerges as a
highly efficient medium, but this is rare."

Mysterious Energies

Do inanimate objects have the power to retain memories—
to be impressed with accurate records of impinging events
from the time of their molecular origins? Is it possible for
objects worn in direct contact with the skin, such as
personal jewelry, a watch or ring, to somehow absorb and
retain the vibrations transmitted by the wearer's thoughts
and feelings? And what about those who subsequently
come into contact with them? Can they unknowingly be
affected by the invisible radiations of internalized benevolent or negative energies?

The late English occultist Dion Fortune wrote of an
experience she had with a nine-inch Buddha statuette
made of soapstone which had been dug up in the jungle on
the ruins of a Burmese city. Often used as a doorstop, it was
kept in an angle of the stairs leading to her apartment.
Disturbed by this casual use of a sacred object, Fortune felt
compelled on one occasion, as she passed by carrying some
flowers, to toss a marigold before it, a traditional act of
Indian devotion. Immediately, she had the strong feeling
that a link had been established between her and the
Buddha, and that there was something very sinister about
it.

Shortly afterward, when returning home late one
evening, she sensed a presence behind her on the stairs.
Looking over her shoulder, she was alarmed to see a golden
light the size of a football separating itself from the
statuette and heading toward her. To neutralize the force,
she automatically made a banishing gesture with her right
arm in the form of a pentagram (a five-pointed star), a
technique common to the occultist. The golden light then
retreated and was reabsorbed into the Buddha.

Reflecting on the experience, Fortune recalled that
sacred objects are sometimes desecrated in black magic

rites through human sacrifice and are thereafter highly
charged and linked with the malevolent forces transmitted
to and embodied in them. A little wiser, she wrote that a
person would be well advised to avoid contacts with sacred
objects with unknown histories. Though they may have
repeatedly changed hands, the initial impressions ritualis-
tically impregnated in them remain indefinitely.

Then there's the peculiar story about a sentry box in
Paris during the reign of Emperor Louis Napoleon. A
sentry on duty committed suicide by hanging. In turn,
three other soldiers assigned to the same sentry box also
committed suicide. Is it possible that the state of mind of
the first soldier when he took his life was so charged with
utter despair and intense negativism that these energies
remained firmly imprinted in the box? Could the subsequent occupants have been subconsciously overpowered by
these energies? When informed of these tragedies, and
growing suspicions that the box was generating a
haunting atmosphere, Louis Napoleon ordered its destruction.

Similar stories abound in occult treatises which caution
us to be wary of the gifts we accept, the money we receive
(particularly old bills and coins), the beds we sleep in,
second-hand clothes and any ceremonial objects we may be
asked to hold. The list is endless. A modern-day equivalent
might even be the grasping of a handrail in a crowded
subway car. Anything, it is believed, can be "magnetized"
by a person's energies, or mentally charged, and may be
harmful if the previous handler was either ill-willed or led a
tragic life.

Are these just zany bedtime stories and fodder for
sensationalistic movie plots? Or have we lost touch with a
world far more awesome and interconnected than our
sense-oriented conditioning has led us to believe? Can the
meaning and dynamics of life be extended to include so-
called inanimate substances as well?

First, let's examine the views of Paracelsus, 16th-
century alchemist and physician. Like other occultists in
his day, foremost among his tasks was to attempt to
systematize the knowledge of ancient peoples; more
specifically, to build the connections between the mind and
the external world. Part of the legacy he had inherited was
the view that the fundamental life-force existed—a spiritual essence—which enabled each substance to dynamically

interact with every other substance. Everything is alive! The Hindus, we recall, call this force prana. The Chinese call it *chi* and the Hebrews, *ruach*. Tribal peoples such as the Iroquois, Eskimo and Australian aborigines have also believed in a vitalistic force, often referred to as *mana* by anthropologists.

Paracelsus, who called the force *munia*, believed it radiated within and around man "like a luminous sphere," and could even be made to act at a distance through mental powers. "Nature, being the Universe, is one," he wrote, "and its origin can only be one eternal Unity. It is an organism in which all natural things harmonize and sympathize with each other."

According to Paracelsus, there was nothing which didn't possess a soul (or *animal mundi*). For example, metals and gems, regarded by occultists as powerful concentrators of energies, were included in this cosmology, though he saw life acting more slowly in them, "since in man, nature has reached the culmination of her evolutionary efforts." While using a different terminology, his vision approximated that found among the early Eastern priesthoods: in all nature there is ceaseless activity and all is interconnected.

John Dee, another well-known occult scholar and prominent intellectual of the Elizabethan era, echoed these beliefs. All things in the cosmos, he said, radiated their forces to all others and likewise received their energies. He believed it possible for these invisible influences to be perceived by the senses through concentration and even suggested that the act of gazing into a crystal as a focus would help.

Inspired by Dee, 17th-century philosopher Gottfried Wilhelm Leibnitz became captivated by the attempts of occult scholars to unravel the mysteries of universal processes and went on to devise a philosophy centered on what he called the *monad* and defined as the fundamental unit of consciousness. He believed all matter was alive and sustained by its monads. However, the more evolved the organism, the better organized and conscious were its monads. For example, a gem would be in a state similar to sleep, but yet very much alive, whereas in man, consciousness had risen to the point of self-awareness.

In 1775, Viennese physician Franz Anton Mesmer published *A Dissertation on the Discovery of Animal*

Magnetism. "Everything in the universe," he wrote, "is contiguous by means of a universal fluid in which all bodies are emmersed." This fluid was the carrier for an energy he called "animal magnetism." Different materials, such as metals, water, stones and glass, absorbed and emanated this energy in varying degrees. An object could be charged by a person and its "magnetism" detected by a sensitive. Magnets, in particular, were seen as natural generators emanating both mineral and animal magnetism.

Much of Mesmer's work was devoted to channeling this magnetism to heal, as he believed it could redress physical imbalances. To pursue this objective, he set himself up in luxuriously furnished quarters in Paris, and had his patients—most of whom were drawn from the ranks of the wealthy—sit in a tub of magnetized iron and glass filings and rub themselves with any number of the thirty or more rods which extruded from the tub's perimeter. Mesmer must have cut a fine figure in his silk robes as he directed the activities, waving a wand. His medical colleagues were, to say the least, displeased, and it wasn't long before a commission charged that "the imagination does everything, the magnetism nothing."

In 1840, pursuing the signposts left by Mesmer and those before him, Baron Karl Von Reichenbach, a German industrialist and chemist, experimented with animal magnetism which he renamed *Odyle* or *Od.* After studying almost two hundred psychics from all walks of life, he concluded that Od was a universal life energy. A human being—a luminous Od container—could, he believed, charge other people and objects with this energy through simple contact.

Certain psychics, he discovered, had a great aversion to the color yellow, others to silverware or heat from stoves. Some had difficulty enduring crowded surroundings. "Their sufferings," he concluded, in his *Letters on Od and Magnetism*," are the consequence of their hitherto unrecognized peculiarity in the sensory faculty." He found that common to all of his subjects was the ability to see a luminous glow around quartz crystals, magnets and people in a darkened room. The north end of a magnet radiated a bluish (or Od-positive) glow, and the south end, yellow-red (Od-negative). The point end of a quartz crystal and the left side of the human body radiated blue, and the yellow or red was a feature of the crystal's base and a person's right side. Od therefore exhibited polarity.

Since some crystals exhibit electrical properties under certain conditions, as, for example, when heated, Reichenbach was careful to control this factor. With or without the introduction of heat, Od emanations were perceived and felt as exciting the nervous system, particularly in those who were ill. All crystals he tested radiated this mysterious energy, and, according to his psychics, the greatest concentration of it issued from the main and secondary axes of the crystals. What did this suggest? That Od was participating in the actual construction of the crystals, corresponding exactly to the direction of their growth.

Closely related are the more recent findings of John C. Pierrakos, a psychically gifted New York psychiatrist and life-energies researcher, who reported that his observations of crystals revealed a pulsating energy field which extended into the atmosphere. What he "saw" was two striated layers (one-eighth and one-third of an inch) surrounding the crystals, varying in color. A quartz, for example, had a blue-gray inner band and a yellow outer band. Pierrakos also observed that the rate of pulsation varied with the orientation of the crystal's leading edge. Pointed west, it's rate was six pulsations a minute; east, fourteen; north, four and south, nine.

The significance of this was revealed during a cruise from New York to Curacao. Continuing his observation of crystals to see whether latitude was somehow related to the rate of pulsation, Pierrakos found that it was. His tourmaline, quartz, sulphur, hematite and obsidian crystal specimens increased their pulsations in direct proportion to higher latitudes and similarly decreased their rate with the lower. Pierrakos speculated that the earth's energy field might in some way interact with the field of crystals.

Before scientists could take these kinds of claims more seriously, some verifiable evidence was needed. Herein lies the importance of the recent controversial discovery called Kirlian photography. It involves placing an object between two electrodes which are separated by a dielectric. A film is then placed next to one of the electrodes and a high voltage is applied. The resulting picture is a variously colored energy field, or aura, which surrounds the object, whether it is a medallion, coin, leaf or fingertip.

Semyon Kirlian and his wife Valentina labored over

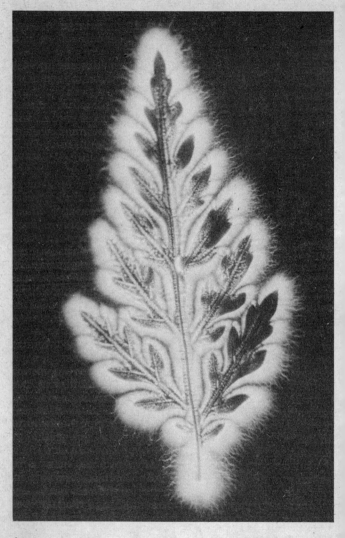

A sprague of leaves using a transparent conductive electrode technique. This photo was taken by a regular camera using an eight second exposure and very fast black and white film. *(Courtesy, Howard W. Mitchell)*

thirty years to develop this system before it attracted the active involvement of other Soviet scientists. One of the first, biophysicist Vladimir Inyushin, of the Kirov State University of Kazakhstan in Alma-Ata, followed the lead of another physicist, V.S. Grishchenko, who had earlier theorized that a plasma body—a fourth state of matter— could surround and interact with a biological organism. Inyushin postulated that the visible energy pattern photographed by the Kirlians was a unified organism sensitive to environmental influences and referred to this organizing radiation as *biological plasma*.

Before long, the essential Soviet research findings were verified by Western researchers. Interestingly, inanimate objects exhibited consistent unvarying energy radiations, and, unlike living objects such as leaves, whose photographed energies faded as they wilted, metallic items continued to emit a steady stream of energy. Could this finding suggest that the Kirlian technique is not simply revealing the physical artifacts of the physics and chemistry involved in the process itself, as some critics have claimed? Are metals continually radiating the fundamental life-force?

Emanations from organic objects were found to fluctuate widely, each species of plant and animal investigated revealing unique characteristics. Photographs of fingertips revealed that energy patterns altered during disease and reflected a subject's biological and emotional conditions. Changes also were affected by cosmic factors such as electrical storms and sunspot activity. When a subject meditated, the energy was more cohesive than when the same subject appeared anxious or jittery. When healers used the laying-on-of-hands method, the energy coming from their fingertips was perceived to focus almost to a fine point, increasing in size and brightness and changing from a bluish color to a yellow-red. After the healing, the energy pattern reduced in size. Patients' auras were observed increasing in size, brightening and remaining that way, indicating that an energy exchange had taken place. Nonhealers did not appear to generate these effects. Incidentally, in the past, clairvoyants who had claimed to see the aura often described the yellow-red energy emanating from a person as "hot," the same sensation felt by many of those being healed.

The great upsurge of interest in Kirlian photography

helped to revive the work of the late Harold Saxton Burr, renowned Yale embryologist, who, along with F.S.C. Northrup, also of Yale, advanced the "electrodynamic theory of life," which proposed that a "field" was necessary to regulate normal maintenance and growth of all living organisms. Electrical in nature, this "Life-Field," or "L-Field," was seen as guiding the organization of physical structures.

Burr later experimented with a micro-voltmeter and claimed that abnormal voltages he detected in subjects preceded disease symptoms, a finding which paralleled the Kirlian evidence of disease patterns photographed in the aura of leaves prior to visible manifestation in the plant. Burr's student and colleague, Leonard Ravitz, of Dartmouth College, demonstrated that the electrical potential found by the voltmeter between the head and chest of his patients closely paralleled seasonal fluctuations. However, it appeared that a person's thoughts could also influence this field, just as a changed state of mind appears to alter the energy patterns observed in Kirlian photography. Ravitz found that the depth of hypnosis and shifting moods and emotions could be measured by the voltmeter.

This latter finding leads us back to the claims of mystics and occultists, such as Dion Fortune, who have long contended that thoughts are things and can assume invisible but nevertheless powerful energetic forms that can be impressed on the fundamental life-force itself and on objects infused by this force. These thought-forms are further believed to be a force field capable of embodying a person's state of mind and even acting at a distance. For example, in the ritual magic of tribal peoples and the occultist, a thought, if dwelt upon with intense, focused concentration, is even believed to potentially have a lethal effect on the unsuspecting target. While to an outsider some of the rituals involved to concentrate this power and give it a charge may appear unnecessarily elaborate and steeped in superstition, it's likely they serve to sustain the state of mind needed to maximize the intensity of the desired thought-form.

The idea of a fundamental life-force, therefore, suggests that an object such as a piece of metal or gem could very well be involved in a dynamic interchange with its owner, and that it may be possible to psychically affect this relationship through the power of thought. Perhaps a precious stone such as the legendary Hope Diamond, infused with the accumulated thoughts of its owners, can in fact "sing" or "speak" in some mysterious fashion, as energy flows between it and its environment. Considering that most people wear some form of jewelry for adornment and that in the United States alone half a billion dollars is spent annually on cut gems, traditionally believed by occultists to be the most powerful accumulators of thoughts and energies, the implications are intriguing.

The recent explosion of interest in psychical phenomena has provided a scientific body of supporting evidence that thoughts can influence physical matter and that physical matter can, in turn, affect the mind.

First, consider PK. Most of the early scientific observations of this phenomenon around the turn of the century were of European spiritual mediums who occasionally influenced heavy objects to move across a table, supposedly through mental exertion. Then, of course, there were the controversial table rappings at seances and the well-known and bizarre poltergeist activities usually characterized by objects seen flying across a room or moving. Accusations of fraud, however, dampened the enthusiasm of some of the early investigators, and it wasn't until the famous Duke University experiments initiated by Joseph Rhine in 1934 that more systematic research got untracked.

Rhine had heard of some gamblers claiming to mentally influence the fall of dice and began to test them. The idea was to see whether the subject could make a desired die face appear at will above what was normally expected by chance. The dice were first tossed by hand and then from a cup. To eliminate the possibility of human interference as a factor in the results, Rhine later used an automatic tumbler apparatus which stopped at regular intervals. The subject's task was to influence the fall of one or more dice in the tumbler when it started up again. In 1942, Rhine published his results. He concluded PK was a fact, that "the mind does have a force that can affect physical matter directly."

To further insure the randomness of the object's movement in PK tests, more sophisticated equipment has now been designed. One notable example is the recent use of an electronic coin-flipper by Helmut Schmidt at the University of Durham in North Carolina. Following a suggestion by psychologist John Beloff of Queens University in Belfast that the random decay of atomic nuclei could be used to activate an object such as a coin so that there would be an equal chance of it turning up heads or tails, Schmidt designed a binary generator powered by the radioactive decay of strontium 90. Nine light bulbs were placed in a circle on a display board near the apparatus, and they were connected so that only one would light up at a time. A "heads" reaction triggered the light to move clockwise around the circle, and a "tails" the opposite way. His subjects were asked to concentrate on moving the light in either direction by affecting the coin in a consistent manner. Results indicated that in thirty-two thousand trials, the odds were ten million to one against chance.

Soviet experimentation in a related but different direction has shown that it is possible to mentally will a small object to move. The most famous of the psychics tested is Nina Kulagina, who demonstrated an ability to levitate a thirty-gram ball and separate the yolk from the white of a raw egg floating about in a saline solution. Scientists who closely observed Kulagina during these demonstrations reported that her concentration was visibly intense, her pulse jumped considerably and she even lost several pounds at a sitting. It was also noted that physiological monitoring showed her to be in a state similar to that of controlled rage, which, incidentally, is the state often believed associated with poltergeist activities, reportedly generated by young children who are experiencing frustration.

Another Soviet woman, Alla Vinogradova, has similarly demonstrated the ability to move a small object on a dielectric surface. While researchers have measured considerable electrostatic energy around the object and electrostatic field pulsations synchronized with her heart, brain-wave alpha-rhythm and respiratory rate, there are no such fields between her and the object. This indicates some action at a distance which violates conventional laws of physics and suggests that an as yet unknown energy is involved.

Physics has certainly progressed to a point which compels a reassessment of the fundamental nature of energy. Albert Einstein's famous equation, $E=MC^2$ has been instrumental in this evolution. Simply translated, it means that everything is energy. Energy is the reservoir or fabric of all universal events. Motion or speed shapes a substance or event. Mass makes it solid. What it also means is that all matter, be it of the mineral, vegetable or animal kingdom, is frozen energy congealed by time. Hardly flattering when we look at our own bodies this way, but nonetheless illuminating.

As mentioned earlier, scientists exploring the underlying structure of matter have found that an electron sometimes behaves like a grain of matter and at other times as a wave in a nonmaterial medium. Humbled by the phantomlike nature of the universe, Einstein had this to say: "My religion consists of a humble admiration of the illimitable superior spirit who reveals himself in the slight details we are able to perceive with our frail and feeble minds."

Some of the more daring and well-known theoretical physicists today such as Jack Scarfatti, Fred Wolff, David Bohm, John Wheeler and Eugene Wigner, who are attempting to deal with the awesome implications of both relativity and quantum physics, speak increasingly of an interconnected universe in which everything influences everything else, where consciousness and energy are one and where there is some degree of consciousness in everything. In other words, at the submicroscopic level, everything in the universe is involved in a continual interchange and is constantly moving, vibrating, growing and changing. Every atom both emits and absorbs energy.

While this rapprochement with the ancient principle of a vitalistic universe continues, there is still considerable resistance within the ranks to throwing the door wide open, for to do so would mean a radical, unsettling upheaval of our most deeply ingrained beliefs about the nature of reality. Our views of a cause-effect daily existence would have to give way to an understanding of a primary energy force in nature which accounts for phenomena such as PK in a reality structure beyond time and space as we know it.

Enter the psi-field. This is an old idea which can be traced back in Western thought to Greek philosopher Democritus, who in 400 B.C. argued that all objects and people continually emitted images or particles at an atomic level, and that these images had a life of their own capable of impressing themselves in whole or in part on anything in the universe. This concept brings us closer to an appreciation of how any so-called inanimate objects might be capable of interacting with people.

Psychical researchers often refer to this field as the

underlying force of all paranormal occurrences such as PK and telepathy. For example, it was once believed that the dynamics of telepathy involved a series of electromagnetic waves, corresponding to thought patterns, rhythmically emitted by the sender's brain. This theory was effectively repudiated by Soviet physicist Leonid Vasiliev, who successfully induced hypnosis at a distance in a subject seated in a metal chamber which effectively shielded him from any possible electromagnetic influences.

The suggestion is that man can affect matter (PK) and other minds (telepathy) via a different pathway than the one usually conceived of in our conventional physical, cause-effect, time-space framework. But what of the other side of the coin—matter affecting mind? Here, too, the prevalent belief in the West has been that the only memories to which we have direct access are our own; only those which have come to us, consciously or subconsciously, through the physical senses. This assumption precludes the possibility that we might have access to memories stored in objects.

Psychical research refers to this interchange as *psychometry*. The term comes from the Greek words *psyche* ("soul") and *metron* ("to measure"). Combined, it refers to the power to "measure the soul of things."

The very first study of psychometry was published in 1849 by J. Rhodes Buchanan, an Ohio physician, who coined the term. He found that some of his subjects were able to "read" the type of medicines concealed in envelopes and could describe with great accuracy the characteristics of people whose letters they were given to hold. Excited by these findings, Buchanan spoke of the possibility of having psychics reach into the past with their abilities to unravel some of the great archeological mysteries.

William Denton, a geologist, took up this task and asked his wife, who seemed to be psychometrically gifted, to hold objects that had a geological history. One was a prehistoric relic that evoked visions of massive beasts roaming the world. Another was a relic from the ancient Roman city of Pompeii which provided vivid impressions of a great city which had been destroyed.

Around the turn of the century, Gustav Pagenstecher, a psychical investigator, decided to focus his attention on one gifted subject, Maria Reyes de Zierold. Using hypnosis to control the flood of imagery that crossed her mind, he gave her a variety of objects to hold. Among them was a piece of pumice that had been kept in a clock, and she responded that she heard a ticking sound coming from it. When given a piece of string which had been attached to some tags worn by a German soldier, she promptly described a battlefield scene which reenacted the terror he had experienced.

Recently, W.G. Roll, director of the Psychical Research Foundation in Durham, took a close look at the bulk of Pagenstecher's data and concluded that, for the most part, the events described by Zierold had occurred somewhere near the object. The first events were usually the first described, and important events which occurred in the object's history came to her attention rather than trivial ones. This suggested to Roll that the objects themselves were generating the impressions. Some psychical researchers, however, argue that the object is simply used as a tool for tuning in, perhaps telepathically, to its owner. Others see it as a combined process. Roll believes that a psychic can receive information directly from the object and simultaneously tap the psi field of the owner.

The fact that only some people have developed a control over PK and psychometric abilities which more or less can be used at will doesn't mean that these extrasensory faculties are the sole property of a gifted few or that they are at any time turned off completely. What it does suggest is that it appears some people can consciously make the connections between themselves and the objects in their environment and others can not.

The Amazing Quartz Crystal

One of the most awesome, mysterious and unusual gems known is not a brilliant diamond, sapphire, ruby or emerald, but an eleven-pound seven-ounce block of clear quartz crystal which has been remarkably and inexplicably fashioned into a human skull. Whatever your personal aesthetics and sensibilities, the skull easily ranks as one of the most exotic and enigmatic objects you can expect to come across.

Beyond any doubt, the Crystal Skull, with its sprinkle of encapsulated bubbles and cloudy veils generated during the natural formation of the mineral, is a masterpiece of optical engineering. It is five inches high, seven deep and five wide. Carefully sculpted concave and convex lenses concentrate light at the base and transmit it to the eye sockets where, prismatically refracted, flashing hues dance a hypnotic ballet. The arches of the cheekbones extending from front to side also shoot light up to the eye hollows. The detachable jawbone, which was, according to mineralogical and morphological studies, carved out of the skull rather than from a separate block of crystal, fits into two sockets and is capable of slight upward and downward movement. In addition, there's an interior prism which, when viewed from above the cranium, magnifies objects placed beneath its base. Imagine the total effect this crystal would have if illuminated by candlelight!

In our conversation with Frank Dorland, the mild-mannered Santa Barbara, California, art restorer and expert on religious icons who for five years meticulously studied this strange gem, he stressed that adequate adjectives to describe it don't come easily to mind. Considering what Dorland discovered—and he still appears awed when he speaks of it—it isn't surprising. The skull's unusual qualities, he learned, are not limited to purely physical effects. While the skull was in his possession, he had the opportunity to study it under a wide variety of conditions. Experiences he had, often shared by guests who were permitted to see the bizarre piece, indicated that the skull appears also to be a powerful catalyst and generator of paranormal effects and experiences.

While gazing into this gem sculpture, Dorland claims to have seen an assortment of unexpected images—faces, temples, fingers, mountain scenery and other skulls. Though its hypnotic refractive qualities would doubtless make it a good Rorschach test, the fact that he often tested the images by moving his position to different parts of the room, focusing on print, then back at the skull—and that others would simultaneously observe the same visual effects—diminishes the possibility of hallucination. And what about the sounds coming from it? Dorland has heard soft human voices chanting, like an a cappella choir, he says. And there have been sounds of bells. And on occasion, Dorland says, the skull emitted a peculiar musky odor.

When in its presence, people reportedly have become very thirsty or trancelike, and those more psychically attuned claimed to have seen an aura or halo of light radiating from it. Yet another dimension of its bizarre character was discovered one morning when, upon awakening, Dorland says he found objects scattered on the floor near the skull as if it had unleashed some mysterious poltergeist force. A prank? Not likely. His home is always securely locked to protect the priceless paintings entrusted to him by museums for restoration work. Given all these unusual traits, perhaps the decision to keep the skull in a vault at a local branch of the Bank of America was based on more than just its estimated value of over one-quarter of a million dollars.

To study the skull, Dorland had borrowed it from its owner, Anna Mitchell-Hedges, the adopted daughter of well-known explorer Frederick A. Mitchell-Hedges, who was a strong believer in the legendary lost continent of Atlantis. While searching with her father along the coast of British Honduras for this mysterious land referred to by Plato, which has had such a strong fascination for many archeologists and adventurers through the ages, Anna, at age seventeen, reportedly found the skull minus its jaw section (in 1927) underneath what had been an altar in the Lubaantun Tomb, part of the ruins of a large Mayan citadel now largely overrun by jungle. Three months later, about twenty-five feet away, the jaw section was found.

But was it really a Mayan relic? While there seems to be little doubt that Anna found it at the site as she claimed in her affidavit, questions have been raised about whether her father had earlier planted it there, perhaps to suggest evidence of a pre-Mayan (Atlantean?) civilization which was technologically capable of creating such an artifact and at the same time, to provide Anna, whom he loved dearly, with the happiness of an important discovery. Mitchell-Hedges' untainted reputation as an explorer would tend to diminish this possibility, but he encouraged speculation by stating in the first edition of his autobiography, *Danger, My Ally*, that he would never reveal how the skull was obtained. Since this reference was deleted in subsequent editions of the book, suspicions were raised about the genuineness of the find.

But, of course, it's always possible that, if Mitchell-Hedges didn't plant the skull in the ruins, someone else at some time in the past did. The highly sophisticated archeological anomaly defies classification in the light of current knowledge of ancient technological skills. And it's impossible to date. Crystal, unlike organic objects such as wood or bone, does not "age"—it can remain unchanged for centuries. The carbon-14 dating method, which is successful only with the latter, is of little use with most minerals. The question of its age and origin will have to remain unsolved until further evidence is accumulated—either through the emergence elsewhere of an identical relic, the discovery of ancient carvings or wall frescos depicting a facsimile or an accurate method of dating the cutting of crystal.

Hoaxes can invariably be exposed, especially if there's evidence that an object is stylistically or technically inferior to the indigenous art forms (in this case, of the Maya)—but this is hardly the case. The skull exhibits considerably advanced craftsmanship. If it's not of Mayan origin, then the obvious questions are: Where did it come from? How did it get to the ruins? Was it used by Mayan Indians in religious ceremonies (which would explain why it was uncovered under an altar) or did it find its way there long after the decline of their civilization, which peaked from 300 to 900 A.D. All worthy questions waiting to be answered.

Making the most of his time with the Crystal Skull, Dorland sought to get some answers. On two occasions in February, 1971, he had it tested at the Hewlett-Packard Company in Santa Clara, California, one of the world's largest electronics manufacturers. They also make quartz oscillators and therefore have a well-equipped crystal laboratory where it was found that the actual carving was apparently done in two stages, as Dorland had suspected. It was roughly chipped out, and then hand-polished, likely with silicon sand and tiny crystal fragments. The absence of concentric scratches indicated that the piece had not been carved with the assistance of metal-age tools. With quartz crystal rating a seven on the ten-point Mohs' scale of hardness, Dorland estimated that it would take about three hundred years of constant work to achieve the high polish and intricate detail in this manner. That it was carved with complete disregard for the axes of the crystal further suggests an unusually advanced knowledge.

Could anyone duplicate the task today? Even though the optical technology is available, it's quite another matter to work the crystal in the same way.

What does Dorland think about the skull's origins? Obviously, he hasn't reached any firm conclusions. He suggests it may be Egyptian, Babylonian or, for that matter, possibly from an ancient and lost civilization which had attained a technology at least equal or superior to ours, such as Atlantis. Dorland also speculates that it may have circuitously found its way into the hands of an occult group such as the Knights Templar, a 14th-century order, having once read that their inner sanctum in London included, "a crystal head with eyes that glow like jewels." If this were the case, of course Anna Mitchell-Hedges' discovery could have been planned by her father. But all this is only speculation and it's possible the truth will never be known.

To add to the mystery, another crystal skull—perhaps a sister skull left unfinished—which is smaller, but similar, and classified as pre-Columbian (most likely Aztec) was discovered in Mexico in 1889 and has been kept at the British Museum's Department of Ethnography. It lacks the fine detail of the Mitchell-Hedges skull and its jaw is attached. Dorland suggests that it's a good example of how the Mitchell-Hedges skull may have looked in its first stage of evolution, lacking the details of the features, lenses and prisms.

Whatever its history, it seems tragic that the skull, now back in the possession of Anna Mitchell-Hedges who brought it with her to England in 1975, should remain by her bedside as it apparently did with her father, rather than be thoroughly investigated in a modern laboratory by a team of qualified scientists. The Crystal Skull is hardly just another gem! Perhaps Dorland is justified in feeling that science may not be ready for it.

It's also unfortunate that, aside from its brief appearance in a 1972 exhibit called "Visions of Mortality: the Skull Motif In Indian Art," held at the Museum of the American Indian in New York, the Crystal Skull has not been available to the public.

Investigations of an "other" nature, however, have not been entirely unproductive. While the Crystal Skull was with him, Dorland was occasionally visited by psychics who had heard about and wished to see the relic, most likely to discover whether they could psychometrize its past. All claimed to sense its powerful embodied energy and felt it had been used in ceremonial ritual. One psychic, James Wilkie, offered that it had been an Aztec ceremonial object used to develop psychic powers and that those who worshipped it as a source of unlimited powers gazed at its frontal lobe and went into trance. It's noteworthy that Mitchell-Hedges' own story had a similar ring to it. He said he had learned from some descendents of the ancient Maya that the skull, which had been rubbed down with sand over five generations, had been the embodiment of evil. The Mayan high priest, they told him, by concentrating on it, had the power to will someone to death.

Like her father, Anna Mitchell-Hedges believes that the skull is a vehicle of destruction only for those who don't handle it with the same attitudes of respect and reverence attributed to the ancient priests. This contention implies that the direction of the skull's embodied power, whether negative or positive, is determined by the motives of those who have access to it. Perhaps it was in reaction to its having been made available to psychics while in Dorland's possession that Anna emphatically announced she would not have the skull used as a crystal ball and ensured this by moving it to her home in Ontario, and later, England. She's been quoted as saying that it could be immensely destructive in the wrong hands.

Frank Dorland is quite convinced that whatever its history, one thing is certain: quartz crystal, which he calls "holy ice," has since ancient times been venerated for its spiritual powers. He believes the ancients may have known of its "inner life" and how to employ it to enhance psychic faculties. But why a crystal *skull*?

The skull has long been believed to represent not only death, as *momento moris* reminding us of the transient nature of life and the common grave that awaits us, but also rebirth and wisdom, particularly among the Central and North American Indians. Traditionally regarded as the center of psychic power and dwelling place of the soul, the skull has been a popular motif in the art forms of most cultures, both ancient and modern. Combining the shape of a skull with the psychic qualities believed to be inherent in crystal would create a powerful magical charm.

In Dorland's opinion, the Crystal Skull was revered and employed by high priests of an ancient culture which understood the hidden powers of quartz crystal—as a "brain box of the universe." He calls this lost knowledge *biocrystallography*, and predicts that we're on the threshold of rediscovering its principles and applications.

The word "crystal" comes from the Greek *crystallos*, meaning "clear ice" or "frozen water." The Greeks believed it was water which had been turned into stone, a view prevalent until the 17th century. In fact, women of ancient Rome even carried crystal balls in their hands on hot days as cooling agents.

Spiritual powers were also attributed to the crystal because of its dazzling hypnotic qualities and the belief that it reflected the Divine Principal—light—which permeated all of Creation. Did it not induce hypnotic trance and visions when contemplated? And was not the eternal part of man, the spirit, also of light? Accordingly, it was believed clear rock crystal could act as a bridge between the microcosm (man) and the macrocosm, opening up dormant psychic faculties.

For example, the Egyptians placed pieces of crystal on the center of the forehead (the mystical third eye) of the dead as a magical aid to the Ka, or spirit, entering the afterlife. In India, Hindu temple priests would wear crystal dangling from the neck in the belief that it enhanced spiritual powers. In Japan, quartz crystal was believed to be the congealed breath of the White Dragon, a powerful symbol of the forces underlying Creation. Also regarded as a symbol of purity and infinite space, they called it *tama*, or perfect jewel. Sorcerers in Africa and in Greece are known to have used crystal in their magical rites, and among the Australian aborigines and New Guinea and Borneo tribes, it was used in rain-making ceremonies. Persian Magi carried a crystal with them wherever they traveled as a continual link with the Divine. This list can go on and on. Like other gemstones, quartz crystal, it was widely believed, was alive, and its energies were seen as interacting with mind and body.

More than for any other purpose, however, quartz crystal was used for divination, or what today is often called *scrying* (from the English, "descry," meaning "to see"), which refers to the practice of gazing at an object which is shiny and has polish in order to induce a hypnotic state and observe paranormal images. Along with gazing at highly polished metallic mirrors and into the reflections of sacred streams, the use of pieces of quartz crystal or crystal balls was prevalent among the Babylonians, Persians, Egyptians and Chinese and subsequently spread to all continents.

In ancient Greece, Aesculapian priests in their healing temples often used large white crystals to elicit prophetic visions and would also place crystals or other precious stones into divining cups, interpreting the relative positions of the gems and their brilliance to provide medical diagnosis. However, the Greeks as well as the Romans seemed to prefer mirrors to crystal. Aboriginal cultures, such as the Australians, Incas and Maya, preferred crystal. The same is true of the American Indians, particularly the Cherokee and the Apache, whose medicine men believed that gazing into a crystal induced visions which would, among other things, lead them to stolen horses. Accurate prophecies of future events were also believed to be revealed in quartz.

Crystal ball gazing became increasingly popular in Europe from medieval times when it was widely believed among occultists that the visions in the crystal were generated by its indwelling spirit. Naturally, to entice this spirit to provide the desired information, it was necessary to invoke its power through magical spells, formulas and the burning of incense and perfumes. The custom at the time also followed the ancient tradition of using a young boy or girl of the greatest purity of both mind and body (virgins, that is) as scryer, while the elaborate conjuration procedure was effected by the occultist. One reason why purity, highly valued as a prerequisite, was particularly favored in Europe is that the clergy needed to be assuaged of their fears that a diabolical force would not infiltrate with its evil influence. It might also be suggested that they may have had at least moderate reservations about opening themselves up to the possibilities of possession.

As mentioned earlier, one of England's most famous advocates of crystal gazing was John Dee, who championed it as a powerful method to tune into the invisible patterns of life and who had a strong hand in making it more respectable. He must have been powerfully persuasive. Fortune-teller to Queen Elizabeth I (who made him Chancellor of St. Paul's and Warden of Manchester), he was occasionally consulted on political matters and found every opportunity to emphasize that his crystal ball (actually he had many), and the insight it provided, was given to him by an angel. No doubt, the watchful eye of the Church, which still considered scrying a diabolical activity, was very much in mind. Protected by his "angel," Dee apparently felt that further purity was unneccessary. His sidekick, Edward Kelly, acted as scryer and interpreted the images while Dee diligently recorded the visions.

A probe of the history of scrying in Europe reveals that the preparations, conditions and technique traditionally required were not taken lightly. In *The Magus* (1801), author Francis Barret quotes Abbot Trithem, the master of medieval alchemist Cornelius Agrippa, advising his student of the quality of the crystal ball and how to prepare it for scrying:

Procure of a lapidary a good, clear, pellucid crystal of the bigness of a small orange, i.e., about one inch and a half in diameter; let it be globular, or round each way alike; then you have got this crystal fair and clear, without any clouds or specks. Get a small plate of pure gold to encompass the crystal round one-half; let this be fitted on an ivory or ebony pedestal. Let there be engraved a circle round the crystal; afterwards the name: Tetragrammaton. On the other side of the plate let there be engraved, Michael, Gabriel, Uriel, Raphael, which are the four principal angels ruling over the Sun, Moon, Venus, and Mercury.

This prescription was closely followed by the Magi and laity alike. The names were believed to provide protection by barring the entry of malevolent powers.

In *Crystal Gazing and Clairvoyance* (1896), essentially a manual which strives to keep the ceremonial aspects of scrying alive and a summary of past knowledge on the subject. John Melville extends Trithem's prescriptions. When not in use, the ball (which must be highly polished) should be stored in either an ivory, ebony or boxwood frame. Glass or crystal is the recommended material for the pedestal. Directions are given for cleaning the crystal. First, it had to be rubbed with soap, rinsed well, washed again in a solution of either alcohol or vinegar in water and then polished with either a soft velvet or chamois leather.

Since Melville was well acquainted with the work of Mesmer and Reichenbach and therefore knew of "animal magnetism" and "Od" and, in addition, seems to have been well-versed in occultism, he paid special attention to the handling of the crystal, warning that it should not be "magnetized" by anyone other than the user and held only briefly by the person who had requested the reading. A mingling of magnetic energies, he believed, could pollute the purity and accuracy of information. Timing was another factor to reckon with. Because of the affinity ascribed by ancient astrologers between the moon and rock crystal, tradition held that the best scrying results would be attained while the moon was on the increase. And, because it was important that the nervous system be at rest, the scryer was advised to maintain a sugar-free diet and either fast or avoid eating for at least two hours beforehand.

In contrast, the actual act of crystal gazing seemed relatively simple. While staring at the crystal at a normal reading distance, the scryer was told to enter a passive-receptive state of calm while focusing on the ball. It was important to be in a relaxed position, free of distracting physical discomfort. Good concentration was absolutely essential. "If the crystal appears hazy or dull," wrote Melville, "it is a sign that you are likely to see; it will afterwards clear and the form of vision become manifest. Immediately before the apparition is beheld, the crystal becomes clouded or darkened, or what some may term 'black.' Presently this clears away and the crystal becomes exceedingly bright..." This was commonly referred to as "the lifting of the veils."

Melville had a basic code for the various images observed in the crystal. If, for example, white clouds were seen, this was an affirmative vision; if black, then obviously the reverse. If violet, green or blue, it meant the coming of joy. Red, crimson, orange and yellow spelled danger, trouble and perhaps sickness. Whatever was seen on the left side of the crystal should be interpreted as real, that is, to be taken literally; if on the right side, it was symbolic.

For those who would approach the crystal with malevolent intent, Melville had a warning:

> A sure and certain law exists, viz.:—That if the seer's purpose be evil when he or she uses the crystal...it will react upon the seer sooner or later with terrible effect; wherefore all are strictly cautioned to be good and do good only.
>
> The aerial spaces are thronged with countless intelligences—celestial, good, pure, true and the reverse. The latter have FORCE: the former possess POWER. To reach the good ones, the heart of the gazer must correspond, and they should be invoked with prayerful feelings.

The most intriguing part of Melville's guide is his emphasis on magnetism and his views on the relationship between the scryer and the crystal. He argues that the surface of the crystal gets magnetically charged; that it "collects [magnetism] there from the eyes of the gazer and from the universal ether, the Brain being as it were, switched on to the Universe, the crystal being the medium." He also mentions that the crystal could be charged by making magnetic "passes" over it with the right hand. Doing so for five minutes, he felt, would strengthen its power, while passes with the left hand would increase the crystal's sensitivity. People of a magnetic temperament (a quality assigned to dark-haired, dark-skin red types, as opposed to blonds, who were considered "electric"), he advised, would probably charge the crystal more quickly but not necessarily any better than those who were fair.

Melville then delves deeper into the issue of magnetism by referring to ancient seers who believed that the magnetic power of the moon was attracted to the crystal due to the presence in it of iron oxide, and similarly to other crystallized substances such as emerald, sapphire and adamantine. He therefore concludes that the fuller the moon, the better it is for crystal gazing, since more magnetism is accumulated.

Reichenbach, we recall, experimented with Od in crystals. One of his discoveries was that the moon appeared to be a source of this all-pervasive life-energy, and that it could magnify the amount of Od there was in crystals and other substances. By extending an eleven-yard copper wire from one of his sensitives, who held one of the ends indoors, and attaching the other end to a four-inch square copper plate outdoors (presumably in the moon-light), he found that she was able to detect feelings of warmth being transmitted, similar to those she had experienced with crystals and magnets. Using other substances to replace the copper plate, she got the same results. Moonlight, concluded Reichenbach, carried Od.

Melville's speculations about the actual role magnetism played in crystal gazing, while admittedly strange, are nonetheless thought-provoking. His argument runs this way: celestial and/or terrestrial magnetism is concentrated in the crystal. Likewise in the body. The ability to concentrate has to do with the activity of what he called the "phrenological brain centre" in the "superior portion of the first occipital convolution of the cerebrum." How well developed and powerful this area was dictated how good a crystal gazer a person would be. Melville refers to Reichenbach's belief that magnetism streams from the eyes to reinforce his theory that the combined power of concentration and magnetic ability was of vital importance to the procedure.

That's only part of the story. Remember the factor of purity? Well, it's crucial. Melville reminds us that the ancients were very particular about the use of young boys and girls in scrying. The phrenologists of his time, he says, "have located the propensity to physical love in the cerebellum, or small brain." Also, "the cerebellum became, as it were, a reservoir of magnetism directly connected with the creative economy, or would at all events, influence the quality of the magnetic outflow through the eyes." So there we have it: an early 20th-century explanation of why the sexually pure in mind and body would be the best scryers.

The quality of blood was also important. The purer, the better. This suggested that since the "purity of the blood is important to purity of power," the entire life fluid had to be cleansed as much as possible. Translation: junk-food addicts and insomniacs, for example, would have been written off by Melville as incapable of crystal gazing. "Clairvoyance depends as much upon air, light, diet, sleep, labour, music, health," he wrote, "as upon mechanically induced magnetism, or mesmerism." In short, interchange with the purity of crystal required spiritual commitment.

While he was a trailblazer in the art of scrying, Melville certainly isn't the last word on crystals.

There's little doubt that quartz crystal has a hypnotic effect. The rituals in scrying no doubt also contribute to inducing a state of mind which would today be described as an altered state of consciousness. Modern psychical research, we recall, has revealed that hypnotized subjects score better in ESP tests, so it's not inconceivable that staring at a crystal might trigger a psychic response under the right conditions.

Around the turn of the century, opinion differed about the nature of crystal gazing. It ranged from the belief that it was all a figment of the imagination or a hallucination to the strong conviction that images really did objectively appear in the crystal. Anecdotes even abound that photographs were taken of these images and that groups of people saw the same image in the crystal. One theory offered by Frederick Myers was that images were projected from the person's subconscious mind, or the "subliminal self." Those appearing images, which seemed totally unfamiliar to the scryer, were explained by Myers as details which had escaped conscious attention. Physicist W.F. Barret, another member of the society, offered that an ESP response was triggered through powerful concentration. The crystal ball, he said, was merely a prop, a point of focus.

Frank Dorland, however, disagrees. "There's no doubt in my mind," he told us, "that the quartz crystal, when charged, begins to interchange energy with a human being. This is done when a person squeezes and then releases it." Quartz displays a *piezoelectric* effect which refers to the positive and negative charge it develops on alternate faces. In a pamphlet Dorland sent us called *Rock Crystal, Nature's Holy Stones*, he expands on this:

> True crystal gazing has been defined as the science of inhibiting normal outward consciousness by intense concentration on a polished crystal. When the five senses are thus drastically subdued, the psychic receptors can function without interference. Exactly why this alteration of consciousness works so well with crystals is not precisely understood. Many scientists and psychologists believe there is an energy interchange between certain portions of the brain and crystal. Thought waves as energy are very similar to radio waves. It is believed that crystal mass acts as a filtering antenna and amplifying reflector to the psychic receptor centers. Waves of energy from the brain trigger the crystal into activity which in return stimulates the sleeping psychic centers to awaken and function.

Does Dorland have any hard scientific evidence for these claims? Not exactly. While he's confident that scientists will eventually realize the powerful qualities of crystals, for the moment, aside from the occasional unofficial support he receives from a scientist that he is on the right track, he has only his own recorded experiences and experiments with crystal to fall back on.

Dorland suggests the existence in the brain of an "absolute sector" where humanity's cumulative memory is indelibly imprinted. Quartz crystal, he says, activates this human property and amplifies it. He expects that in the future, human-crystal interchange will be an important method for amplifying a wide variety of paranormal experiences such as PK, telepathy and even levitation. This will, he believes, mark the gradual revival of an ancient science which may have existed when the Mitchell-Hedges Crystal Skull was created.

Psychic Archeology

Digging up the past is hard, grimy work. While the archeologist in charge of a dig acts as an overseer, directing the efforts of the diggers, often students, who get down to the nitty-gritty, he or she is continually and intimately involved with every phase of the work.

There are false starts, for example, knowing exactly where to dig. Sometimes many square yards of ground are carefully combed, yielding no or very meager finds. Major discoveries are often made on the basis of an intuitive hunch or stem from vital clues stumbled across quite by accident.

And when the spoils are in, the real work has only begun. Often working from fragments or stains in the soil, as well as the particular location of these clues, the archeologist proceeds, piecemeal fashion, to classify and date objects, and map and draw layouts in an attempt to accumulate sufficient data to reconstruct a living portrait of life in ancient societies.

An archeologist must live with ambiguity, loose ends, unanswered questions. The ghosts are silent. Most of the material remains have perished. Metals, pottery shards, stone and bone, ash and charcoal markings in the soil are frequently the sole remnants of ages past. Intuition is often all he or she has to go on.

Norman Emerson, an eminent senior archeologist at the University of Toronto, however, has found something better than intuition: the assistance of George McMullen, a psychic who is able to psychometrize sites and the history of their inhabitants merely by tuning in to held objects yielded by a dig. In doing so, McMullen says, he is able to hear and see past events in relation to the object, often eliciting very vivid impressions.

Talking with Emerson about this psychic enterprise

gives the impression that he is not at all concerned about
his unusual alliance. In fact, he visibly enjoys what he's
doing, appears to still be amazed that McMullen and his
working relationship with him emerged in his later years
as an archeologist and treats it all with a sense of humor. "I
don't really understand what's going on," he shrugs, "but it
surely can't be ignored." Understandably skeptical at first,
Emerson now believes that his psychic collaborator is a
potential prototype of the future archeologist's chief ally in
reconstructing the past.

"It all began casually, as fun and games," he explained.
"George and I had fished and played cards together with
our wives for some time before my discovering that he
apparently had psychic abilities. So on New Year's Day,
1971, I handed him an object, a pipe stem I had discovered
in 1948 on a dig, and asked him to hold it."

McMullen concentrated for a few moments with the
object in hand and then not only told Emerson it was part
of a pipe, but proceeded to draw a picture closely resembling
a traditional Iroquois pipe indigenous to the time and
location of the site. He described the pipe-maker as
toothless, between thirty and forty years old, having a
fleshy face, high cheekbones, black dirty hair, unkempt
and wearing an old patched garment which reminded him
of a skirt.

"George proceeded to pinpoint the location where I
found the pipe stem," Emerson continued. "And George
knew almost nothing about archeology. He's an intelligent
man, but rarely reads anything academic. Most of his spare
time is spent fishing and card playing."

"But couldn't he have somehow picked your mind?" we
asked.

"Possibly—I can't completely reject that hypothesis, but
the strongest argument against telepathy is the fact that a
good chunk of George's statements relate to a very distant
past and touch on things I often know little or nothing
about."

Emerson offered an example. At the annual banquet of
the Canadian Anthropological Association, Jack Miller,
an amateur archeologist, presented George with a black
argillite carving, dug up while digging a posthole on the
Queen Charlotte Islands of British Columbia. McMullen
surprised everyone by saying that it had been carved by a
black man from Port-au-Prince, Haiti. Emerson was

convinced that this time McMullen's judgment was off.
Later, when a longer reading was given, McMullen said
that the carver was born and raised in Africa, and had been
brought to the New World as a slave, where he worked in
the Caribbean. He was later taken to British Columbia on
an English ship, eventually escaped, mixed with the
natives and married, lived and died there.

"Well, I couldn't report on that without some sort of
verification," Emerson said. "I got it in a peculiar fashion.
Soon after the banquet, I met Sandy, my daughter's friend,
who claimed to be able to read tarot cards. So I asked her to
psychometrize the carving, volunteering nothing, and she
came up with very much the same story."

Emerson then handed the carving independently to six
other clairvoyants, got their readings down on tape, and
after weeding through the transcripts, came to the
conclusion that the readings were so similar as to preclude
chance. Shortly after, a former student who was well versed
in African art came to visit and, when shown the article,
told Emerson that the carving had all the qualities of a
West Coast African carving. "So I had established what I
then called a psychic team approach," Emerson said.

McMullen, it turned out, also had an uncanny ability to
turn up data while on the actual site of a dig. "I took him to
the site of a prehistoric Iroquois village located in Pickering
Township, just east of Toronto, which a colleague of mine,
Paddy Reid, had been investigating for two years without
having produced any evidence of a palisade.* In a matter of
minutes, no doubt to Reid's consternation, McMullen
pointed out where he believed the palisade had been. Reid
marked out the line with metal survey pins. When he later
dug it, archaeological traces of where the palisade had been
correlated almost exactly with the line George had
indicated. It should be understood that this particular site
was a field covered with grass, weeds, brush and gravel,
giving no visual indication of its former occupation. How
did McMullen do it? Quite simply, he told Emerson and
Reid: he was able to see the site as it once was.

Encouraged by this success, Reid asked McMullen
whether he might attempt to outline where a longhouse had
been. Without hesitating, McMullen proceeded to walk

---

* A palisade is a protective wall of upright posts that surrounded many
Indian villages. Evidence of these walls is indicated by circular stains in
the subsoil where the posts once were.

along where he psychically felt it had been. Reid again followed, carefully marking the line of the walls. Six weeks later, after the area had been cautiously and scientifically dug, McMullen's directions were proven accurate.

"When George comes to a site," Emerson continued, "his behavior reminds me of a bird dog scenting his prey. He walks around briskly to orient himself and then proceeds to describe the people who once lived there, their dress, their economy—it's really quite amazing."

"Isn't he ever wrong?"

"He seems to have some difficulty at times with estimating the age of a site, and is reluctant to deal with burial sites, but he's been 80 percent accurate on data I've been able to check out."

Initially, McMullen appeared to be a specialist in Indian sites and artifacts, but a trip to Egypt and Iran, despite an initial lack of confidence, changed this evaluation.

"We got the opportunity to test out some of the Edgar Cayce readings in these countries," Emerson recalled. Cayce, famous as a clairvoyant who gave readings on health and personal problems, had also provided a large body of trance data on prehistory, including some on the legendary lost continent of Atlantis.

"Hugh Lynn Cayce (son of Edgar, and director of the Association for Research and Enlightenment) was quite impressed with George's readings of eight small artifacts from Mediterranean sites and invited us on an expedition to see whether George could verify some of Cayce's statements. It was hoped that George might locate some of the sites which could provide the basis for excavations."

McMullen was initially resistant. He psychically felt a powerful surge of loneliness as if the expedition was somehow threatening. When they reached Egypt, he felt that he really shouldn't have been there, that the area wasn't his territory and that his powers were somehow being controlled. "George had been psychically counseled against visiting the king's chamber in the Great Cheops Pyramid," Emerson noted in his account of the trip. "When he did go there, he said it felt as if the top of his head was being drawn upward; he was only able to tolerate staying a very short amount of time."

After a five-day immersion into Egyptian archeology, McMullen gave a summary reading on the pyramids. He said that there had been "a system of water channels, pools, fountains and bath houses replete with luxurious vegetation in the area immediately adjacent to the Sphynx."

"There's little you can do with this kind of information," Emerson said, "without actually digging to verify it."

When the expedition arrived in Iran, a search was made near the village of Shushtar for the City of the Hills and Plains. Cayce had referred to himself as having spent an incarnation at this location in Persia, which had then been a gathering place of peoples from many different lands.

McMullen located twenty-five significant cave sites in the vicinity of Shushtar; one now caved in and obscured had been a healing center, he said. A man who was an early incarnation of Jesus had lived there. If the cave were to be dug up, tablets would be found. He also said that excavations of the area around the other cave sites, thought to have been the City of the Hills and Plains, would turn up cultural debris which would indicate that the site had once been a great coordinating center for caravan activities from many areas. A great tent city, he said, had once been there.

The party moved on to Teheran. At a research site called the Caravansary, New Teheran, the chief archeologist of Iran asked George what general feeling the site gave him. George answered:

> Ah ... very old, very old and somewhat sad, too. My immediate impression was that things I had learned in my country about the Bible and things that they had taught me in church ... about Christianity—all of a sudden was a pile of chaff. Because, I'm sorry to say—because I could suddenly see that everything they said in the Bible was just stories that they had got from here, you know, and I suddenly realized that this was where it happened, not in the so-called Holy Land.

Emerson points out that the discovery of the Dead Sea Scrolls had established early Christian writings in an ancient Near-Eastern tradition. "It occurred to me," he notes in his journal, "that we were faced with a situation where further Christian traditions might be finding themselves set back in a Persian cultural setting."

Emerson is relatively new to the psychic field. He was

irrevocably drawn to it as his work with McMullen progressed. He now looks to possible explanations of the dynamics of McMullen's readings from work being conducted on a variety of psi phenomena. He sees these various research paths as converging toward a new science of humanity and feels that archeology is only one of the sciences to be affected by changes in scientific thinking.

"How do your colleagues feel about your work?" we asked.

"There's been a bit of flack, but there's definitely a growing interest. Just think of the money that could be saved in locating features on sites ... in any case, the proof is going to be in the digging. There is a great deal more of this that must be done."

Emerson, however, sees the psychic as a helper, not a substitute for the rigorous methods of the archeologist. McMullen has raised a bold issue about the nature of archeological work itself: how many archeologists could learn to develop and professionally employ their latent psychic abilities?

"It's my impression," Emerson said, "that many field archeologists have had brushes with the psychic during their field investigations, but have preferred to leave them unexplored, though I have had hints that perhaps one or two have put this kind of ability to practical use."

How Did You Get Into My Mind?

Clout.... You need it if you're going to make an impact on your profession. And it doesn't hurt if you belong to the right clubs, have impressive academic credentials and a cautious demeanor.

You don't get clout by screaming. That only alienates potential allies. A gentle but firm stance gets the point across, and, if you've already done your share of work with the accepted ideas, then you may be able to successfully introduce new ones.

This is University of Miami psychiatrist Stanley R. Dean's personal formula for getting his American Metapsychiatry Association off the ground. At the last four meetings of the American Psychiatric Association (APA), Dean, a pioneer in the treatment of schizophrenia, has organized a panel attended by overflowing crowds called "Metapsychiatry: The Interface between Psychiatry and Mysticism." The participants have largely been medical people interested in studying altered states of consciousness, meditation, biofeedback, mysticism and varieties of ESP.*

The definition of metapsychiatry is the base of a pyramid whose other sides are psychiatry, parapsychology, philosophy and mysticism. Dean got the term from G.W. Kleinmaeir, a California physician who began applying it in his practice. The term has since found its way into the glossary of the American Psychiatric Association.

"We psychiatrists," Dean asserted, "are conditioned to equate hallucinations with schizophrenia and other psychoses, but throughout history there have been instances of nonpsychotic individuals—many people includ-

---

* Stanley R. Dean has edited and compiled these talks in *Psychiatry and Mysticism*, Chicago: Nelson-Hall, 1975.

190

ing sages and seers—who have heard voices, seen visions and experienced supernatural phenomena." Psychiatry, says Dean, should become more willing to encourage people to disclose paranormal experiences and respond to such disclosures in an open-minded spirit.

It's becoming increasingly evident that ascetics don't have the patent on mystical, or "peak," experiences. According to a national survey by sociologists Andrew Greeley and William MacCready, four out of ten Americans claim to have had one. The experience is generally described as a sudden powerful inner illumination which transcends daily reality, flooding one's consciousness.

Mainstream psychoanalysis and psychiatry, in the spirit of the Protestant work ethic, have traditionally brushed aside reports of these experiences as irrelevant, if not harmful, escapes from reality—not unlike schizophrenia—a retreat away from constructive problem solving, a regression....

Dean begs to differ. He believes the mystical experience is genuine, a factor of human growth. Quite often it catalyzes a healthy restructuring of consciousness and self-image, compelling an appreciation of life deeper than allowed for on the wheel of endless material acquisitions. And no, it's not simply a temporary reorganization of brain functioning (and therefore not illusory).

Dean gets some of his inspiration from Richard Maurice Bucke, the early president of the American Medico-Psychological Association. In 1894, Bucke wrote a paper called "Cosmic Consciousness," in which he argued that higher levels of consciousness had sporadically been experienced throughout the ages, and that this was a natural phenomenon, latent in all of us. It was evolutionary and would eventually raise humankind to a higher plane of existence. Bucke also ventured that psychical research would one day become a major concern of psychiatry.

Dean adds to this. "The developing human mind undoubtedly harbors a rudimentary awareness of cosmic evolution, more manifest in some than in others, which may ultimately evolve into an aggregate understanding of the origin and the nature of the universe." He calls this summit of experience the *ultraconscious*, to bring the idea more in line with psychiatric language (e.g., conscious-unconscious). When this state is achieved, Dean says, "the mind, divinely intoxicated, literally reels and trips over itself, groping and struggling for words of sufficient exaltation and grandeur to portray the transcendental vision."

Many people, he says, fear experiences of this nature, experiences which violate consensus reality. When he sees people who appear to be schizophrenic in his clinical setting, he probes to see whether in fact their apparent lack of self-control is related to a previous mystical experience, one which may have pulled them over the emotional edge. This isn't difficult to understand considering the nature of the experience. Dean gives these examples:

* The individual is bathed in emotions of super-charged joy, rapture, triumph, grandeur, reverential awe and wonder.
* an ecstacy so overwhelming that it seems little less than a sort of super psychic orgasm.

* An intellectual illumination occurs that is quite impossible to describe. In an intuitive flash, one has an awareness of the meaning and drift of the universe, an identification and merging with Creation, infinity and immortality, a depth beyond depth of revealed meaning—in short, a conception of an Over-Self, so omnipotent that religion has interpreted it as God. The individual attains a conception of the whole that dwarfs all learning, speculation and imagination and makes the old attempts to understand the universe elementary and petty.

* There is a feeling of transcendental love and compassion for all living things.

* Fear of death falls off like an old cloak; physical and mental suffering vanish. There is an en-hancement of mental and physical vigor and activity, a rejuvenation and prolongation of life.

* There is a reappraisal of the material things in life, an enhanced appreciation of beauty, a realization of the relative unimportance of riches and abundance compared to the treasures of the ultraconscious.

* There is a sense of mission. The revelation is so moving and profound that the individual cannot contain it within himself, but is moved to share it with all fellow men.

It's usually the last characteristic of the experience that can get someone into trouble. "While I want those patients who have had this experience to know that it is widely shared by great numbers of sensible, rational people in all walks of life, there's an important qualifier, particularly if psychic phenomena begin to come through as well." Dean says some people feel compelled to start sharing their psychic experiences with the public; they'll call the FBI when they seem to tune in to voices sounding conspiratorial and will generally make a mess of things.

"Once you get these abilities," he said, "you must maintain control over them. You have to remain in contact with the everyday world. Even if there is another world to experience, a person has to aim at having the best of both."

This is when the right kind of therapy can help. Otherwise, a person might seek salvation and reinforcement from misguided, sensationalistic cults. Dean hopes that greater acceptance of metapsychiatry will serve as a viable deterrent.

The metapsychiatric push is, in part, a throwback to the early days of psychical research which dealt with trance states, multiple personality and possession phenomena. The medical and psychology members of the Society for Psychical Research in London were especially interested in the relationships between various nervous disorders and psi. They studied hysteria in the hope of throwing light on the often bizarre muscular reactions evidenced in mediumship. The study of multiple personalities, it was hoped, would give rise to a theory of consciousness.

Frederick Myers proposed a theory of personality which could incorporate psi experience. He called one aspect of the unconscious the subliminal self, an organized personality structure which was always active but could only in certain circumstances break through to consciousness. It could, for example, be tapped via hypnosis. In that case, he said a deeper level of mind would be capable of independently relating to other minds. Clairvoyance was an example of the result of the subliminal self becoming more active in waking consciousness. Telepathy could occur if a person's sensitivity became much more acute. In short, the subliminal self was always there, ready to be used, ready to rise to the surface.

The relationship between the unconscious and conscious mind, of course, came of age with the emergence of Freudian psychoanalysis. Freud, incidentally, was a member of both British and American psychical research societies, and had once even written to psi researcher Hereward Carrington that if he had his life to live over again, he would devote it to psi.

Freud, however, did a fancy two-step—he had to be cautious. Psychiatry was quickly becoming established as a branch of modern medicine, and in the United States, where his work received the greatest respect, playing around with psi was for many tantamount to professional suicide. So while Freud was seriously interested in the paranormal, particularly in telepathy, he stopped short of making any firm statements.

Why especially telepathy? Because it was a behavior which seemed to frequently emerge in the analyst-patient relationship. Aside from the common occurrence of correctly anticipating a therapist's question, patients would report dreams of a telepathic nature, detailing some of the analyst's behavior. While later psychoanalytical writings made repeated mention of this, the more skeptical therapists wrote it off as the patient's subconscious wish fulfillment.

Not everyone, however. Analyst Jan Ehrenwald suggested that a schizophrenic could be a "sensitive" deluged by telepathic information, who couldn't cope with or control the psychic assault. More recently, psychotherapist and dream researcher Montague Ullman has asserted that telepathic rapport can occur in the clinical setting. He attributes this to a loss of effective symbolic contact between therapist and patient. When the patient really desires the contact, he or she may use a telepathic maneuver. Considering that almost sixty percent of people interviewed in a recent poll by the National Opinion Research Center said they believed they had had at least one telepathic experience, the possibility of it occurring in the clinical setting wouldn't be that unusual.

Aware of this history with its occasional foreward stabs and the current impact being made by Stanley Dean and others to bring the question of psi and mysticism to the forefront of psychiatry, Howard Eisenberg, a young

Toronto physician and psychotherapist, is involved in a brave therapeutic-telepathic adventure.

Telepathy certainly isn't new to Eisenberg. When a student at McGill University, he conducted a major study for his master's degree. Telepathy testing by and large has been a boring business. A receiver continually guesses what cards a sender in another room is concentrating on. Eisenberg made it more interesting. He used film sequences as "targets." Twenty-four senders. Twenty-four receivers. A sender watched a randomly selected film sequence (e.g., from *The Boston Strangler*) and a receiver seated in another room relaxed and tried to tune in to the image being transmitted.

The results: the odds against their being due to chance were about 100,000 to one.

Now Eisenberg makes use of telepathy in his clinical practice. "One woman patient," he told us, "was unreachable. She was what I would call a boderline schizophrenic. I knew that many like her often turn out to be good psychics who seem to be suffering from information overload. Society tells them they're crazy and this itself drives them further into psychosis. There were a few behavioral patterns which gave her away. I noticed that she always wore dark glasses, and I suspected that his wasn't for optical reasons. When in one of our earlier sessions I asked whether I could check them to see if they were prescription lenses, she refused. She also avoided direct eye contact, tending to cast her eyes down.

"Later sessions," he continued, "revealed that from childhood she had been sensitive to the thoughts of others. People seemed to sense this and she was repeatedly told that she had a discomforting way of looking at people, as if she were seeing through them. So, she eventually took to wearing glasses, to conceal her eyes and, in effect, hide behind them."

Eisenberg tried to communicate with her telepathically. "Her mind needed company," he said. "She needed to be told that someone understood, someone really cared for her, that she wasn't crazy, that, on the contrary, she was psychically gifted."

He concentrated, gazed directly at her, relaxed and imagined himself mentally merging with her, thinking of caring and helping. He was following what seems to be a basic prerequisite for being a telepathic agent: you have to be relaxed and make yourself a center of attraction, drawing the receiver mentally toward you. According to one view, held by Andrija Puharich, a psi researcher and medical scientist, the sender doesn't actually send but creates a form of mental vacuum toward which the receivers mind is drawn. "The sender," writes Puharich, "by his need and desire prepares a mental stage; the receiver in turn populates the stage with his own symbols and images." Concentration clears the sender's own mental screen and allows the desired image to be projected onto that screen.

Is there an energy bridge of some kind?

B.B. Kazhinsky of the Ukrainian Academy of Sciences proposed that rhythmic electrical currents emanate from the brain, and, therefore, the brain of a sender may send a series of electromagnetic waves which correspond to thought patterns. Leonid Vasiliev, a Soviet researcher, thinks not. He investigated this viewpoint by successfully inducing hypnosis at a great distance. The subject was in a metal chamber which shielded him from electromagnetism. Some researchers are therefore hoping to eventually discover some subatomic particle which may somehow telepathically transmit information. Others speak of Carl Jung's notion of a *collective unconscious* as the universal force which binds us together at a deeper level of Self.

Whatever the explanation, the process seems to have worked for Eisenberg in therapy. "She sat there," he said, describing his patient, "unmoved for a minute, and then glared at me, demanding, 'How did you get into my head?'"

In future sessions, she sensed a probing, an invasion. This naturally frightened her, a fear which subsided as she began to feel that there was friendly company in her mind. Reassured, her armor of inhibitions began to soften. Eisenberg then gradually proceeded to encourage her to develop her psychic abilities while stressing the need to willfully control and manage them.

"She got well," he said, "and still is well, and an exemplary university student. You have to wonder how many people there are in psychiatric wards who got there because they were psychic.

"All that's necessary sometimes," he continued, "is someone who understands, someone who is open to unusual mental powers, who can reduce the level of fear of these experiences and help to channel them into constructive behavior."

The view that empathy, warmth and genuine concern is basic to psychiatric healing has been repeatedly demonstrated in a variety of studies. Those therapists who exhibit these characteristics consistently and convincingly get better results than those who lack them.

Stanley Dean is even more emphatic:

The entire gamut of psychotherapy—from the native witchdoctor at one extreme to the academically trained psychiatrist at the other—hinges upon two constructs: the therapeutic personality (charisma) of the therapist, and the expectant faith of the patient, both of which apparently involve a suprasensory, suprarational level of mentation (the ultraconscious) as yet little understood.

Dean with clout, Eisenberg with dare both as physicians who care deeply about the well-being of their patients are helping to refocus attention on the possibilities of mind in modern psychiatry.

Helping Children with Mind

When Marilyn Rossner, an educational therapist specializing in the guidance of emotionally disturbed children, first saw eleven-year old James, psychiatrists at the Montreal Children's Hospital had already clinically diagnosed him as schizophrenic. He was so disturbed that his condition was seen as hopeless. The most he would be capable of accomplishing would be to write his own name. They were convinced he would spend the rest of his life in mental institutions.

Rossner didn't "see" it that way. Not at all.

"When I first saw him," she told us, "he was sitting on the windowsill, rocking back and forth, flailing his hands and just repeating, 'The big round bus goes round and round and the wheels on the bus go round and round.' When I looked at him psychically, I knew that his condition had been misdiagnosed, that one of his major problems was a motor one which would not be apparent to anyone judging him purely by externals."

This is what she saw:

* There were very erratic energy patterns behind his head, and around his entire body.

* Little colorful arrows and dots of energy were radiating from him like lightening bolts.

* His spine appeared to be crooked in her clairvoyant perception, but when she looked at his back physically, it proved to be perfectly straight. The message was a symbolic one; that there was something wrong with his ability to move.

Marilyn Rossner's psychic abilities are multifaceted.

"When I look at someone," she explained, "different colored energy patterns start coming over the body. If there is something physically wrong with a person, I will see a color of a very light hue over that particular part of the body. Then the distance that this color of the aura is from the body tells me whether it's a past, present or future condition." If it's on the body, she knows it's a present condition, if behind, then past and if in front, then future.

She offered an example. "If I'm looking at a person who in the past had a problem controlling temper, but eventually learned to do so, I see a red color with arrows darting from it behind the head. Then I'll see the red turning into a pink and eventually coming over the person's face. But if the person hasn't been able to control his temper, I'll see red and pink intermingled."

Rossner, of course, isn't unique in her claimed ability to read auras. The psychical literature has repeatedly referred to the ability of some psychics to see "subtle energy bodies" interpenetrating the physical. Disease, it's been said, first manifests itself in these prephysical energies before it becomes physically embodied. And as previously discussed, recent work in Kirlian photography has given the aura a new lease on life.

Rossner, however, is not about to wait for conclusive scientific proof. She's confident of her interpretations of what she sees, having had these experiences since she was a child. "I would see a rainbow of colors around people and thought it quite normal until I reached the age of fourteen, when I discovered I was unusual, that others didn't have this ability."

Over the years, she's developed a comprehensive clairvoyant system of diagnosis. "After I see the aura," she continued, "I may get a clairaudient sound, a voice saying something like, 'When you were sixteen, this is what happened.' I then might hold the person's hand and get further impressions of the emotional state and problems hovering around that person."

"Can you just turn these abilities on when you want?"

"At will," she responded. "But most of the time, I look quite normally at someone with one exception; I always see an energy pattern in the solar plexus region. I see energies moving, and, if they are erratic and in a turmoil, I know right away that the person is tense or has problems. This tells me how to relate in a more sensitive way."

Rossner, also a Spiritualist, says she's able to tune in to spirit communicators and actually hears and sees them behind people. By deeply inhaling and concentrating, she can make them advance before the person to whom they have been attracted. These spirits will often provide her with further information. "I can see them when I choose to," she said. "They can't be permitted to spontaneously intrude without my wanting them to come through and I'm careful to maintain continual control. When I want a particular entity close to someone to come through, I extend an invitation, but that doesn't necessarily mean they'll accept."

How does she know whether the impressions she receives are literal or symbolic?

"When I hear something [clairaudience], I've learned to interpret it literally. But when I get a visual impression, it's almost always symbolic."

James (her "very special boy") appeared to have some psychic abilities of his own. When Rossner "listened" carefully to his conversations with imaginary people, she quickly realized he was really "seeing" and "hearing." Often, she found, James received clairvoyant impressions. Once he said: "Bump, bump, bump, mommy down the stairs. Whirr the siren." Rossner later learned from James's mother that she had fallen down the stairs at home and was taken to the hospital, and that it happened at about the time that James got the impression.

Rossner became aware that the emanation she saw around James resembled the aura of highly gifted psychics. "Usually when I see the aura around a person," she explained, "what I first see is a dark, thick energy band around the head and shoulders, and then the colors appear. But with highly developed psychics, I rarely see that dark pattern. It's almost as if everything is transparent and translucent and moving at a much greater vibratory rate than with most people."

The vibrations of a very psychic person, she says, closely resemble those of a schizophrenic. "Also, when I touch a schizophrenic's hand, I feel energy shooting out, and when I look at the eyes, I see a shade of yellow. So I've learned that a schizophrenic has a very specific auric pattern and vibratory rate."

In James's case, Rossner also got the clairvoyant impression that he had a chemical imbalance. When she sent him to a cooperative physician, her suspicions were confirmed; he was immediately placed on a megavitamin program. In addition, whenever Rossner communicated with James, she would always tell him that she believed that he was really "seeing" and "hearing" things. "But I wanted to teach him how to control these impressions," she said. "I would tell him to close his eyes and that when he opened them again, the impressions would stop, and he'd only see me and the book I had given him or whatever he was playing with. Whenever I felt him going off into a psychic state, I would either ring a bell or use a light flasher attached to his desk. I'd say, "James, here's your token [reward] for doing your work," and I'd bring him back, because once he went into that state it took a long time to bring him back."

Rossner was certain that if she used this form of behavioral therapy combined with exercises to develop a greater sense of body mastery along with her psychic intuition, that he'd recover and be capable of doing at least seventh grade work and get around the city on his own. "The psychiatrists," she said with some exasperation, "were concerned about my optimism, and warned me I was in for a big disappointment."

James is now eighteen, drives a car, has completed seventh grade at a high school for slow learners, and is about to work in his father's restaurant. "He's fine," Rossner said with a broadening smile. "He's not like other eighteen-year-olds, but absolutely not severely emotionally disturbed nor retarded. I'm convinced that if we had gotten this kid when he was five or six, he'd be perfectly normal now."

As for the further development of her own psychic abilities, Rossner credits her teacher, Mamie Brown, a Philadelphia medium and minister of the Spiritualist church, now eighty-six, for having carefully guided her over the past ten years and with whom she enjoys an ongoing relationship.

Rossner also has an extensive background in yoga, having studied closely with Swami Vishnu Devananda and often employs yoga techniques in teaching children to develop their motor skills and how to relax. "Regardless of a person's age, background and intellectual capacities," she insists, "everyone has needs on several levels: physical, emotional, social and spiritual. Any program we provide for children must be all-encompassing."

Doesn't she get any flack about using her unorthodox abilities?

"When I began, I was very cautious not to broadcast my abilities, but gradually physicians and psychiatrists I worked with began to see that some of the so-called hopeless and difficult kids I worked with were being helped. Aware of how my hunches were being repeatedly vindicated, they weren't, however, about to define them as psychic. They looked at me as someone who was a little way out but highly successful—regardless."

Here are two more of Rossner's correct hunches:

1. Ruth

"Ruth was diagnosed as retarded and epileptic. However, when I looked at her, I saw her aura was yellow, and I had learned that children with brain damage don't have yellow auras.

"I began wondering whether it might be a good idea to get her off the antiepilepsy pills. I was quite surprised shortly after I had this thought when Ruth came up to me and confided that she had flushed her pills down the toilet and asked me not to tell her mother. I promised to persuade her mother not to punish her but felt she should be informed.

"Ruth was then taken to a doctor who agreed to take her off the pills. She didn't show any signs of epilepsy."

2. Brian

"Brian was an in-patient of the Montreal Children's Hospital's psychiatric unit and was diagnosed as having a severe character and behavioral disorder."

"When I saw him psychically, I saw the number three before him. I then sent out a mental question and got a clairaudient answer that his problem stemmed from frustration relating to his inability to read and that in three reading lessons he would learn how, and his problems would subsequently dissolve."

"After his third lesson, he began to read a bit and was encouraged. He's now sixteen, and has finished the tenth grade in a regular high school."

Rossner is concerned about the rampant misdiagnoses by physicians. "Too often, medical people respond to external symptoms," she said. "When I see a person, I can psychically perceive the root problem rather than its external manifestation. Sometimes, if the problem is of a psychic nature, the child will lack control over it. In many cases I can teach them to learn control and function effectively in both worlds, consensus reality and the psychic."

One event which emphasizes the number of patients in psychiatric wards who may be psychics out of control is very clear in her memory. When visiting New York's Bellevue Hospital in the 60s, the resident chief of psychiatry took her on a tour through some wards, and he said, "This is what happens to people who play with psychic abilities. Many of these people are here because they've had bum drug trips; they've abused their bodies, or they've tried to develop too quickly and ... they're a little bit schizophrenic."

Rossner, therefore, strongly asserts that if physicians would become aware of the psychic factor by developing their own intuitive abilities, many people could be helped. Instead, all too often, they are given up on or their potential is perceived in limited terms. For example, rather than simply dismiss someone's reported "visions" as hallucinations, closer examination might often reveal actual clairvoyant perceptions.

"One day, a mother and father came over with their child," she recalled, "and as soon as I looked at him, I knew that he was seeing clairvoyantly, but I also knew he was hallucinating. The child had continually told his mother he was communicating with three entities. I got a vision of one of them, who he said was able to go through walls, as being real [that is, in spirit form]. But when he described the other two, I psychically saw two children and arrows going from his mind to them. I knew right away that these two had been created by his own mind.

"Now, this is the kind of child," she continued, "who could very easily become schizophrenic, but with proper therapy, this situation can be brought under control."

Rossner believes the boundary line for many children is a tightrope, that negative attitudes from parents, teachers and therapists can push a child over the edge.

"All words," she explained, "are created by thought. The

thought precedes the word. I can psychically see these words forming when people are talking. I see the vibrations, as though they are coming off a typewriter going from one person to the next, and, if there's anger or frustration, these vibrations are jagged; when they're loving, they are smooth and have a curved motion."

She believes that if those therapists who deal with children with emotional problems would learn to control their own minds and react positively (rather than focus on, and thereby reinforce, bad behavior), this in itself would have a beneficial transforming effect on the child.

The same is true about family members and teachers. "I often wonder why there aren't even more disturbed children. If you look at the negativism of family members and the way that some slow-learning kids with emotional problems are persecuted in the school system by insensitive teachers, you can understand how the attitudes of these people are dragging them down."

Her hope, then, is to persuade more people to recognize the psychical level of our existence, and how health disturbances can be generated and reinforced by the thoughts and attitudes of our peers.

"I believe the day is coming," she said, "when people will go to psychics for preventative measures. I personally 'see' so much around children when I visit hospitals—what kinds of things will happen to them. Sometimes it's just a matter of whether a child should be sent to a foster home or to unit A or B in the hospital. I might get the impression that they should be sent to B. You see, it might not matter all that much to the authorities where the child is sent, but a psychic may be able to see the incredible difference it would make."

Healing Energies

OOMMM...OOOOMMMMMMmmmmm...The chanting reverberates throughout the small, poorly-lit auditorium. Our bodies feel like tuning forks. Three hundred strong, some sitting, some standing, everyone's attention is riveted to the front.

Draped in a yellow sari, Hilda Charlton, elderly Manhattan yogini, follower of the Indian holy man Sai Baba, holds a woman's hand. The chanting is being directed somewhere across rain-drenched New York City to the woman's brother. He has cancer.

Hilda's eyes are closed in concentration, her body a transducer for the sounds and energy level building in the room. She opens her eyes, the OMs subside. Does anyone else have a friend or relative they would like to have healed? Three people walk up to join the small line beside her.

Each person in turn describes the physical or psychological problem of the person being petitioned for. Hilda repeats it for our benefit and the OMs begin again.

This healing is the finale to the group meditation class Hilda leads each Thursday night (traditionally guru night in India) in the Greenwich Village basement of St. Luke's Church on the corner of Hudson and Barrow.

We're sitting in the coffeehouse of the Sheraton Mount-Royal Hotel in downtown Montreal with Ethel DeLoach, a healer highly regarded by the professional psi community and founder of the New Jersey Society of Parapsychology. By tuning in to the universal energies that surround us, Ethel says, she is able to channel it through her to heal. In the course of our talk with her, we question her about the range of physical afflictions she had successfully healed.

Among those cited are cases with multiple sclerosis, inoperable eye conditions and arthritis.

Ethel doesn't practice the usual "laying on of hands" to heal, but performs an extraordinary finger dance— movement over a person's body. Her hands, she explains, appear to be guided by invisible forces. Describing Ethel's healing procedure, her patients say they feel needlelike sensations where her dancing fingers pass, as if she's performing invisible acupuncture. Curiously, acupuncturists who have observed her healing sessions report that her fingers deftly follow meridian lines and pulses well known to practitioners of the ancient Chinese art.

In 1957 at the Allan Memorial Institute of Psychiatry in Montreal, Bernard Raymond Grad began to experiment in his leisure hours with Oskar Estebany, a healer, to determine whether the laying on of hands could measurably influence biological systems.

A group of laboratory mice were made goitrous by being fed a diet low in iodine and were later given thiouracil, a drug which prevents even the smallest amount of iodine from reaching the thyroid gland. The thyroids of the mice were expected to enlarge several times their normal size. Grad wanted to see whether Estebany could, through the laying on of hands, prevent or retard this growth.

The mice were placed in cages and divided into three groups, two of which were controls. One was given a heat treatment because Grad wanted to test the possibility that heat coming from Estebany's hands might have an effect on the development of the goiter. The other control group was not touched at all but the mice were removed from their cages whenever the other groups were moved. Mice in the experimental group were held by Estebany for fifteen minutes twice daily.

The result: the mice which had been held by Estebany had a significantly slower rate of goiter development than the others in the two control groups.

If Estebany could have this effect, Grad reasoned, could he also heal wounds? Mice were anesthetized and an area of skin about the size of a quarter was surgically removed from their backs. After introducing appropriate experimental controls in three experiments, the results were the same: mice held by Estebany healed significantly faster than control groups.

Grad was persuaded by the evidence that he was onto something important. Some unknown healing energy appeared to have been transmitted.

Grad next set up a series of plant experiments. He knew that plants could be put into a state of need if they were given a saltwater solution. This would inhibit their growth. Could Estebany's treatments diminish the salt solution's inhibiting effect on plant growth?

Estebany was handed an open beaker of the solution and instructed to hold it for fifteen minutes. The barley seeds Grad had chosen for the experiment were then watered with Estebany's solution and the controls with an untreated control solution. Those watered with Estebany's solution came up through the soil faster and grew higher than the control group. To insure that this wasn't a chance occurrence, Grad found that when two groups were given the same solution, this time untouched by Estebany, there were no significant differences between them.

Convinced by the results that Estebany's hands had somehow produced a physical effect, Grad concluded in a paper published in the *Journal of the American Society for Psychical Research*:

> Although little can be said about the nature of the force that is producing the biological effects ...or the mechanism whereby it acts, the experiments on wound healing and plant growth have demonstrated that the so-called laying on of hands, at least when done by certain individuals, has objective, demonstrable effects which, because it was done on animals and on saline poured over plants, can hardly be explained as being due to the power of suggestion....

After the Hungarian Revolution in 1956, Oskar Estebany immigrated to Canada. He brought with him an unusual history. He was known in Hungary as a healer, a man who had the power to cure in his hands. It began when he had cradled his twelve-year-old son, who was feverish with diphtheria, in his lap for two days. The child dramatically recovered. Later, when teaching in a military academy, Estebany noticed that his horses never tired after long rides, nor did they become lame. His students' horses did, however, but quickly regained strength when he rubbed them down. Word spread. Estebany had healing hands. Estebany could cure. Laying his hands on other animals had the same beneficial effect. And with people as well, he discovered, when he agreed to treat patients with a variety of illnesses in a Sopron hospital after physicians had given up on them.

While Estebany's career as a healer was in the making, Grad was exploring the theory that a life energy exists, interpenetrating all animate and inanimate matter. Not a recent idea, but one which goes back through the centuries.

Grad first became aware of the presence of this life-energy in his teens. When ill, he felt that at a certain point of the day, a tide of energy would flow through him, and, at other times, it would leave. These feelings, he says, were almost subliminal and yet tangible. He assumed everyone had them and left it at that.

In 1948, after earning a Ph.D. in biology, Grad came across the work of Wilhelm Reich, the German-born Freudian psychoanalyst who later turned to a controversial preoccupation with a life-energy he called *orgone*. Reich said it was everywhere, in varying degrees, and was the basis for all life. Each species metabolized this energy according to its own species potential. The *bion*, he proposed, was the tiny carrier or orgone, a basic unit of all living matter.

Reading Reich's ideas, Grad's earlier subjective energy experiences found a context. The lightbulb flashed. In September, 1949, he traveled to Rangely, Maine, where Reich was conducting his orgone experiments with "accumulators." These were boxes made of metal and organic materials which Reich believed captured and concentrated orgone. By spending time in one of these human-size accumulators, he believed, the infusion of orgone into the body had healthful effects, even on degenerative diseases such as cancer.

Grad witnessed many of Reich's experiments, became a friend, regularly visited him in his laboratory and stayed by him throughout the tumultuous trial period. Reich was eventually sentenced to two years imprisonment for having violated an injunction to cease experimentation— with animals—with the orgone, and died in Lewisburg Penitentiary in 1957 after serving less than a year.

The trial had a major impact on Grad. People who had new ideas had best keep their lips tightly sealed—at least so he felt at the time. Exploration, however, should never cease. It had to be done quietly. Working in the Gerontological Unit at the Allan Memorial Institute, he went on to produce over eighty scientific papers on the aging process, including some on cancer. Throughout his work, life-energy and its potential remained in the back of his mind, and then....

"I met Estebany through a Hungarian lab technician working with me," Grad told us in his office. "The technician told me that the wife of a friend had been suffering with arthritis of the hip, and a man who had just arrived from Hungary had alleviated her condition by simply putting his hands over the afflicted area. Well, I was interested immediately and thought that maybe we should get together and talk."

He asked Estebany when they first met how he thought his healing worked. "I feel an energy traveling through my hands," he had replied.

"Now that really caught my interest," Grad said. "My interest in energy had never died and here was a chance, I thought, to pursue it further. And soon after some preliminary trials, the major experiments began."

During the time of the experiments, Estebany often treated Grad's common colds. "He'd just put his hands on my nose and the cold would be gone the next day; it just wouldn't develop any further, and I would feel my energy level go up almost immediately. An energy seemed to be passing from him to me. It was the same feeling I had experienced when I was younger."

Grad speaks of Estebany's work and the experiments with a tinge of sadness. "You know, it's a bloody shame. So much could have been done if we had been given the means to continue this work."

Grad's experiments with Estebany did stimulate wide-spread interest and further research. In 1966, when he lectured on his work at Rosary Hill College, Sister Justa Smith, a biochemist and enzymologist, was impressed with the findings. Rather than work on goiter, wound healing or plants, Grad suggested that if she were to work in this direction, she might attempt to determine whether or not Estebany could influence the activity of an enzyme called trypsin. This was an area in which she already had considerable expertise. She had experimentally demonstrated that magnetic fields increased the trypsin's activity. The question was: could a healer do likewise?

In 1967, Sister Justa Smith's work with Estebany began. He was handed a test tube filled with the enzyme and instructed to hold it. To insure that heat alone wouldn't be a factor, she measured it by taping a thermistor to his hands and got continuous readouts via an electronic thermistor. Fresh crystallized trypsin solution was divided into four samples, one of which was the control. The second was held by Estebany for periods of up to seventy-five minutes. The third was jolted with a damaging ultraviolet light which reduced enzyme activity and which Estebany also held to determine whether he could restimulate enzyme activity. The fourth solution was exposed to a high magnetic field to see how it would compare with Estebany's effect. Throughout the experiment, Justa Smith withdrew tiny samples of the solutions for analysis.

Trypsin activity can be measured in several different ways; Smith made it cleave a colorless chemical (BAPA) to form a new compound which is yellow. The greater the enzyme activity, the more intense the yellow.

The result: Estebany was doing something to the trypsin—dramatically. The enzyme activity had accelerated. The sample which had been exposed to the damaging ultraviolet light also responded significantly to his touch. Some unknown, invisible and powerful force had influenced the enzyme solutions held by the Hungarian healer. The effect measured was equivalent to a magnetic field sixteen thousand times more powerful than the earth's magnetic field. But magnetic energy had not emanated from Estebany's hands. Gauss meters don't lie. The energy—call it Energy X—was unknown.

Grad believes that there are different kinds of healers. Their ranges of efficacy appear to differ. "Estebany," he said, "could treat thyroid problems, but he knew an Austrian who was a tremendous healer who couldn't. But Estebany definitely also had his limitations.

"Healers differ considerably one from another in the range of diseases with which their healing effect appears to work best. Ethel DeLoach's technique, for example, like Estebany's, also involves the use of the hands; but in her case, I feel, the method is better described as a form of acupuncture than laying on of hands. She says she works on a person's energy field, or aura, and on the basis of my very limited experience with her, I believe that her healing may as much involve the redistribution of energy in the body as the adding of energy by the laying on of hands. Too, Ethel believes that while healing, she is assisted by healers in the spirit world who guide her fingers along the body."

Estebany did not appear to believe that he had spirit guides helping, and had Grad met Ethel first, it would have all been much more puzzling to him. Estebany's approach was less complex and as such allowed for a more direct connection with the work of Reich.

"I'm not claiming here that one healer was better than the other," he added, "just comparing their approaches to healing."

One recent view of how healing takes place is expressed by psychologist Lawrence Leshan. After studying the claims of a wide variety of healers, he put them into two basic categories. The Type I healer, he wrote, appears to enter a state of consciousness in which the patient is seen to merge with him as a part of a single reality. When the healer knows or feels certain that this unity has taken place, healing is then possible. The Type II healer views the healing process as originating from himself in the form of a current of energy. Laying on of hands is an example of the latter.

Leshan says Type I transcends a purely sensory reality and operates beyond his or her five basic senses. He calls this a clairvoyant reality where the Self becomes merged with and an active part of a universal consciousness. Through an extensive regimen of disciplined meditation, visualization and also certain exercises, such as dancing, which can be employed to help alter a person's state of consciousness, the clairvoyant reality, he says, can be induced.

Did Grad agree with this dichotomy? "To me," he replied, "the simplest explanation lies in the common denominator to all types of healing, which is life-energy. Healers are manipulators of energy—whether they heal by some variation of the laying on of hands or heal at a distance." He referred to a story about the late renowned healer, Ambrose Worrall. He once received a letter from a young woman in India who was ill. Worrall described how, when he thought of the girl, he distinctly felt something—a ball of energy—leave from his solar plexus and travel to the girl.

What role does the mind play in all this?

"Some people say that the mind is involved," Grad said, "but what is mind? A marvelous organizer of energy. 'In the beginning' ... there was Energy. The world didn't begin from the moment that brain cells appeared. These came a long time later. What we call mind, I feel, is a highly evolved form of this primordial energy. So no matter how you want to phrase it, a healer—whether he be type I or II or whatever—manipulates this energy in some way.

"This life-energy," he continued, "can be seen as carrying information. It is information in action. In our thyroid experiments with mice, we found that Estebany's hands inhibited the growth of the thyroid. That means goitrous cells were prevented from multiplying and growing larger. But in our wound-healing experiments, Estebany accelerated the proliferation of cells, because the wounds of his mice healed faster. How did the energy know in one case to hold back and in the other to speed up the multiplication of cells in order to achieve the original healthy state of the body as a whole?"

Grad speaks of an energy union between healer and patient.

"How can healer and patient form a union at a distance? I assume that they accomplish this as a result of the healer's ability to transmit energy to the patient—to, in effect, form an energy bridge. If the healer is here and the patient is far removed from him, it is certainly not the healer's physical body which unites with and heals the patient. What is it, then, which forms the union, if not energy? But don't ask me to draw a more detailed picture," Grad summed up, smiling. "A great deal of further study in this area is required."

Recently, Olga Worrall, wife of Ambrose, who has continued her husband's work in healing, demonstrated that she could have a physical effect over a delicate instrument at a distance of six hundred miles. In experiments conducted at Agnes Scott College in Atlanta, Georgia, by Robert N. Miller and his associates, Worrall was asked to demonstrate a measurable effect of energy leaving her hands. The target was the interior of a cloud chamber used in atomic laboratories. Miller's report in the magazine *Science of Mind* describes its complex structure:

It consists of a cylindrical glass chamber 7 inches in diameter and 5 inches in height, which has a sheet aluminum bottom and a viewing glass across the top. The unit is operated by covering the floor of the chamber with a quarter-inch layer of methyl alcohol and placing the entire unit upon a flat block of dry ice.

When the liquid surface of the alcohol is in contact with a closed volume of air to form a vapour, some of the molecules of the liquid evaporate into the air. Equilibrium conditions are reached when the rate of evaporation from the liquid surface is just balanced by the rate of reentry of the alcohol molecules from the vapour state into the liquid.

When the bottom of the chamber is chilled by the dry ice, a supersaturated zone about one inch in height is created in the chamber. Condensation through the chamber ionizes molecules of air and vapour and produces a trail of positive and negative ions along its path. The alcohol vapour preferentially condenses on these nuclei and a visible trail of droplets is formed. A spotlight mounted at the side of the chamber provides the lighting necessary for photographing the tracks.

Worrall was asked to place her hands at the side of the chamber, not touching the glass. As she did so, she visualized energy leaving her hands as she does when treating a patient. This had the effect of creating a wave pattern in the mist inside the chamber, waves which were parallel to her hands and the direction of motion perpendicular to her hands. When she shifted her position ninety degrees, the waves inside the chamber also shifted.

Two months later, the experiment was repeated, but this time at a distance. Worrall was in Baltimore, about six hundred miles away. At 8:50 P.M. she was instructed to visualize her hands held in the same manner as before. At 8:53 a change occurred within the cloud chamber. The mist pulsated and dark waves became visible, continuing in this manner for seven minutes. At 9:10 P.M. the experiment was repeated. This time the observed effect was more turbulent. Miller summarized his report, writing, "The results of the second experiment, in which she was 600 miles away from the cloud chamber, indicates that *'thoughts are things'* and *visible manifestations in the physical world can be produced mentally at a distance.*" (our italics)

Who can become a healer? Do we all have this potential? In Grad's opinion, everybody might have the ability to a limited extent, but there are some people who appear to have it to an extraordinary degree.

What, then, about healing classes? Could they teach someone to heal, or was that fool's gold?

"I want to emphasize this," he said. "I think that the problem with a lot of people is that they run around looking for powers as a kind of overlay to their personalities. They say to themselves, 'I don't want to change as a person, but I want these "powers" so that I can more effectively cope with the world.' They seem to say, leave my faults alone, let me remain as I am, but maybe give me a bit of healing or some clairvoyant power so that I can manipulate the world at my whim.

"You'll notice, for example," he continued, "that there are many clairvoyant and healing experiences described in the Bible, Koran, the Vedas and so on, but these gifts are not cited as the primary thing. These ancient healers and psychics were people who, it seems to me, always said, 'Live right, develop moral and ethical responsibility—and if you do, you might get the other things. They're part of the package but not available until certain prerequisites are met. 'To acquire special powers without the wisdom of how to responsibly use them is to augment, not lessen, the dangers in the world."

Grad doubts that many people will emerge from healing courses with any significant ability. Sure, it may help a few who have learned to meditate, to alter their states of consciousness, and if the potential is there...

"If the oil is there," Grad believes, "the course is just a little pipe that's been drilled to tap it. All of a sudden—boom—it floods to the surface. But if there's no oil, you can do all the drilling you want. But you won't be a healer."

A healer, Grad says, must be psychologically well integrated, not disturbed, if a healing bridge or rapport is to be established with the patient. This was demonstrated in one of his experiments. A psychotically depressed man was instructed to hold a saline solution which was poured on a container of barley seeds. Plant growth, compared to the control, was significantly inhibited. In the same experiment, a woman who was somewhat less depressed than the man learned about the aim of the experiment and immediately brightened at the prospect of helping plants to grow. Her emotional turnaround, Grad suspected, may very well have influenced her effect, which was better than that of the control group but not as extensive as that of a man who had a "green thumb."

We thought of the three hundred OMers in Hilda's group. If tuned correctly, that was a lot of tapped energy. But was it? Might some of it, if transmitted, work at cross-purposes? Especially if some of the participants were depressives?

"Can you imagine how much energy is generated in a class like that?" Grad echoed. "But I wonder about the quality of the energy in that kind of situation. Those who have the ability to heal, I've noticed, have a certain compassion and love for others—but this is a detached kind of emotion. And they must be able to control their hang-ups, to essentially become 'clear channels' when it's time to heal. Remember what happened in my experiment with the depressives. There is so much more we need to know, however, before drawing firm conclusions."

What does this qualifier mean for medical practice? Grad shook his head. "Some physicians may be very good healers and not know it. Here, I refer to something which is beyond the knowledge learned in medical school, or the experience they acquire later still. I refer to a quality which is a part of their personal charisma and which has long been recognized as the 'bedside manner,' which, however, is just the tip of the iceberg. But there is another side to this.

"Physicians, being human like the rest of us, may become disagreeable and carry with them all manner of negative attitudes. Under such circumstances, they should be quite careful not to negatively influence the patient—because they can, in some cases, potentially worsen the patient's condition through their attitude at the time. Psychiatry has, to some extent, been aware of this interaction between patient and physician, but not to the extent which I feel is warranted. Being aware of and sensitive to the depth to which such influences can operate can enormously enhance the physician's ability to heal.

"One other point," Grad continued. "To my mind, there

is no contradiction between conventional medicine with its logical, mechanistic bent and methodology and the unconventional healing methods with their intuitive approach. The contradiction exists only in the minds of those trained to see things so exclusively in a restricted manner that any information which doesn't easily fit with their preferred, ingrained bias is automatically dismissed as ridiculous and irrational. The broadest understanding of the body's functioning and healing requires a cooperation between and synthesis of both approaches. When that occurs, medicine will have entered a Golden Age.

"As for the importance of life-energy for science, the trend these past few centuries was to mechanize biology and psychology—that is, to inject the principles discovered in physics and chemistry into the life sciences. This has had some good effects, but it has unfortunately been too one-sided. I believe that one day the fertilization process will go in the other direction—from the life sciences to physical science. And at the core of this process will be the life-energy."

Dowsing at Danville

A young woman who appears to be concentrating is slowly and purposefully walking across the lawn. She's holding, at chest level, two thin nylon rods tied together at one end, forming a Y-shaped instrument. Suddenly, some mysterious kinetic force seems to be activated, forcing the rod to dip.

Out of a cluster of people watching her progress, an elderly man in baggy pants begins to walk toward her holding two rods with six-inch right angle bends for handles. As he nears the spot where her Y-rod dipped, his own angle rods cross. "Very good," he reinforces. "There's definitely a water vein there."

Nearby, another group is gathered watching a white-haired man. He's observing the movement of his pendulum, a glittering bob suspended from a chain held between his thumb and index finger. As he asks himself whether the woman before him has a vitamin B deficiency, the pendulum gyrates in a counterclockwise direction. "A personal code I've established," he explains, "is that a clockwise rotation means 'yes' and a counterclockwise, 'no.' She, therefore, doesn't have a deficiency. If I wanted to give a complete medical diagnosis, I would ask myself questions about her heart, circulation, respiration, the state of her mental health and so on."

Beside a tree soaring well above the others on the parklike expanse, an elderly man explains to his audience that he believes one cause of arthritis and perhaps even cancer is the emission of noxious rays from underground streams and fissures in the earth. He claims that when two streams cross each other, the human body can be dangerously exposed to these rays. He has made it a practice to use a Y-rod to detect them (particularly underneath houses) and has repeatedly found that when a bed located directly over two crossing underground streams is moved, a person suffering from arthritic pain gets almost immediate relief. If an entire house is located over one of these areas, its occupants may be more susceptible to illness.

To rid a house of these noxious rays, he suggests placing a sixteen-inch rod, about one-half inch in diameter upright over the area in the house with the positive end up (i.e., the end which attracts the north end of a magnet). Another neutralizing method is to deflect the rays from the areas where most time is spent, especially the bedroom, by placing either metal bars or blue fiberglass tape at opposite ends of the noxious zones. He says these reflecting materials dispel the underground rays.

Huddled around a picnic table, five people are intently watching a man who's holding a Y-rod over a map of a person's farm. He's attempting to determine the exact spot on the farm which would be the most productive for a well. Moving the Y-rod back and forth over the entire map until it finally dips, he explains that he often uses this technique to search for water, oil and minerals at a distance. He has even had success in locating missing persons for the police. All he needs is a detailed map and the Y-rod.

"How do you do it?" someone asks.

"Just as I've demonstrated," he responds with confidence. "I ask myself specific questions and keep my mind focused on what I'm looking for. Usually I begin by eliminating large areas on the map before narrowing my focus. Maybe it's ESP."

The art of divining with instruments, or *dowsing*, as it is generally called today, can be traced back to ancient times in China, Egypt, Greece and Persia where it appears to have been used to locate water. During the Middle Ages, there were references to its use for mineral prospecting, particularly in the Hartz Mountains in Germany and then later in Cornwall, England.

Often associated with the world of the occult and witchcraft, its popularity persisted, particularly among rural peoples who applied it as a practical tool to find water. Gradually its use spread throughout Europe, flourishing in France where it was championed by a number of priests.

Today in North America, dowsing has met with the same reproach and criticism as have palmistry, astrology and other occult activities. At the turn of the century, the

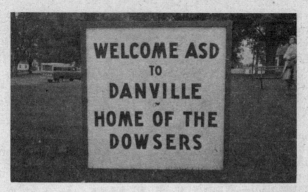

Danville, Vermont, site of the annual dowsing convention
of the American   Society of Dowsers. *(Courtesy, the
authors)*

U.S. Geological Survey, in its pamphlet *The Divining Rod:
A History of Water Witching*, described dowsing as a
fraudulent and curious superstition. Another critic speculated that the dowser's ability to locate water basically
resulted from a subliminal awareness of surface clues to
underground water, among which he listed soil composition, the sounds of vibrations of underground streams,
outcroppings of rocks and even the temperature of the
surrounding air.

Refusing to be the apathetic targets of such criticism, a
group of dowsers who had been meeting and exchanging
experiences for several years decided in 1961 to incorporate
and form the nonprofit and educationally oriented American Society of Dowsers in the hope that their collective
efforts would serve to:

1. Give dowsing a stature of dignity and authority.
2. Win for it prestige and respectful recognition of
   its great growth.
3. Help members with their dowsing problems.
4. Give assistance, guidance and encouragement to
   beginners.
5. Disseminate dowsing knowledge and information to as large a group as possible so that
   dowsing may become more universally accepted
   and used.

With the expansion of its open membership and increased circulation of its quarterly journal, *The American Dowser*, word of the society has spread. Each year, dowsers, the curious and media people converge on the tiny, picturesque mountain village of Danville, Vermont, to attend the convention. Experienced dowsers lead workshops held in the village's churches, lodges and high school. You can learn to use various types of dowsing instruments from crudely fashioned forked sticks (Y-rods) to a wide variety of pendulums and rods and explore techniques to search for water, oil and mineral deposits, locate downed airplanes, pipe blockages, missing persons—anything you want to find.

The physical response which is triggered by the aid of an instrument or prop in the search of something is defined as an *autoscopic* activity. It matters little what the instrument is. Some dowsers are content to use pendulums made of thread and any of a wide variety of bobs. One dowser even uses a blade of grass the same way another might use a Y-rod.

But how, and from where, does the signal or information originate which activates the muscles involved in holding the instrument?

It was once widely believed that some external force—perhaps demonic—acted upon the instrument itself causing it to move. Few dowsers would agree today. They are more aware than ever before of scientific research on dowsing. One research direction has been to determine the possibility of the dowser being influenced by electromagnetic fields given off by the objects sought by the dowser. Yves Rocard, a French physicist, claimed dowsers were capable of detecting magnetic fields with 85 percent consistency. Dutch geologist Solco Tromp arrived at the same conclusion, finding that when a sensitive dowser was hooked up to a cardiograph, he or she registered a reaction to an artificial magnetic field one two-hundredths the strength of the earth's magnetic field.

Charles Buffler, a consulting physicist living in New Hampshire, picked up on this work and conducted a test to see whether dowsers registering reactions to a magnetic field might, in fact, be responding to suggestion. He found that while about eighty percent of his subjects could detect the field when they knew it had been turned on, only one in fifty was capable of registering a dowsing reaction when they didn't know whether it was on or off.

The debate over the possible electromagnetic factors in dowsing recently has been contributed to in grand fashion by physicist Z.V. Harvalik. He's chief of the U.S. Army's Scientific Consultants Staff of the Advanced Material Concepts Agency and has extensively tested dowsers' responses to artificial electromagnetic fields.* Harvalik was interested in finding the sensor, or area in the body which was instrumental in activating the dowsing response. He says he found it in the renal gland of the kidney. The incoming signal is transferred from the renal gland to the brain and in turn triggers muscular reaction, activating the dowsing instrument. The strength of the reaction, he suggests, is due to the dowser's ability to still the mind and focus on the object of his search, as well as on the force of the electromagnetic emission from the object.

Harvalik's research shows that when he blocks off the kidney area with a metallic shield, there is no dowsing reaction. If he blocks off the brain, no reaction. But interestingly, if he blocks off both at the same time, there is a reaction. Conclusion: more research is necessary.

There's another problem with an electromagnetic explanation. How does it explain map dowsing? It doesn't. This is why more dowsers are listening to an ESP explanation for dowsing. One major view has it that dowsing is only one of many forms of natural ESP—a form of systematic mental dissociation. It's believed the human organism continually operates at an extrasensory level. All we need do is become conscious of it and use it.

With an instrument in hand, the mind focuses in pinpoint fashion on a specific question. This intensifies the level of expectation and activates the latent ESP ability. This view holds that in any search where concentration is maximized, the intuitive capacity is extended. To dowse well, then, requires using the mind in a laserlike fashion or as a focused searchlight while it's simultaneously cleared of the usual bombardment of imagery. The dowsing instrument magnifies a subliminal physiological response to a given question which might otherwise go undetected.

Intruding thoughts unrelated to the quest (say, to find

---

* The tests have included exposing dowsers to polarized electromagnetic fields, to artificial alternating magnetic fields in a frequency range from one to one million cycles per second and to D.C. magnetic fields.

water) are called "monkey thoughts." It's essential, dowsers stress, to clear the mind and allow information to come through. These monkey thoughts are akin to the uncontrolled images that flood one's mind when learning to meditate, and so similar discipline to quiet the mind is essential.

Some dowsers are experts in given areas (water, oil, etc.). Technical knowledge of the subject matter, such as having a thorough understanding of oil locations, is a must. Otherwise, you won't know what questions to ask yourself.

The key to dowsing, according to the ESP view, is the mind of the operator. The instrument is merely a tuning device to help amplify and visually register the "signal," or response to the dowser's questions.

Of all the abilities believed to be psychic in nature, dowsing seems to be the most readily accessible. But while almost anyone seems to be capable of achieving some sort of dowsing reaction, to be good at it is something else. It takes practice, lots of it. You need a positive attitude and the ability to still the mind. The Danville dowsers especially stress that proficiency in dowsing requires integrating the technique into your own evolving life philosophy. There are no instant routes to success—at least for most of us.

What better way to discover whether you have dowsing ability than to try it? Here is a chart telling you how to construct your own dowsing instrument, and a few simple exercises gleaned from the instruction at Danville.

Dowsing Instruments

INSTRUMENT	CONSTRUCTION	HOW IT WORKS
1. *Y-Rod* Made for centuries from a forked branch. Some dowsers still believe that a particular type of wood such as a willow, apple or Chinese elm is the only suitable material. Any flexible material will	Recommended material: plastic tubing, at least 1/2 inch thick 1. Bend about two feet of plastic tubing in the middle. 2. Securely tie or tape the folded end (use masking tape).	1. Hold the free ends of the Y, one in each hand, with hands in front of you, knuckles toward the ground. 2. By grasping the rod firmly, bend the ends outward, creating a tension in the rod.

work unless you
believe otherwise.

3. The apex of the rod
   should point
   upward.

4. When you cross a
   water vein, the rod
   will swing away
   from you and
   down.

---

2. *Pendulum*

Any weight on the
end of a light chain
or string.

Select a small weight
(e.g., a fishing
"sinker") and tie it to
a length of string or
light chain

1. Hold the chain or
   string between
   thumb and index
   finger.

2. Establish a
   a personal code, e.g.
   back-and-forth
   movement means
   "yes," a circular
   movement, "no."
   Or clockwise
   movement, "yes,"
   counterclockwise,
   "no."

---

3. *L- or Angle Rods*

Two metal rods bent
to a 45 degree angle
at one-third their
length.

Needed: 2 metal
coathangers and
metal shears.

1. With the average
   coat hanger
   having a 16-inch
   base, the "handle"
   will measure about
   5-1/2 inches.

2. With the shears,
   sever the hanger
   at the left base
   corner and on the
   right, 5-1/2 inches
   toward the apex.

3. Bend the shorter
   end until it is at a
   right angle.

1. In each hand hold
   an L-rod in a level
   position, parallel
   to the other, before
   you.

2. Ask the rods to
   cross each other
   over the target you
   are seeking, or to
   signify a "yes"
   answer to a
   question. No
   movement
   signifies "no."

The authors leading a dowsing search for a hidden bucket of water.
(Courtesy, The Mike Douglas Show)

Exercise #1: Dowsing For Water

Indoors:

It's best to begin with a water source you know exists as
you can verify what you've found. You can begin at home
locating water pipes running under the floor surface
Referring later to a blueprint of your home or apartment
you can compare the location of dowsed water pipes to
those indicated in the plan.

1. Your question must be focused with your mind
   concentrating in a relaxed manner on the object
   of your search (water, water pipes), erasing all
   interfering thoughts. Try this: "I am looking for a
   water pipe presently feeding this house (apart
   ment) with water." This will eliminate the
   finding of pipes no longer in use.
2. As you walk slowly across the ground, holding
   your angle rods or Y-rod, instruct them to cross (or
   if a Y-rod, to dip) when you have crossed a
   functioning water pipe.

Outdoors:

Once you've developed confidence, you can search for underground veins of water, sewer lines, underground cables, etc., using the same method described. If you're looking for drinking water, try to focus this way: "I am looking for a vein of good drinking water, not more than twenty feet down, flowing at least five gallons a minute, which will never go dry."

To determine depth, stand directly over the spot where you received a dowsing reaction and ask either aloud or mentally to yourself, "How deep is this vein?" Then start counting, "one foot, two feet, three feet, etc., until your rods cross or your Y-rod dips.

To determine rate of flow, ask, "How many gallons a minute are flowing right now through this vein?" Then start counting, "One gallon a minute, two gallons a minute," until the dowsing instrument reacts.

Exercise #2: A Dowsing Game With Pendulum

1. Get twelve small identical opaque boxes or containers.
2. Arrange them on the floor in a semicircle, about six inches apart.
3. Have someone, when you are not in the room, put an object inside one box.
4. Enter the room and suspend the pendulum at the center of the semicircle; mentally instruct it to swing in the direction of the box containing the object.
5. Repeat this as often as you like, scoring your "hits."

Pyramid Power?

Tired of meditating near a gentle rolling brook, to music or by repeating a mantra? How about meditating inside a one-person pyramid tent? People have described a sensation of being surrounded with energy while inside the shape. Comparisons have been made with Wilhelm Reich's orgone energy accumulator. The pyramid shape seems to serve a similar function. Whatever the explanation, something seems to be happening inside the pyramid shape. Is it real or imaginary?

The man who introduced us to pyramidology is Bill Cox, a southern Californian in his sixties who is the editor of the monthly *Pyramid Guide*, a newsletter covering everything

Pyramid tent meditation. *(Courtesy, George E. Cooper)*

you ever wanted to know about pyramids—energy research, experiences and theories. Bill was touring the continent conducting workshops on pyramid power and dropped by to visit for a couple of days.

Among his display items were pyramid shapes to be placed over plants to energize them, small cardboard replicas of the Great Cheops Pyramid on the Egyptian plateau of Giza to sharpen razor blades and mummify meat and connector-joint components to make an approximate four-foot high replica of the Great Pyramid. All we needed, he said, was some nickel-plated tubing to assemble it. No side panels required.

The pyramid craze began shortly after the publication of *Psychic Discoveries Behind the Iron Curtain* by Sheila Ostrander and Lynn Schroeder, who reported on the discovery of Antoine Bovis, a Frenchman. When visiting the Great Pyramid he noticed that dead cats and other small animals who had apparently wandered in and died had not decayed. Bovis speculated that the pyramid shape may have been responsible for the mummification effect. To explore this possibility, he built a wooden replica of the pyramid, oriented it to true north, placed the body of a dead cat and then other organic materials inside and observed that, as he had suspected, after a few days they hadn't putrified.

Soon after, Karel Drbal, a Czech radio engineer read Bovis's conclusions, experimented further and concluded there was definitely a relationship between the shape of the space inside the pyramid and the physical, chemical and biological processes going on inside that space. Drbal also claimed that the pyramid's shape was responsible for accumulating some mysterious energy, and when he placed a used razor blade in a Great Cheops model, he found the blade's sharpness had been restored. Drbal was able to convince the Czech patent office to grant him patent number 91304 for "Cheops Pyramid Razor Blade Sharpeners," since this phenomenon could be observed with some regularity.

Serge King of Huna Enterprises in Los Angeles says the pyramid shape speeds up a natural process in the blade. The metal on the edge of a blade, he explains, has a crystalline structure. It is, therefore, a dynamic structure. Leave the blade alone for a few days and it will regain some of its original cutting power.

No one these days, it seems, would bet too much either way. It might all be subjective wish fulfillment. How sharp is sharp?

Bill's newsletter carries some of the ongoing arguments but blades are hardly the "in" thing. People who spend time meditating inside a pyramid form report that they can relax better and attain higher levels of self-awareness. Among the sensations are an increase in body energy, feelings of weightlessness, intense body heat and easing of pain, particularly headaches. Some have perceived brilliant flashes of white light. Some have claimed their ESP improves. Observing a pyramid meditator some people have claimed to see energy fields surrounding the body inside the tent becoming more compact. Blue flashes have also been seen around the pyramid form itself.

Others report in the *Pyramid Guide* that when they place eggs, meat and fish inside small Cheops replicas, dehydration (about fifty to seventy-five percent) occurs. Flowers, too, are mummified; wine tastes better and so does coffee. Put a silver coin inside, and, twenty-four hours later, the tarnish can be wiped away with a finger.

Bill understands what he's up against as a believer in the pyramid effect. Scientists haven't exactly been over-whelmed by these tales and some even call the pyramid researchers "pyramidiots." One reason is that they are no persuaded by the lore surrounding the Great Cheops. The dominant archeological view has it that the pyramid was built as a tomb for the Pharoah Khufu, or Cheops. This would mean that the 481-foot-high structure, spanning over thirteen acres and comprised of some two million stone blocks weighing about 5¼ million tons, was a colossal, ego-gratifying monument. This kind of argument makes Bill Cox smile. He has visions of a Cecil B. De Mille epic of Egyptians pulling blocks of stones on wooden rollers. When another oft-cited argument that the pyramid was built to keep workers preoccupied during the annual flood pops up, Bill becomes devilishly animated. "Where's Khufu's tomb? Why hasn't it been found?" he asks. "When did they get the logs for rolling the blocks to build it? Did they materialize forests in that area?"

Bill is somewhat more comfortable with the idea that the Great Pyramid was somehow connected to the Egyptian "mystery" schools, those initiated in esoteric principles who understood that the pyramid was a "book in stone" containing the creative principles of nature in its very form. But the key, he maintains, is the pyramid's mathematical structure.

Among the more intriguing statistics is that the Great Cheops appears to be a compass of sorts, one of its sides almost facing true north. Its estimated weight is approximately 5,273,000 tons. Some claim that if you add fifteen zeros to this, you'll get the estimated weight of the earth. And try this one:

> Distance from the earth to the sun is 91,837,484 miles
> Height of the Great Pyramid is 5,813.01 inches
> Multiply the height by two and you get 11,696.02
> 11,696.02 divided into 91,837,484 is 7,909.7, the exact polar diameter of the earth in miles.

Impressed? Well, here's something to cool your heels:

> The height of the Washington Monument is 555 feet 5 inches.
> Its base is 55 feet square.
> Windows are exactly 500 feet from the base.
> Multiply the base measurement by 60 (five times 12 months) and you get 3,300.
> 3,300 is the weight of the monument's capstone in pounds.
> And if you multiply the base times the weight of the capstone, the result is 181,500—a figure close to the speed of light in miles per second.

This bit of doodling with the Washington Monument comes from the mathematical shrewdness of Martin Gardner, author of *Fads and Fallacies in the Name of Science* and a notorious skeptic of psychic matters.

This kind of criticism may daunt some of those who are less confident, but the new breed of pyramidologists allows it to bounce off. Gardner can have his doodles, they say. Too much remains unexplained about the Great Cheops. Even in the *Timaeus*, Plato held that its shape is a key to the physics of the cosmos. That's Bill's feeling. He says there is too much to learn about the pyramid structure to worry about critics. He's convinced that its shape serves as a generator for an as yet unknown life-force and that the ancients were aware of it.

Recent research at Huma-Tech Industries in San José, California, manufacturers of biofeedback equipment, has revealed that the brain-wave activity of people meditating inside a pyramid tent differs from that of the same subject who had meditated a few minutes earlier outside. The amplitude and abundance of alpha waves increased three fold along with a significant increase in theta wave production which is often associated with deep tranquility and a state of euphoria. There were also wider extremes of the quicker beta brainwaves. Their conclusion is: another (Cosmic) force comes into action, created by the form itself—subliminally enhancing a person's ability to voluntarily, or involuntarily, develop heightened states of consciousness.

Pat Flanagan, a physicist and one of the more active pyramid researchers, has recently experimented with some of the observations of both Bovis and Drbal. He has concluded that the energy content in a pyramid varies with environmental factors, such as the time of day, the season, weather, phases of the moon and especially the quantity and polarity of ions (positively or negatively charged) and the alignment of a pyramid's side to magnetic north. He believes the pyramid shape creates an electrical vacuum inside and that the cavities in the brain and the body's interior accumulate *dielectric energy* (a reflection of the electrical charges on the surface of matter). He concludes that the distribution of these charges is concentrated at the apex of the pyramid.

These speculations and preliminary experimental results have since generated a boom in pyramid homes, office buildings, churches, greenhouses and backyard hideaways. Those who believe mystical experiences can be triggered inside the pyramid are planning month-long vigils inside.

All this, says Bill Cox, is an indication that more people are interested in tuning in to the energies of the cosmos and in making maximum use of their minds and bodies.

After Bill left, we stuck one of his pyramids over a spider-mite-infested plant (a palma bella) in our apartment. Two weeks later, the plant was surviving and the mites, which resemble white powder, had turned yellow. New shoots were healthy and not infested. It certainly wasn't a controlled experiment, but who knows....

Pyramid experiments are simple, especially to attempt sharpening a used razor blade or to preserve food (but don't use an expensive steak):

1. Cut four triangles with dimensions in the following ratio: 9⅜ x 8⅞ x 8⅞.

2. Use the longer side as the base. Placing the triangles flat on a table with sides adjacent, simply tape them together and fold them into a pyramid. Tape the open sides shut.

3. Place whatever you want inside.

4. Try putting, say, a piece of meat at various levels inside on top of a matchbox. There's some controversy about the best location, so try one-third of the way up and two-thirds.

5. You have to orient the pyramid to either true north or magnetic north (again more controversy, so try both). If you want true north, you will have to scan geodetic charts at your local library, which will indicate how many degrees of magnetic declination exist in your area of residence.

Meditating inside a pyramid tent is another matter. If the pyramid shape is in fact an energy accumulator, then it's entirely possible the effect may not always be beneficial, at least that's what some more conservative pyramidologists are saying these days. We know too little about our own psychophysical systems and how they may react to an infusion of some mysterious energy force. That's why we didn't build our own pyramid tent.

FOUR

Mind, Magic
and Cosmos

Astrology, Talismans, and Magic

A vaporetto ride through the Grand Canal brought us to Piazzo San Marco, the pigeon-packed heart of the old merchant city of Venice. On the square is St. Mark's Basilica, sometimes called "the Church of Gold," (because of its interior wealth of golden mosaics) and inside its presbytery is one of the most awesome religious jeweled treasures—the "Pala d'Oro" (or Golden Altarpiece). Made in 976 A.D. in Constantinople, it describes the life of Jesus and serves as a sacred jewel for the most solemn of liturgical ceremonies. The total number of jewels decorating the forty-eight enameled panels is a staggering 2,486. Among them are three hundred pearls, four hundred garnets, ninety amethysts, three hundred sapphires, three hundred emeralds and eighty rubies.

We left the presbytery with a sense of awe, but the impact is surprisingly fleeting. When touring Europe, you are repeatedly offered one staggering view after another of extraordinary gemstone collections. In the Old Castle of the Hofburg in Vienna, for example, once the official residence of the Habsburgs, is the Jewel Room containing the Ecclesiastical Treasure Chamber and the crown jewels. Gemstones glitter hypnotically, silently vying for attention everywhere you look. In Munich is the Schazkammer of the Residenz, the former official palace, one of the world's greatest treasure houses. Jeweled swords, crosses, crowns and statuettes glisten with diamonds, pearls, gold, ivory, rubies and emeralds. A miniature of St. George slaying the dragon is completely inlaid with precious stones. Moving from piece to piece, it becomes difficult to fathom the magnitude of the display of wealth, which doesn't stop short of diamond-studded dishware. And then, of course, there is the Tower of London, home of the English crown jewels. On display there is the pear-shaped Great

Star of Africa, a 530.2-carat diamond, one of the nine major gems cut from the famous Cullinan Diamond, the largest ever discovered, which in the rough weighed 3,106 carats. It was discovered quite by accident in 1905 when the superintendent of the Premier Mine in South Africa noticed a huge mass protruding from the wall of a diamond gallery, and thinking a prank had been played, discovered otherwise.

Museums like these are scattered throughout the world. Their jeweled treasures are enduring reminders of the pomp and pageantry of emperors, kings and queens; their jewel-studded ceremonial regalia and glittering religious reliquaries and altar vessels symbolize the importance and power of secular and spiritual rulers, while ornamental jewelry in the form of rings, tiaras, brooches and necklaces anticipate the eventual prominence of precious stones in the realm of fashion.

However, the accessibility of gems has now been democratized. Once the exclusive reserve of royalty and the Church, they are now worn for personal adornment by greater numbers of people; clever advertisements such as "Diamond's are a girl's best friend" helped to usher in the new era. Incidentally, the reason behind this particular claim, according to gem lore, can be traced back to the time of King Charles VII of France, who was attracted by the sensational appearance of Agnes Sorel wearing a necklace of the many diamonds which she had borrowed from her male friends in the hope of winning the King's heart. Until that time, diamonds had only been worn by men. Score one for liberation.

Other than as sound investment, personal enhancement and status, people desire precious stones simply because they're beautiful and captivating. If you've ever gazed into the deep green of the emerald, admired the iridescence of opals and pearls, the ruby's likeness to smouldering coal, the fire of a diamond or violet brilliance of a sapphire, you will have, at least for a moment, experienced the excitement of a silent, dynamic interchange.

What makes a gem precious is its rarity, beauty and durability. Rarity basically refers to just how much the supply fulfills the demand. In short, precious stones are scarce. Most are minerals, being both chemically and physically homogeneous and natural constituents of the earth's crust. In addition, because their basic elementary particles are found to be arranged in "lattices," or definite geometrical forms, which create multiple faces on the exterior, they are considered to be crystals. Rays of white light which play on the gem are transmuted into varied colors by its mineralogical and chemical structure. Those wavelengths which are not absorbed by the gem are reflected, and experienced by the human eye. White light magically becomes colored. As for durability, in the case of the diamond, the slogan "a diamond is forever" refers not only to the expressed desire for the relationship between two people to be infinite, but also characterizes the fact that the diamond, as the hardest known substance, is made for eternity. Other minerals follow in its footsteps on a scale of one to ten, with ten being the hardest. Those classified from eight to ten, such as the ruby, emerald and diamond, can withstand abrasion, scratching, corrosion and the bleaching action of light. Their beauty survives the test of time. Others, with proper care, can be equally enduring.

This is one reason why ancient peoples believed that only the gods could have created precious stones. Offered in ceremonies to the gods, they were also extensively used in burial rites. Excavations in 1922 by a team of archaeologists from the British Museum and University of Pennsylvania at the Chaldean ruins of the biblical city of Ur, for example, turned up a tomb of the Queen U-Abi. Found was a mantle of beads made of gold, silver, lapis lazuli, carnelian, agate and chalcedony. The hem border was lined with small tubes of alternating carnelian and lapis lazuli. Recently, in China, one of a series of remarkable archaeological discoveries unearthed the 2nd-century, B.C., tomb of Princess Tau Wan. Her burial shroud was made of 2,156 jade tablets sewn with gold threads. And in ancient Egypt, the decoration of the dead with gemstones was accomplished with equal devotion, as evidenced by the excavations of the tombs of the pharoahs. For the most part, these tombs had been vandalized long before the appearance of archaeologists, yielding only fragments of the wealth which had been ceremonially interred with the mummified remains. An indication of the lost splendors was provided by the excavation, early in this century, in the Valley of the Kings at Luxor, of the tomb of Tutankamen, a young 18th-century, B.C., dynasty ruler. Somehow having eluded thieves through the centuries, it had remained relatively undisturbed. This fortuitous find yielded 146 pieces of meticulously crafted jewelry, decorated mostly with fine specimens of rock crystal, green feldspar, amethyst, garnet, carnelian, turquoise and lapis lazuli.*

In each of our examples—that of Queen U-Abi, Princess Tau Wan and King Tutankhamen—the intriguing question is what did these gemstones and pieces of jewelry symbolize?

While even in ancient times jewelry signified social status, it also represented a belief in the magical properties of gemstones. Seen as sacred and embodying divine qualities and powers, gems were widely used as amulets and talismans. Simply defined, an *amulet* (from the Latin "amuletum") is believed to be any object which inherently has the power to dispel or neutralize negative, harmful influences. It's worn as a general form of protection. A *talisman* (from the Greek "telesma"—to consecrate) refers to an object believed to be capable of attracting specific favorable influences—either through its intrinsic qualities or because of energies ceremonially transmitted to it. The two terms have often been confused and used interchangeably, but as E.A. Wallis Budge, the late Egyptologist of the British Museum offered, the talisman can be thought of as a sword, and the amulet as a shield.

Since ancient times, precious stones have been regarded as the most powerful forms of amulets and talismans. In fact, if we consider the ancient Greek and Roman literary references to gems, in particular, the surviving works of Heroditus and Pliny—which considerably influenced the gem treatises of medieval scholars—almost all gems, regardless of their monetary value, were used as amulets and talismans to induce desired psychological characteristics, perhaps equanimity, courage, persuasiveness or compassion; for their specific healing qualities and to avert susceptibility to misfortune and disease. Their color, physical structure and inherent mystical properties were the main factors determining the virtues and powers

---

* However, recent examinations by gem experts from New York have astonished Egyptologists in reporting that many of the stones once believed to be carnelian and lapis lazuli are, in fact, expertly cut and polished pieces of glass. The reason for this "heresy," offered by Thomas Logan of the Metropolitain Museum in New York, is that trade interruptions between Egypt and Afghanistan (which supplied these stones) necessitated the departure from tradition.

attributed to them. Interred with the dead, linked as they were with invisible Cosmic forces, they would continue to attract favorable influences to the spirit in the nether areas.

Gems were also extensively worn as astrological talismans, to attract the favorable influences of the planets, sun and moon, catalogued by the ancient astrologers. As a link between humanity and the creative life-forces, they were believed to mediate with the planets, evoking desired virtues latent in the soul.

The usual reaction to these ancient and medieval claims is one of fascination, but little more. Most gemologists categorically charge that the extravagant uses of precious stones for magical purposes leads to the tyranny of superstition and are the last vestiges of a primitive worldview. And so, with a cursory review of ancient magical beliefs, and a brief reference to amulets and talismans, our historian is curiously eager to move on to consider the development of styles and form in jewelry and the uses of ornaments in ancient times, to make brief historical forays into the world of famous gemstones (meticulously citing the kings, queens and aristocrats who possessed them) and the obligatory scrutiny of modern jewelry design and retailing practices. On the other hand, we find at the other extreme numerous volumes which have compiled lists of the manifold uses of gemstones throughout the ages by various cultures, often without consideration of the need to distinguish between outright superstition (the lack of understanding of the original concepts behind the practice) and what may be the vestiges of a lost ancient wisdom. Lumping them both together only confuses the issue and makes it exceedingly difficult to understand the cosmology of which the ancient use of talismans forms an integral part.

With this background in mind, let's ask some questions about the modern use of gems as astrological talismans.

Can a talisman actually be used to attract the positive and neutralize the negative influences of your astrological sign? If, for example, you happen to be an Aries, will wearing a diamond and jewelry made of copper make you more courageous, enterprising and simultaneously curb an inclination towards selfishness and aggressiveness? If you're a Sagittarius, will wearing topaz and tin-alloy items enhance your jovial and optimistic nature while squelching capriciousness?

An unlikely proposition? Not according to what we discovered in a wide variety of modern astrology books which claim to represent the teachings of ancient civilizations said to have possessed a much deeper understanding of the relationship between humanity and the cosmos than we have today. Gemstones and the noble metals, we learn, were believed to be uniquely sensitive to certain planets or groupings of stars, and an understanding of their inherent properties and, hence, their correct astrological use brought protection and success. The implication is that we, too, can benefit from their use by drawing upon this ancient knowledge. The following composite chart provides a modern example of the zodiacal signs, their positive and negative characteristics and their gem and metal correspondences:

It's all very neat and tidy. The probability is that if you look elsewhere, you'll come across other charts which will, with equal confidence, assign a widely varied assortment of gems (the metals are usually consistent). So, if you want to buy a zodiacal stone, whom are you to believe?

That's not all. Sun signs are only a part of astrology. Before buying our opals, sapphires and amethysts, a brief look at some of the key elements of this ancient art is in order.

First, an astrologer needs the correct date, time and place of a person's birth, the *sidereal* time (which provides the exact length of the day) and all the corrections made for time zone, longitude and latitude. The Zodiac, an imaginary belt across the heavens, provides a backdrop for describing the exact positions of the planets, sun and moon as they are viewed moving across the heavens. Divided into twelve equal sections, this belt gives us the twelve signs. The sun enters each of them in turn around the 21st of every month. This gives us our sun sign, which is one of the numerous calculations required. Each sign is ruled by one or more planets which are believed to influence its characteristics.

In addition, the signs are divided into *quadruplicities*: Aries, Cancer, Libra and Capricorn are *cardinal* signs marking the beginning of each of the four seasons as the sun enters them; Taurus, Leo, Scorpio and Aquarius are *fixed* signs, meaning that the season has already been launched and is "fixed" by the time the sun enters; Gemini,

SIGN	POSITIVE	NEGATIVE	GEM	METAL
Aries	Pioneering, courageous	Selfish, pugnacious	Diamond	Copper
Taurus	Practical, reliable, solid	Possessive, lazy, boring	Sapphire	Copper
Gemini	Versatile, adaptable, lively	Restless, two-faced	Agate	Mercury
Cancer	Kind, sensitive, tenacious	Hypersensitive, unforgiving	Pearl	Silver
Leo	Generous, creative, dramatic	Dogmatic, pompous, power-mad	Ruby	Gold
Virgo	Discriminating, analytical, modest	Worrier, fussy, hypercritical	Sardonyx	Mercury
Libra	Charming, romantic, idealistic	Indecisive, frivolous, gullible	Sapphire	Copper
Scorpio	Persistent, powerful feelings	Obstinate, secretive	Opal	Iron
Sagittarius	Jovial, optimistic, sincere	Tactless, extremist, careless	Topaz	Tin
Capricorn	Ambitious, reliable	Rigid, pessimistic	Turquoise	Lead
Aquarius	Humanitarian, intellectual, inventive	Unpredictable, fixed in opinion	Amethyst	Uranium
Pisces	Compassionate, humble, intuitive	Careless, vague, weak-willed	Moonstone, bloodstone	Tin

Virgo, Sagittarius and Pisces are the *mutable* signs representing the end of the seasons and the beginning of the new. The astrologer will want to know how many of the planets at the time of a person's birth are in a particular quadruplicity. For example, if all the planets at the time of a person's birth are in the mutable signs, this would suggest very powerful mutable characteristics, or, in other words, basically a very changeable, adaptable personality. If you're a cardinal person, it suggests restlessness. Fixed indicates stability but not adaptability.

Then we have the *triplicities*, represented by the four ancient elements: fire, earth, air and water. The fire signs are Aries, Leo and Sagittarius; earth, Taurus, Virgo and Capricorn; air, Gemini, Libra and Aquarius; and water, Cancer, Scorpio and Pisces. Again the astrologer determines the planetary distribution. The characteristics of these signs jump out at us. Fire suggests fiery, and so on.

Also of great importance in preparing a chart is the *ascendent*, or rising, sign, which refers to the constellation zone which at the moment of birth is rising up over the eastern horizon. This is not the same as the sun sign, since it is based on the earth's twenty-four-hour rotation on its axis (passing through the same celestial influence as the sun does in one year) and thus provides a corresponding division of the Zodiac, referred to as *houses*, numbered one to twelve, beginning with the rising sign. Characteristics have been assigned to each, such as physical appearance to the first house, family ties to the third and the professions to the tenth.

A person's chart may be further qualified by investigating the characteristics of the angles between sun and planets, moon and planets and between the planets themselves. When, for example, a planet is in "opposition" to another, that is, at an angle of 180 degrees, this could spell trouble; similarly at 90 degrees or the "square." But at the "trine," or 120 degrees, and the "sextile," or 60 degrees, the influence will be beneficent.

The astrologer's task is to gauge the importance of all the variable celestial positions on the chart at the moment of birth and arrive at an interpretation. Reaching into an extensive system of relationships said to have been compiled in ancient times and refined through the ages, the task requires considerable skill in manipulating the complex combinations of influences.

Given the importance, then, of considering the entire horoscope to determine the multiplicity of factors to which a person is predisposed, the relationship between gems and metals and the sun signs appears much too casual. Furthermore, since this kind of information is usually presented with little or no explanation of the nature of its derivations, it only contributes to the voluminous clutter and glib superficial nonsense of pop astrology—the kind usually found near comics in daily newspapers.

The crucial question, of course, is whether there is any validity to astrology in the first place, and whether the use of gems and metals as astrological talismans is merely a fanciful extension of ancient superstition that has managed, over the centuries, to pull the wool over the eyes of the gullible.

According to most historical accounts, the foremost early astrologers were the Chaldeans, descendents of the Sumerians who lived in Mesopotamia around 3000 B.C. Like other peoples of the ancient civilized world such as the Chinese, Indians, Egyptians and Central Americans, they are believed to have inherited the legacy of sky watching from our prehistoric ancestors who—as modern interpretations of primitive cave art suggest—attempted to catalogue the night sky and relate phases of the moon to the seasonal availabilty of game.

We are informed that Chaldean priests would sit day and night in their watchtowers, or *ziggurats*, meticulously charting the movements of the stars and planets. Then, in a childlike consciousness, they related events in the sky to those transpiring on earth. In short, while possessing advanced mathematics, the Chaldeans also thought and lived magically: all of nature was seen as interconnected. Events on earth stemmed from the will of the gods, represented by the stars and planets. Over the centuries, the Chaldeans devised a detailed astrological system based on their characterizations of the heavenly bodies and life on earth. Examining the rhythmical movement of the planets in relation to each other, they looked for omens to determine the future of their country, such as the possibility of famine and war and the well-being of the king.

Particularly godlike to the Chaldeans were the five planets known to them (Mercury, Venus, Mars, Jupiter and

Saturn) and the sun and moon. It is usually suggested that probably as a result of their apparent color, extensive observation of the predictable course of these planets in the heavens, and fortuitous or malefic events on earth with which they happened to coincide, they were assigned specific attributes (that is, qualities and powers) believed to be reflected in and capable of influencing everything, visible or invisible, in the cosmos. Some of these attributes, we learn, appear to follow a simple logic based on imaginative associations. Let's go through the list.

Mercury, home of the god Nabu, doubtless appeared to be a speedy and elusive trickster because of its proximity to the sun which made it difficult to observe. So this quick-footed planet was seen as the cunning messenger of the gods and was given dominion over trade and travel. Venus, home to the goddess Ishtar, reigned over fertility and fecundity. She was the goddess of nature and love. Mars, home to Nergal, also ruled over discipline and judgment. The very large Jupiter, home to Marduk, could unleash holocausts and was perceived as a dangerous planet. Slow-moving Saturn, dwelling place of Ninurta, was sometimes dangerous, but also old, thoughtful and wise. The sun appeared as the fiery essence of the symbol of truth and divine insight, and the moon, often viewed as the sun's consort, ruled over the rhythms of life.

The Chaldeans, we're told, diligently charted the relationships between these bodies and their paths through the heavens. They are credited with having invented the Zodiac and, as early as 600 B.C., to have established accurate *ephemerides*, or tables of planetary movement. By the 5th century B.C., personal horoscopes for the king and members of the royal family were charted primarily from observations of the rising and setting of the stars and planets. A critical appraisal of some of the predictions that were recorded and that survived through the centuries places them in the same league as the sun-sign column advice in daily newspapers. If, for example, a child was born when Jupiter was rising and Mars was setting, he would be expected to vanquish his enemies, but if the god of war was found to be rising and Jupiter setting (a truly unfortunate alignment), the reverse was predicted.

From the trailblazing Chaldeans, we move briskly to ancient Greece. The Greeks are usually credited with extending the scope of astrology, and, because of their developing scientific acumen, mathematically refining it. In the process, they substituted their own pantheon of gods, greatly elaborated the Chaldean interpretations of relationships and completed the naming of the twelve zodiacal signs. They are also credited with emphasizing the hour of birth (horoscope means "view of the hour"). After all, there were only so many signs to go around and many people were born on the same day. Since the Chaldeans are said to have provided forecasts for only king and country, presumably this democratic compulsion to extend astrology to the masses hadn't been a problem for them.

The general consensus is that astrology as currently practiced in the West is a legacy from ancient Greece, exhaustively consolidated in the Tetrabiblos of Ptolemy in 140 A.D., which has survived almost intact through the centuries. It is, therefore, directly linked to the ingenious but "magical" Chaldeans through the refinements of the more rational but yet mystically inclined Greeks. Rooted as it is in what is usually referred to as an ancient, primitive way of perceiving and interpreting cosmic events, modern astrology is derisively dismissed as a convoluted labyrinth of updated ancient ignorance, perpetuated by those who are entirely lacking scientific sophistication (not to mention scruples).

Little wonder that the same process of ancient, primitive perception is attributed to the relationships catalogued between talismans, especially gems and metals, and the heavens. The idea that a gem is ruled by a specific planet or zodiacal sign and can, therefore, be used to attract specific influences is viewed as the absurd product of a lofty, albeit charming, childish imagination.

Here, for example, is one scale of correspondences generally characteristic of both ancient and medieval times showing what metal, gem and color each planet was believed to control.

The underlying magical logic is viewed as naively simplistic and based on an associative system of analogy. What better metal was there to characterize the golden glow of the sun than gold? The topaz, sometimes mistaken for a yellow diamond, fits in well. The silvery appearance of the moon gives rise to silver metal, and, because the moon controls the seas, the pearl in the oyster shell makes sense.

PLANET	METAL	GEM	COLOR
Sun	Gold	Topaz	Gold, yellow
Moon	Silver	Pearl	White
Mercury	Quicksilver	Amethyst	Gray
Venus	Copper	Emerald	Green
Mars	Iron	Ruby	Red
Jupiter	Tin	Sapphire	Blue
Saturn	Lead	Onyx	Black

As for the fleet-footed Mercury, it rules over quicksilver, the most mobile of metals. When quicksilver is boiled, it gives off a violet vapor. Therefore, the amethyst.

The correspondences of Venus are perhaps a bit more complex. Aphrodite, to the Greeks, for example, was associated with Cyprus, the chief supply of copper, and it's noteworthy that copper salts are green, so we get the emerald or its look-alike, green beryl. Venus is the mistress of nature and again this signifies green. As for Mars, the red planet, it is associated with the reddish rust of iron and accordingly rules the red gems. The silvery or tinlike appearance of Jupiter, god of the blue sky, rules the blue sapphire. And the leaden, slow-moving, sometimes violent Saturn (referred to as the Lord of Death) rules the black onyx.

If a ring was to be worn to attract the influence of a planet, the gem would be set in the corresponding metal; topaz in gold, pearl in silver, and so on. The gem could also be engraved with the figures representing the planets.

The selection of gems and metals to correspond with a particular planet is certainly not consistent throughout the ancient and medieval world. Among the Hindus, for example, the diamond was dedicated to Venus; perhaps, it is suggested, because as the goddess of love, it was believed she deserved the most brilliant gem. And, according to some reports on Chaldean custom, the sapphire was believed to be ruled by Saturn, the diamond by the sun and the agate by Mercury. Each culture, while sharing some of the analogies, then, added its own. Modern gem correspondences differ as well, and there is no one system accepted by all astrologers as the correct one—a feature often emphasized by critics.

The same can be said about zodiacal correspondences. Here's an example from classical Greek mythology:

SIGN	RULING DEITY	GEM
Aries	Minerva	Sard
Taurus	Venus	Carnelian
Gemini	Apollo	Topaz
Cancer	Mercury	Chalcedony
Leo	Jupiter	Jasper
Virgo	Ceres	Emerald
Libra	Vulcan	Beryl
Scorpio	Mars	Amethyst
Sagittarius	Diana	Hyacinth
Capricorn	Vesta	Chrysoprase
Aquarius	Juno	Rock Crystal
Pisces	Neptune	Sapphire

The following represents a typical modern occultist chart:

SIGN	GEMS	METAL	COLOR
Aries	Ruby Bloodstone Red jasper	Iron	Red
Taurus	Golden topaz Coral Emerald	Copper	Yellow
Gemini	Crystal Carbuncle Aquamarine	Mercury	Violet
Cancer	Emerald Moonstone	Silver	Green
Leo	Ruby Sardonyx Amber	Gold	Orange
Virgo	Pink jasper Turquoise Zircon	Mercury	Violet
Libra	Opal Diamond	Copper	Yellow

Scorpio	Agate	Iron	Red
	Garnet		
	Topaz		
Sagittarius	Amethyst	Tin	Purple
Capricorn	Black and white onyx	Lead	Blue
	Beryl		
	Jet		
Aquarius	Blue sapphire	Lead	Indigo
Pisces	Diamond	Tin	Indigo
	Jade		

A glance at the correspondences in the modern chart opening this chapter, then, can hardly inspire confidence, and exponents of the modern-conventional version of the development of astrology, therefore, feel justified in arguing that we are indeed being had. Since astrology is seen as originating in the minds of people inclined to fanciful leaps of the imagination and as a spurious association of ideas to make sense of the universe, it only follows that any claims for the powers of gems and metals as astrological talismans used to augment or neutralize celestial influences is yet another example of ancient superstition, transformed into a modern commercial exploit.

While the confusion can hardly be denied, astronomer Johann Kepler (1571-1630), who was also deeply immersed in astrology, issued a plea to his contemporaries "not to throw the baby out with the bathwater." Indeed, there is another side to the story.

Proponents of what will be referred to as the *Western magical tradition* would argue strongly that the modern-conventional view demands serious qualification. While there is little argument that much of what is astrology today, particularly the brand spewed out by the mass media, is an odious junkheap, references are made to a deeper level of understanding that can be attained.

Modern historians and archeologists, they assert, have shafted us with Cecil B. De Mille-like ancient pageantry similar in quality to those amazing scenes which depict a multitude of Egyptian slaves moving the gigantic blocks of stone for the Great Cheops Pyramid on wooden rollers.

They further argue that we've inherited from them a chauvinistically constructed history of the past which portrays all ancient peoples as superstitious and primitive in their thinking and that there has been a serious failure to distinguish the original knowledge of the ancients from the meandering stream that has been progressively polluted through the centuries.

The argument continues that, as a result of this historical folly, we have been woefully severed from our true Cosmic nature and have difficulty distinguishing between superstition and the true nature of magical consciousness. The reference to the uses of astrological talismans as based on superstition and primitive imagination is interpreted as typical of the shallow level of understanding which permeates conventional scholarship: of course using a gem to attract the specific powers of a planet or sign will be an exercise in self-delusion if done in a total vacuum! When superstition prevails, magic becomes a philosophical hodgepodge. The trick is to separate the wheat from the chaff, and only then will the Cosmic powers of precious stones offer far more in purpose and in quality than something akin to the medieval practice of placing a moonstone on a fruit tree to attract the influence of the moon to reap a more plentiful harvest.

The main point of reference, or the roots of the Western magical tradition, is frequently attributed to ancient Egypt. The Egyptians are often portrayed by Western scholars as having been crudely polytheistic, worshipping a wide variety of gods. This is correct, but only partially so. For example, according to E.A. Wallis Budge, the late curator of Egyptian and Assyrian antiquities in the British Museum, "The priests and educated classes who could read and understand books adopted the idea of One God, the creator of all beings in heaven and on earth, who, for want of a better word, were called Gods." In short, the Egyptians believed the entire universe, both visible and invisible, to be conscious and to possess intelligence in varying degrees. Monotheism and polytheism went hand in hand.

More specifically, we find it emphasized in the Egyptian Book of the Dead (essentially a guide for spirits entering the nether regions) that a person's constitution or nature incorporates all the universal essences which include an echelon of spirits, angels and gods. Not one part of our being can be seen as apart from these essences. Stated yet another way, a person is a miniature image of the universe itself. How to allow these essences to unfold, to harness and employ their powers, was the focal point of an Egyptian spiritual science.

By attempting to invoke these forces in religious ceremony, the energies of these essences could be called upon for help in directing life. Recorded in art and architecture, it is believed the symbols for these forces became the triggering agents of an entire cosmology which could be used to activate a person's magical potential. Peoples of the ancient world are therefore not viewed as having arbitrarily attributed characteristics to their gods; the contention is that the ancients never created their gods but systematically determined over long periods of observation how they symbolically revealed aspects of the Divine.

And so it's also suggested that given the deep magical understanding of the Egyptians, it seems unlikely, as generally claimed, that they had a vague and unsophisticated astrology since the principal beliefs underlying astrological correspondences are first and foremost magical. One argument is that the high priests passed astrological knowledge to others via an oral tradition in the same way that architectural knowledge may have been handed down.

In any event, exponents of the magical tradition suggest that the Egyptians and their mystery schools were responsible for the dissemination of an advanced wisdom which included astrology and which has been passed on through the centuries by schools of adepts in the mystical arts comprised of individuals trained in the "hidden knowledge" who did not confuse the widespread and increasingly vulgarized aspect of this knowledge with the real thing. We are, therefore, advised to be leery of accepting outright the conventional version of the childishness of astrological origins and the almost exclusive emphasis on its pop aspects throughout history to modern times. Budge, for example, explains tht the Greeks and Romans didn't fully understand the basic underlying philosophy of Egyptian magic and began to mimic some of its purely outward ritualistic forms.

The same can be ventured about the uses of gems and metals as talismans and amulets. Once seen as part of an

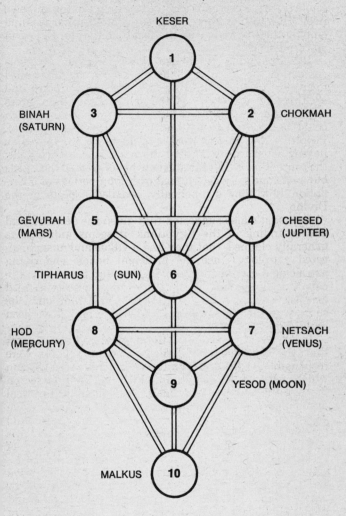

The Tree of Life

attempt to symbolically represent and activate a fundamental occult force of nature—a form of profound spiritual
communication with the Divine—this art would bear little
resemblance to modern superstition. Perhaps the best way
to exemplify this viewpoint is to briefly describe the general
flavor of the use of the Tree of Life of the Cabala, a highly
sophisticated Western magical system. We say "briefly,"
for it can certainly be described as having the same
complexity as any major science.

Cabala means "tradition" and refers to a body of
knowledge believed to have been systematized by the
Hebrews and perhaps to have originated in ancient Egypt.
In its totality, it stresses the underlying unity of the
universe and suggests that this unity can be experienced
inspirationally. These universal forces are represented on
the Tree of Life, whose branches symbolically spread
throughout the cosmos and incorporate every aspect of it. It
also represents the central Cabalistic view that the inner
spirit of man's immortal Self can be liberated through
ascending the Tree. The concept—which is also central to
astrology—is that the soul descends before birth through
the celestial spheres and acquires their essential properties. The goal of the adept is to accomplish the ascent during his or her lifetime.

Looking at the Tree of Life, we can see that it has ten
spheres called *Sephiros* which correspond to the earth, the
seven ancient planets, the Zodiac and, at the summit, the
trinity of supernals referred to as *the sphere of the prime
mover*. Think of these as Cosmic forces which function in
the macrocosm as well as in the microcosm. The adept's
task is to cultivate an understanding of the nature of each
of these Sephiros by focusing attention on their correspondences and perhaps, through meditative techniques, yoga
or breathing exercises or whatever other forms of induction, to sharpen the powers of will and imagination,
enabling him to nurture qualities previously deficient in
some part of the soul. The pursuit of this objective may
necessitate voyages to what is called the *astral plane*, the
world in which the products of the imagination are believed
to have their reality. Correspondences, however, such as
the ones in the chart below, can also be used in magical
rituals as in the case of capturing the influence of a planet
through its numerous correspondences.

SEPHIRO*	PLANET	COLOR	PRECIOUS STONE	METAL	PERFUME	PLANT	DIVINE NAME
1. Kesar Ptah		White	Diamond		Ambergris	Almond in flower	Eheieh
2. Chokmah Thoth		Gray	Star ruby, turquoise		Musk	Amaranth	Jehovah
3. Binah Isis	Saturn	Black	Star sapphire, pearl	Lead	Myrrh, civet	Cypress, opium poppy	Jehovah Elchim
4. Chesed Maat	Jupiter	Blue	Amethyst, sapphire	Tin	Cedar	Olive, shamrock	El
5. Gevurah Horus	Mars	Red	Ruby	Iron	Tobacco	Oak, nux vomica	Elohim Gibor
6. Tipharus Ra, Osiris	Sun	Yellow	Topaz, yellow diamond	Gold	Olibanum	Acacia, bay, laurel, vine	Jehovah Elch ve Daes
7. Netsach Hathor	Venus	Green	Emerald	Copper	Benzoin, rose red sandal	Rose	Jehovah Tsavoos
8. Hod Anubis	Mercury	Orange	Opal, especially fire opal	Mercury	Storax	Moly, annal, lewinii	Elohim Tsavoos
9. Yesod Shu, Pascht	Moon	Purple	Quartz	Silver	Jasmine, ginseng	Manyan, damiana, yohimbe	Shaddai el Chai
10. Malkus Seb		Black	Rock crystal		Willow, lily, ivy	Dittany of Crete	Adonai Melech

* The second name is the Egyptian counterpart

These rituals are in many cases quite extensive and demand meticulous preparation in establishing the correct frame of mind right up to the minutest detail in clothing and, as we can see from the chart, color, precious stone, metal, perfume, plant and the invocation of divine names. These symbols are believed to represent the language of the subconscious mind itself. The influence of a planet, therefore, can be magically captured through the use of things which are linked with it. An example is the use of red clothing, iron and a ruby to tap the forces of Mars.

By knowing the exact details of his or her horoscope charted by a competent astrologer, it is believed that the ritual can even be timed to maximize the benefits. This is one reason why serious astrologers today who are acutely aware of the magical roots of their art would not recommend the use of a gem which corresponds to a person's sun sign as an astrological talisman. They would want to know all the details before recommending the appropriate gem. For example, if a chart reveals that there are too many planets in fixed signs (Taurus, Leo, Scorpio and Aquarius), it may be recommended that, to help balance the chart, Mercury be attracted to gain greater versatility. Accordingly, all the correspondences attributed to Mercury would be employed in ritual.

This naturally brings up the question of who can use this magical system. According to Israel Regardie, an eminent authority on the Cabala and Western magic, the ritualistic aspect of magic is not for dabblers:

> ... There can hardly be a real understanding of the rationale of Magic and certainly no realization of the complexities taking place within and without the constitution of the Magician, if the corner stone of philosophy is not firmly laid in his mind. If there is danger in the pursuit of Magic, that danger only arises where the Operator has no precise knowledge of what it is that he is doing. It is upon an intelligent understanding of the meaning of the occult symbols and the realities that they are primarily intended to convey, that the efficacy of the rites largely depends. The symbols and the appurtenances of Magic in the profane hands of one not acquainted with the foundations of the art, would most assuredly fail to

produce the proper thaumaturgic results. The mere intellectual familiarity with these arcane principals, however, is of little avail if there is no spiritual experience. On the other hand, magical investigation of the universe, and its consequent spiritual realization in consciousness, assumes a greater dignity and a richer implication and profundity when well buttressed by a theoretical understanding.

In sum, then, the message is quite direct: the magical use of symbols such as gemstones to attain greater control of universal forces should not be a flippant pastime. Why bother in the first place if the intention is not spiritual? According to the Western magical tradition, man, as a bridge between the earth (microcosm) and spirit (macrocosm), contains within his body and psyche, elements, powers and characteristics operative throughout both realms. To varying degrees, all aspects of creation are believed to be influenced by the vital forces inherent in nature, linking them with those in the heavens. Gemstones, metals, colors, herbs and plants, acting as transmitters of the planets ruling them, can then be critically employed to strengthen or neutralize certain qualities inherent in man. The key concept is that a vital energy links all that is above with all that is below—and man, who is intimately interconnected with and involved in an ongoing dynamic interchange with all aspects of his total environment, can learn to harness and control these forces. The mass of humanity might, from the magical position, be compassionately likened to helpless pawns of the impersonal, ever-revolving Wheel of Fortune. Lacking an understanding of the laws operative throughout creation, we are nonetheless subject to them. In learning the nature of the complex correspondences between matter and Cosmic forces, the magician strives to gain control of and direct them to further his spiritual evolution. As part of a social organism, in so doing, it is believed he raises humanity with him—and, if propelled by a desire to employ powers attained to the betterment of mankind, is better equipped to do so. Metaphorically, the magician strives to sever the chains which bind him to the wheel, to increasingly become the master of his destiny.

The Modern Trajectory

One of the major reasons why the magical cosmology is so elusive is that most of us in the Western world have, from childhood, been conditioned to a rational, materialist way of perceiving and interpreting information. To open to another way of perceiving reality requires considerable motivation and conscious effort—a process of systematic deconditioning. The impatient researcher who demands easy and instant understanding would probably be unwilling to make this effort and would likely withdraw exasperated, heaping abuse on the intricate subject. Those who persevere and apply themselves to fully exploring the system, we are assured, will be rewarded with an ever-deepening understanding of themselves and their ultimate purpose in life—to fully realize their maximum psycho-spiritual potential, with access to a comprehensive "map" which will guide them to this end.

Generally, however, we demand and are totally geared, from television toothpaste commercials to new reports on the environment, to a scientific language—even though most of us, much of the time, find it just as difficult to get what the scientist is speaking about. Still more alien, magic is often accused of deliberate wooliness. We have to remember, of course, that scientists are often guilty of speaking as if they were members of a secret brotherhood and might keep this in mind when we think back and try to imagine what intellectual exchange might have been like in ancient Egypt among the sacerdotal priests. They no doubt also had their scientists and various levels of knowledge dissemination. What kind of vulgarized interpretations of their knowledge has survived and filtered down to us, must, short of stepping into a time capsule, remain an open question.

The fact of the matter is that even if detailed analyses of

early Egyptian symbolism eventually vindicated the claims of Western magicians and other schools of occultists who also claim to receive their inspiration from the Egyptians, this would by no means sway scientific sentiments about the basic principles of the magical cosmology.

Astrology, which, as we've discovered, is but a part of a larger archaic magical world view, quickly fell from public grace during Roman times because of the absence of a satisfactory physical explanation for the "how" of it. Renaissance and medieval interest in symbolism played a significant role in keeping it alive, but by the late 17th and 18th centuries, when science advanced its systematic attempt to unravel the workings of the universe, astrology was again challenged to defend and explain its validity from a physical rather than symbolic position. Astrologers have since made little progress and, in our time, are routinely condemned by many scientists as charlatans, as they have yet to explain how a specific planet or constellation may physically affect a person. Before dealing with the proposition that a talisman, such as a ruby, can be used to attract the physical and subtle influences of Mars, through a magical link between it and the planet, the scientists would argue that there must first be evidence that Mars does in fact have a physical influence on the earth and its inhabitants.

This is the nature of the impasse—and is a major reason for the eagerness on the part of astrologers to immediately seize upon and celebrate the advent of any scientific research which appears to support or be sympathetic to the contention of the ancients that the stars influence physical and mental states. Let's take a look at some of this data, generally referred to as part of a new cosmobiology.

In 1946, John Nelson, an electrical engineer, was hired by RCA Communications to study sunspots. The largest shortwave radio communication organization in the world wanted a forecasting system which would reveal when magnetic storm interference, believed to be caused by sunspot activity, would disrupt their communications.

When Nelson began his research, work in this area had been going on for years with little progress. After two years of gathering all available data, provided in part by a six-inch refracting telescope at the RCA Observatory in New

York, he reached the conclusion that sunspot activity was only part of the problem. Something else was triggering magnetic storm interference, which he suspected might be some kind of planetary activity. After several years of exploring this possibility, Nelson concluded that sunspot activity, the behavior of shortwave radio signals and certain planetary arrangements were interrelated in such a manner that it was possible to predict the behavior of shortwave radio signals by studying the angles made between the planets as they circled the sun.

An RCA news release on April 12, 1951 reported the following findings:

1. When two or more planets are at right angles to each other, or in line on the same side of the sun— or in line with the sun between them—magnetic disturbances occur more frequently on the earth's surface.

2. That the most disturbed twelve-month periods will be those preceding and following the positioning of Saturn and Jupiter in such a configuration with relation to the sun.

3. That the most severe disturbances occur when Mars, Venus, Mercury and the Earth are in critical relationship near points of the Saturn-Jupiter configuration.

4. When Saturn and Jupiter have moved away from their critical relationship, there is a corresponding decline in the severity of magnetic weather, although storms of shorter duration result from the critical combinations of smaller planets.

5. That the least disturbed periods occur when Saturn, Jupiter and Mars are equally spaced by 120 degrees.

Astrologers who have long believed that the "square" (90 degree angles) and "opposition" (180 degrees) give rise to disharmony and disruptive influences and that the "sextile" (60 degrees) and "trine" (120 degrees) gave rise to harmony and benevolent influences, were, of course, delighted.

Nelson's work, seen in relation to a variety of statistical studies, has intriguing implications. In the 1930's, Soviet historian Alexander Chijevsky had already reported correlations between sunspot activity and events on earth. He concluded that wars, revolutions and migrations from 500 B.C. to 1900 A.D. correlated seventy-two percent of the time with peaks in sunspot activity and merely twenty-eight percent otherwise. A similarly high correlation appeared for the plagues of the Middle Ages, European cholera and diphtheria outbreaks, typhoid fever in Russia and smallpox epidemics in Chicago. Chijevsky even discovered that the great financial fiasco of 1929 coincided with a period of peak sunspot activity. Displeased with this flagrant digression from their institutionalized system of thought, the Soviets were quick to reward his efforts by shipping him off to Siberia. It was much more difficult in those days to conceive of human events being somehow influenced by subtle forces.

Research presented in a book published in 1962 called *The Chemical Basis of Medical Climatology*, written by Giorgi Piccardi, a highly regarded Italian chemist, offered a clue to the significance of the Chijevsky findings. Piccardi's initial intentions were orthodox enough, having begun with a commission to devise a way to prevent the formation of crust on industrial boilers. The usual method of dissolving the calcium deposits with an acid solution of distilled water and bismuth sulphide was not, for some reason, always effective. Previous chemists, lacking Piccardi's ingrained curiosity, had habitually written this off as an aberration and had not explored the reason behind it. Piccardi, however, rose to the challenge.

Thirty years of meticulous research revealed that cosmic factors were involved. He discovered that the rate at which the bismuth sulphide became a colloid* in activated and normal water varied with sunspot activity. It appeared that even an inorganic compound could be affected by fluctuations in solar activity. The implication was that the human body, which largely consists of water, could

---

* A colloid solution is characterized by the fact that the dissolved particles are of sufficient molecular weight so that each molecule's surface tension is capable of influencing the solution's behavior. Colloids are found in glue, gelatin, milk, egg white and blood.

similarly be affected. In addition to this, Piccardi found that water conductivity could be affected by a small magnet, a fact corroborated by the Atmospheric Research Center in Colorado, where it was demonstrated that electromagnetic fields had similar effects. These findings are further heightened by the fact that, while surprisingly little is known about the structure of water, it is now believed by some chemists that the fragility of its hydrogen bond is rendered even more precarious by the normal temperature of the human body. Humans may, therefore, be even more susceptible to electromagnetic fields in space.

This brings us to the "Takata reaction." Maki Takata, professor of medicine at Tokyo University, discovered that the formation by white blood cells of bacteria-fighting cloudlike aggregates (a process called *flocculation*) varies with sunspot activity. He also found that this process slowed in the evening and rose sharply just before sunrise, and that it could not be interfered with by keeping a subject within thick walls or complete darkness. Only during a full solar eclipse, he found, or when patients were rested 600 feet underground was the influence of sunspot activity neutralized. The startling implication is that the strength of part of our bodily defense system against disease is influenced by cosmic radiations.

While solar activity adds to the mysteries of daily life, the moon also weaves a fascinating plot. In 1959, Frank A. Brown, Jr., an eminent Northwestern University biologist, challenged the hypothesis that organisms have, through natural selection, evolved internal biochemical timing mechanisms, or "biological clocks," which parallel geophysical* rhythms. After detailed experiments in which he sealed off organisms such as the potato, oyster and rat from light, pressure, temperature and humidity, Brown found that their behavior was modified by lunar rhythms affecting the geophysical environment. To further test this correlation, he brought oysters to Evanston, Illinois, from New Haven, Connecticut, and discovered that after two weeks of opening their shells at the time of high tide on the East Coast, they adjusted to what would have been high tide in the Midwest. The environment appeared to be

---

* Geophysics is the study of the earth and its atmosphere by physical techniques including seismology, meteorology, hydrology, terrestrial magnetism.

generating clocklike signals, which Brown believes is strong evidence for the *cosmic-stimulus* hypothesis. He argues that organisms are dependent for their timing on cues from the geophysical environment which is, in turn, affected by these cosmic stimuli.

Other research has focused on the ways in which human behavior might be affected by cosmic activities. At the Douglas Hospital in Montreal, for example, psychiatrist Heinz Lehman, who was curious about the periodic incidence of sporadic violence and bursts of intense activity on psychiatric wards, placed his patients under around-the-clock surveillance for several months. The outbursts were timed and compared with such environmental factors as humidity, temperature, barometric pressure, as well as changes in diet and medication. Lehman's investigations left him with a morass of statistics, but little of special interest. When, however, his findings were later compared with sunspot data at the United States Space Disturbance Forecast Center in Boulder, Colorado, the effects of "peak activity" in the wards correlated significantly.

Another study by orthopedic surgeon and researcher Robert Becker and his colleagues revealed a positive correlation between days of geomagnetic intensity and numbers of people admitted to a psychiatric hospital.

How can this effect be explained? We know that the magnetic field of the earth, which extends around the planet and is believed to be generated by the flow of molten metals in the earth's core, while weak, produces a pulsation (about 7.5 cycles per second) known as the Schumann Resonance. The vibration of this resonance synchronizes with the vibration of cosmic electromagnetism. Interference in the cosmic electromagnetic patterns—due, perhaps, in part to planetary alignments—may directly or indirectly affect life through the earth's field. Becker suggests, for example, that changes in the geomagnetic field intensity affect the nervous system by altering the body's own electromagnetic field. And according to George N. Chatham of the National Aeronautics and Space Administration in Washington, D.C., "Careful and precise studies of magnetism and its effect may open up a new approach to biology, since the entire body is an electrical organism, basically, owing to the characteristic electrical charges and valences of atoms of bioelectrical energy in nerves, organs and tissues."

As a result of work done with the scanning electron microscope, there is new information about the body's cellular structure. Biologists once believed that a cell was a simple bag of fluid. Now it appears likely that cellular components include organic semiconductors (such as liquid crystals) which are very sensitive to magnetic and electrical fields and radiations.

It's becoming increasingly evident, in the light of the above data, that cosmic radiations influence a variety of mass and individual behavioral phenomena on earth. This, however, should not be stretched to infer—as some astrologers have been tempted—that astrology as it is practiced has been vindicated by science.

Michel Gauquelin, a French statistician and psychologist, has this to say:

> ...How can this vast vague conception of a microcosm analogically related to a macrocosm be put into concrete form? How can it explain the detailed and highly specific prescriptions of Greek astrology? This Olympus of pre-established harmonies is soon lost again in the attempt and honored astrologers of the past, like contemporary ones, are either at a loss to do so or founder in a morass of half-baked analogies.
> ...The loftiness of fine symbolic doctrines soon collapses into a comforting pop-astrology when our own small persons are involved.

As an exponent of the conventional history of astrology, however, Gauquelin fails to distinguish between superstition and magical consciousness, so one might reasonably infer that a deeper understanding of symbolism escapes him. Ironically it is his own work which began in 1950 and continues today that has lately been advanced as evidence—by astrologers—of the validity of astrology.

Poring over birth registers which provided the exact time of a person's birth in France, Italy, Germany, Holland and Belgium, Gauquelin discovered correlations between those who had risen to prominence in professions and those planets which were rising or culminating in their path through the horizon at the time of birth. His first study, which compared 576 French Academy of Science members and planetary positions, revealed that a large number (well above chance) were born when Mars and Saturn were rising or culminating. Extending his research, he consistently found that scientists and physicians were positively linked with Mars and Saturn. Soldiers, politicians and team athletes were linked with Jupiter; artists and painters always seemed to avoid Mars and Saturn. Writers seemed to favor the moon and rarely any of the planets.

While Gauquelin's statistics have been checked and verified by the Belgian Committee for Investigation into Phenomena That Are Reportedly Paranormal, a highly critical body suspicious of any unusual claims, the debate continues over his statistical methods. Gauquelin has meanwhile sought an explanation for his findings. He wondered why, for example, a child born under a rising Mars appeared to have a better chance at becoming a physician. Rejecting the idea that some "ray" from the planet at the time of birth somehow influenced an individual's genetic makeup—because if such a ray did exist, he reasoned, it would have to affect the genetic endowment at conception and not at birth—Gauquelin wondered whether a case could be made for the idea that a child might be predisposed to be born when a certain planet was over the horizon. In other words, is a person born at a time when cosmic conditions correspond to his genetic endowment?

After another five years of hitting the birth registers, matching over fifteen thousand births of parents with their children, and calculating 300 thousand planetary positions, Gauquelin discovered that the positions of the planets under which a person is born (notably those of Mars, Jupiter, Saturn and Venus) correlate highly with those of the parents. The correlation was stronger when both parents were born under the same rising or culminating planet, and it was the mother's planet which most generally corresponded with the child's.

While this by no means proves his planetary heredity hypothesis, Gauquelin speculates that his data nonetheless presents an electrifying direction of research. This is his reasoning:

> The planetary effect would...make no alteration in [the child's] constitution, would not imprint

any influence on it at birth, and would provide no
lucky or unlucky predestination in addition to the
natural predispositions of the newborn child. In
short, the birth would only be a reaction of our
organism more easily indicated according to
certain terrestrial conditions, and this reaction
would probably not be the only one. It would still
be nothing but a statistical datum whose value
would be relative. It would not have permanent
meaning, unlike the pronouncements of astrology
concerning each aspect of the sky.

Gauquelin further concludes that "there is not, and there
never will be any planet of the professions, nor even a
planet of character, but only cosmic clocks or time-keepers
which operate in a way which is still unknown but seems to
be connected to the earth's rotation."

Despite his protests, Gauquelin's brand of cosmobiology
has been lauded by astrologers while the scientific
community has for the most part dismissed him as an
advocate of the practice and questioned the validity of his
findings. His desire to avoid this guilt through association
by insisting on a strong distinction between cosmobiology
and astrology appears—at least thus far—to have failed. A
deeply embedded resistance to anything remotely connected with astrology's central axiom, "As above, so below," is
largely to blame. It remains, however, entirely possible
that this "new science" will one day be vindicated and
prove to have much more in common with the magical
knowledge symbolically codified in the art forms of ancient
peoples than with modern astrology taken in isolation.

What implications, then, concerning the astrological
use of talismans can we draw from all of this data?
Regardless of how the growing body of cosmobiological
data and knowledge of cosmic influences is interpreted—as
either the first stage of research which may eventually
vindicate the basic principles of astrology or as pointing to
an entirely different direction—there is at present no
scientific justification for the claims made for the astrological uses of talismans. Modern astrologers who refer to
correspondences (which are ultimately rooted in an ancient
magical cosmology) and attempt to extend the inherent
logic to the realm of physical influences (often this is done
very casually) only help to confuse the issue. As we already

discovered, there is increasing reason to suggest that gems and metals might interact with both mind and body, but it would be unreasonable from a scientific standpoint to suggest that specific gems can attract specific Cosmic influences.

EPILOGUE:

The Mind Trajectory

The Mind Trajectory

A small group of scientists and philosophers calling itself The Committee to Scientifically Investigate Claims of Paranormal and Other Phenomena recently declared that too much fantastic theory and poorly conducted psi research abounds. Its aim? To critically wade through many of the claims and present summaries of what can be supported with scientific evidence. Among the group members are L. Sprague de Camp, an archeologist who has written books debunking what he calls pseudo-science; B.F. Skinner, father of modern behaviorism (a school of thought which negates the existence of the human mind); Bark Bok, an astronomer who spends some of his spare time publicly railing against astrology and science-fiction writer Isaac Asimov.

Strange bedfellows indeed! All a bit quick on the gun and determined to strike down the irrationalism, superstition and obscurantism lurking around every corner.

While there's little doubt that you don't have to open too many closets to discover the skeletons of the mind revolution, to assume that certain High Priests of Academe are qualified to pass final judgment on all matters of mind ranks with the best in the annals of self-deception.

If anything, this sudden committee consciousness can be seen as an important sign of the times. More "authorities" are finally taking note of the mind revolution that has been barking, even howling, at their doors.

In our MIND-SEARCH, one thing above all else became abundantly clear to us: the mind remains a mystery. No one has unraveled its secret code and no amount of sabre rattling will prevent those stimulated by mysteries to seek solutions. Cochis, the Magus, in the novel of the same name written by John Fowles, has this to say:

...Mystery has energy. It pours energy into whoever seeks the answer to it. If you disclose the solution to the mystery you are simply depriving the other seekers of an important source of energy.

These few words have a subtle power, for they reflect what each of us needs: the freedom to pursue and attempt to unravel our own mysteries as we see fit. To presume that science or any other body of knowledge can unilaterally arbitrate the opening and closing of doors to these mysteries is to greatly misjudge the emerging modern consciousness. To refer to the growing desire of great numbers of people who seek to probe their inner realms of Being—to search for a greater understanding of the powers of mind—as the emergence of irrationalism is a vital clue to the fact that many scientists have not adequately kept pace with major changes in thinking in our society.

Throughout our MIND-SEARCH, we spoke with people who had grown weary of waiting for scientists to investigate claims made in the name of the mind. Granted, there are dangers in this, for it's difficult, if not naive, to conceive of a mind revolution in a consumer society without mind merchants. So the rip-offs abound and the exploitation syndrome rears its ugly head time and time again. And it's not always easy for those pursuing mysteries to separate the wheat from the chaff if well thought-out perspectives are lacking, as they often are. But these are growing pains that accompany any widespread social upheaval and should not be seen as the Great Return to superstition.

One conclusion we've reached in surveying the impact of the mind revolution is that the generally accepted view of how science changes its patterns of thinking must be partially modified. The traditional scenario has been explained this way: scientists work within specific frameworks, or *paradigms*, of what is acceptable to research and what isn't. New ideas emerge slowly as new scientists enter the fold and the old guard dies off. Therefore, when it comes to the issue of mind, one dominant paradigm says the brain can explain everything; there is little need to involve something as abstract as mind.

While this basic understanding of how science evolves may still apply, another element must be addressed: the power of the mass media. Here are a few examples.

During one segment of the 1976 National Hockey

League playoffs, the mass media rage in North America for about one week was pyramid power. It all began very suddenly when the wife of the coach of the Toronto Maple Leafs heard an announcement on the radio that pyramid models could be used to cure a variety of physical ailments. She promptly purchased one and claimed to have used it to cure her daughter of a severe migraine. Before you could say "Great Cheops," the entire Toronto team was reported basking beneath a huge pyramid model suspended from the dressing room ceiling before each game, and pyramid models were observed lined up in a neat row beneath the team bench.

"It energizes them after they lose energy," the Leafs' coach asserted with a stonelike seriousness during a television interview. "It's some form of magnetic energy."

Little would have been made of this had the Leafs lost all their games to the Philadelphia Flyers as the experts had expected. But no, the Leafs won three games, bringing the series to a seventh and deciding game. By then, pyramid power had already become a household word. Articles hit the newspapers, and television and radio talk shows had a new toy.

If only the Leafs had won the final game. It would have been a bonanza for the pyramid-power entrepreneurs. But they didn't. They were soundly thrashed and a good story killed. An infectious media backlash was generated and gained momentum almost overnight. Time to get back down to earth. Time to get away from these kinds of rip-offs. Had the Leafs won, it's likely the media would have escalated its interest, and, for a couple of months, pyramid models would have become the in craze.

But herein lies an important lesson. Something like pyramid energy, at this time, too far extends—is alien to—how we have learned to see ourselves in relation to our total environment. While serious research is being done in this area, it will be some time before the findings are incorporated into our educational process. Because it's alien, it's all too easy to dismiss. So when the media spotlight fell on pyramids as it did, in a relative vacuum or lack of knowledge, it could only approach it on a level of entertainment.

But how about something which has practical implications for us in the here and now? An example is the rise of TM. Basing its initial claims on a very small body of scientific data, it became a super phenomenon spurred on by the mass media. Only after its extensive claims had been accepted by people from all walks of life did an increasing number of scientists begin researching the entire phenomenon of meditation. A few years ago, many of these same scientists probably wouldn't have been caught dead wiring up people to machines and asking them to repeat various mantras.

The point is simply this: science, more than ever before, must compete with other sources of information, particularly word-of-mouth, and the mass media's power in further capitalizing on a growing phenomenon. But it will only compete if it becomes evident that we the public have a real need to pursue something. And in this manner, subtle changes within the dominant paradigm begin to take place. It would be a mistake to argue that TM's popularity is solely built on its scientific justification. It has certainly helped, but TM's rebirth was timely. We need techniques to help us deal with stressful life conditions.

Another example. Anyone seriously scrutinizing the research on laying on of hands conducted by Bernard Grad will have to wonder why more follow-up research has not been done. After all, the data has been available for almost two decades. Grad's opinion is that when his work first appeared, there was, in addition to its being outside the dominant scientific paradigm, little practical need for alternative methods of healing in the West. The medical profession, while increasingly mechanistic in its approach to patients, nevertheless has had things well under control. Conventional medicine, Grad says, has been coping with illness in the West unlike the situation in Third World nations where illness is widespread, doctors scarce and cultural norms allow for unorthodox healers.

But now the situation is beginning to change. More people are growing dissatisfied with orthodox medicine. In particular, well-publicized scares about the side effects of drugs abound, and malpractice suits are soaring. While in the past, people would resort to unorthodox forms of healing only as a last-ditch effort, more are now turning to healers for less complex and serious ailments.

Doubtless, the soaring costs of medicine have also made alternative forms of healing more attractive. In addition, more information has become available via the mass media about the ways we can learn to take better care of ourselves in the preventative sense. Innovative work such as the cancer therapy offered by Carl and Stephanie Simonton addresses the question of how our thoughts may decrease resistance to disease.

While all this becomes a greater part of our consciousness, the unorthodox healing trajectory becomes more visible. It isn't as easy to dismiss it, and more physicians and scientists are beginning to show interest. Greater commitment to studying new forms of healing will undoubtedly follow. This doesn't mean, however, that more unusual forms of healing, such as medical dowsing, will gain immediate acceptance as legitimate areas for research. They will have to wait their turn. It seems likely that there will be more immediate investigation of the kind of work the Simontons are doing and the ground already charted by Bernard Grad.

How does the psychic explosion fall into this perspective? For almost a century, psychical research has been accumulating data on telepathy, clairvoyance and the like. Orthodox science has generally dismissed or ignored most of these findings, even though the research has been conducted in a methodical, experimental fashion by qualified scientists. There is now evidence that a shift in thinking is taking place, but, significantly, it is the more practical aspects of the psi explosion which are beginning to make inroads. An example is the work of Stanley Dean and Howard Eisenberg we described. By introducing previously neglected concepts into psychiatric practice, more heads are turning. The same is true of Marilyn Rossner's clairvoyant diagnosis of mentally disturbed children. Norman Emerson's research in archeology, aided by his clairvoyant friend, is also geared to practical aims. All these pursuits have discernible benefits, and the results are beginning to attract the attention of their colleagues.

It's revealing that the committee mentioned earlier stated that their topics for investigation included things like astrology, UFOs, out-of-body experiences and predictions made by well-known psychics who often appear on national television. That's fine and dandy, but the essence of the psi trajectory is already geared toward the practical applications of unfolding powers of the mind. Few of the mind explorers we mentioned in this book are interested in psi for psi's sake, and the same can be said for the lay public in search of practical benefits.

As for the many psi-related courses stressing self-development, they're a strong reflection of widespread public interest in developing and applying latent human potential. Granted, many of these courses are makeshift and prey on the misguided expectations of those desiring instant revelation or power. But just as there now is a greater professional need to put psi to practical use and to get beyond psychic showmanship and gimmickry, many of these courses will likely be forced to adopt a more sophisticated regimen or lose out in the marketplace. As the mind revolution continues to grow in scope, more people will better understand that self-development is an ongoing process, not a one-shot deal.

In this book, we've presented what we feel is a cross section of the mind revolution, a revolution we believe is here to stay. From our observations, it should be evident that there is little security in closing the door on any mystery. Our conversations with Alfred Tomatis concerning TM are an important example. While there is no conclusive evidence for his views, his research on the effects of sound on the body should give anyone pause who has categorically accepted the claims of mantra meditation. Those who gain energy pursuing the solutions to mysteries will no doubt be motivated to reexamine the benefits of all forms of meditation.

As we have suggested, things are not always what they seem, and it's likely that better understanding of the complexity of our psychophysiology will propel us to readjust many of the prevailing self-development techniques.

And so, our MIND-SEARCH continues.

BIBLIOGRAPHY

Bagnall, Oscar. *The Origin and Properties of the Human Aura*. New York: University Books, 1970.

Baker, Penny M.E. *Meditation: A Step Beyond With Edgar Cayce*. New York: Pinnacle Books, 1975.

Bancroft, W. Jane. *The Lozonov Language Class* (a pamphlet). Scarborough College, University of Toronto, 1975.

Barber, Theodore Xenophon. "Who Believes in Hypnosis?" *Psychology Today*, July 1970.

Barnett, Lincoln. *The Universe and Dr. Einstein*. New York: Bantam, 1968.

Barrett, Francis. *The Magus*. 1801.

Barrett, William, and Besterman, Theodore. *The Divining Rod*. New York: University Books, 1968.

Batcheldor, K.J. "Report on a Case of Table Levitation and Associated Phenomena." *Journal of the Society for Psychical Research* 43 (1966): 729.

Beal, James B. "The Emergence of Paraphysics: Research and Application." In *Psychic Exploration*, edited by John White and compiled by Edgar Mitchell. New York: G.P. Putnam's Sons, 1974.

———. "Bioelectric Fields." *Theoria to Theory* 7 (1973).

Beard, Paul. *A Field of Enquiry: The College of Psychic Studies*. London: The College of Psychic Studies, 1971.

Becker, Robert O. "Electromagnetic Forces and the Life Process." *Technology Review* 75 (1972): 2.

_____. "The Effect of Magnetic Fields Upon the Central Nervous System." In *Biological Effects of Magnetic Fields*, edited by Madeleine F. Barnothy. New York: Plenum Press, 1969.

Bell, A.H., ed. *Practical Dowsing: A Symposium*. London: G. Bell and Sons, 1965.

Besant, Annie, and Leadbeater, C.W. *Thought-Forms*. Wheaton, Illinois: The Theosophical Publishing House, 1969.

Besterman, Theodore. *Crystal-Gazing*. New Hyde Park, New York: University Books, 1965.

Bloomfield, Harold H. et al. *TM: Discovering Inner Energy and Overcoming Stress*. New York: Delacorte Press, 1975.

Bohm, David, "Quantum Theory as an Indication of a New Order in Physics." In *Quantum Theory and Beyond*, edited by Ted Bastin. New York: Cambridge University Press, 1971.

Bova, Ben. *The Fourth State of Matter*. New York: Mentor, 1974.

Boyer, David G. and Tiller, William. *The Colors in Kirlian Photography—Fact or Artifact?* Stanford University: Dept. of Materials Science, 1974.

Brena, Steven. *Yoga and Medicine*. Baltimore: Penguin, 1973.

Brier, Bob et al. "Experimental Tests of Silva Mind Control Graduates." Paper read at Parapsychological Association Convention, Charlottesville, Virginia, 1973.

Brown, Barbara. *New Mind, New Body: Biofeedback: New Directions for the Mind*. New York: Harper & Row, 1974.

Brown, F.A., Jr. *Biological Clocks*. Boston: American Institute of Biological Sciences, 1962.

Brown, Slater. *The Heyday of Spiritualism*. New York: Pocket Books, 1972.

Bucke, Richard Maurice. *Cosmic Consciousness: A Study in the Evolution of the Human Mind*. New York: E.P. Dutton, 1969.

Budge, E.A. Wallis. *Osiris: The Egyptian Religion of Resurrection*. New Hyde Park, New York: University Books, 1961.

————. *The Mummy*. New York: Collier Books, 1972.

————. *The Book of the Dead*. New York: Dover, 1967.

————. *Egyptian Magic*. New York: Dover, 1971.

Budzynski, T. and Stoyva, J., "An Instrument for Producing Deep Muscle Relaxation by Means of Analog Information Feedback." *Journal of Applied Behavior* 2 (1969).

Burr, Harold Saxton. *Blueprint for Immortality: The Electric Patterns of Life*. London: Neville Spearman, 1972.

Campbell, Anthony. *Seven States of Consciousness*. New York: Harper & Row, 1974.

Campbell, Joseph. "Seven Levels of Consciousness." *Psychology Today*, December 1975.

Cavanna, Roberto and Ullman, Montague. *Psi and Altered States of Consciousness*. Proceedings of an International Conference on Hypnosis, Drugs, Dreams, and Psi at Le Piol, St. Paul de Vence, France, June 9-12, 1967. New York: Parapsychology Foundation, 1968.

Cavendish, Richard, *The Black Arts*. New York: Capricorn, 1968.

Chari, C.T.K. "Psychophysiological Issues About EEG Alpha Activity and ESP." *Journal of the American Society for Psychical Research*, 64 (1970): 4.

Chaudhuri, Haridas. *Integral Yoga*. Wheaton, Illinois: The Theosophical Publishing House, 1965.

Chijevsky, A.L. "L'action de L'activité Periodique Solaire sur les Phénomènes Sociaux." *Traite de Climatologie Biologique et Medicale*. Paris: Masson, 1934.

Collin, Rodney. *The Theory of Celestial Influence*. New York: Samuel Weiser, 1973.

Cone, C.D., and Tonguer, M., Jr. "Control of Somatic Cell Mitosis by Simulated Changes in the Transmembrane Potential Level." *Oncology*, 25 (1971).

Crow, W.B. *Precious Stones: Their Occult Power and Hidden Significance*. New York: Samuel Weiser, 1968.

Dean, Stanley R. "Metapsychiatry: The Confluence of Psychiatry and Mysticism." *Fields Within Fields* 11 (1974).

_____. ed. *Psychiatry and Mysticism*. Chicago: Nelson-Hall, 1975.

Deikman, F. Ned. "Biofeedback and Self Regulation." *Medical Electronics and Equipment News*, July 19, 1974.

Denes, Peter B., and Pinson, Elliot N. *The Speech Chain: The Physics and Biology of Spoken Language*. New York: Doubleday, 1973.

Ebon, Martin, ed. *The Amazing Uri Geller*. New York: Signet, 1975.

Eccles, Sir John C. "The Physiology of Imagination." *Scientific American*, September 1958.

Edwards, Harry. *A Guide for the Development of Mediumship*. London: The Spiritualist Association of Great Britain, N.D.

Ehrenwald, Jan. *New Dimensions of Deep Analysis: A Study of Telepathy in Interpersonal Relationships*. New York: Grune and Stratton, 1955.

_____. *Telepathy and Medical Psychology*. New York: Grune and Stratton, 1966.

Einstein, Albert. *The Meaning of Relativity*. Princeton,

New Jersey: Princeton University Press, 1945.

Eisenbud, Jule. *Psi and Psychoanalysis*. New York: Grune and Stratton, 1970.

Ellis, A. "Telepathy and Psychoanalysis: A Critique of Recent Findings." *Psychiatric Quarterly*, 21 (1947): 4.

Ellis, Arthur J. *The Divining Rod: A History of Water Witching*. Washington, D.C.: Government Printing Office, 1917.

Emerson, J.N. "Intuitive Archaeology: Egypt and Iran." Department of Anthropology, University of Toronto, November, 1975.

————. "Intuitive Archaeology: A Developing Approach." Department of Anthropology, University of Toronto, November, 1974.

————. "Archaeology, Parapsychology and One White Crow." Department of Anthropology, University of Toronto, April, 1975.

————. "Intuitive Archaeology: A Psychic Approach." *New Horizons* 1 (1974): 3.

Fagan, Cyril. *Astrological Origins*. St. Paul, Minnesota: Llewellyn, 1971.

Ferguson, Marilyn. *The Brain Revolution*. New York: Taplinger, 1973.

Fernie, William T. *The Occult and Curative Powers of Precious Stones*. Blauvelt, New York: Rudolf Steiner Publications, 1973.

Flanagan, G. Pat. *Pyramid Power*. Glendale, Calif: Pyramid Publishers, 1974.

Forem, Jack. *Transcendental Meditation*. New York: E.P. Dutton, 1974.

Fortune, Dion. *Psychic Self-Defence*. New York: Samuel Weiser, 1930.

Fowles, John. *The Magus.* New York: Dell, 1973.

Freud, Sigmund. *Studies in Parapsychology.* Edited by Philip Rieff. New York: Collier Books, 1963.

————. "Dreams and Telepathy." *Imago* 8 (1922).

Friedman, Howard et al. "Geomagnetic Parameters and Psychiatric Hospital Admissions." *Nature* 200 (1963).

Gallert, Mark, L. *New Light on Therapeutic Energies.* London: James Clarke & Co., 1966.

Gardner, Martin. *Fads and Fallacies in the Name of Science.* New York: Dover, 1957.

Garvin, Richard. *The Crystal Skull.* New York: Pocket Books, 1974.

Gauquelin, Michel. *Cosmic Influences on Human Behavior.* New York: Stein and Day, 1973.

Glueck, Bernard C. and Stroebel, Charles F. "Biofeedback and Meditation in the Treatment of Psychiatric Illness," *Comprehensive Psychiatry*, 16 (1975): 4.

Grad, Bernard. "Laboratory Evidence of the 'Laying-On-Of-Hands.'" In *The Dimensions of Healing.* Los Altos, Calif.: The Academy of Parapsychology and Medicine, 1972.

————. "Orgone Treatment of Cancerous Rats," Esalen Institute Symposium on Reich and Orgone, San Francisco, August, 1974.

————. "A Telekinetic Effect on Plant Growth," *International Journal of Parapsychology*, 6, 1964.

————. et al. "The Influence of an Unorthodox Method of Treatment on Wound Healing of Mice," *International Journal of Parapsychology*, 3, 1961.

Greeley, Andrew M. and McCready, William C. "Are We A Nation of Mystics?" *The New York Times Magazine*, January 26, 1975.

Green, Elmer E. "Biofeedback for Mind-Body Self-Regulation: Healing and Creativity," In *The Varieties of Healing Experience*. Los Altos, Calif.: The Academy of Parapsychology and Medicine, 1971.

――――. "How to Make Use of the Field of Mind Theory." In *The Dimensions of Healing*, Los Altos, Calif.: The Academy of Parapsychology and Medicine, 1972.

Green, Judith A. "The Mind-Body Hyphen." *Social Policy*, March/April, 1974.

Griffith, F. and Thompson, Herbert, eds. *The Leyden Papyrus: An Egyptian Magical Book*. New York: Dover, 1974.

Hansel, C.E.M. *ESP: A Scientific Evaluation*. New York: Scribner's, 1966.

Hartmann, Franz. *Magic: White and Black*. Hollywood, Calif.: Newcastle, 1971.

――――. *Paracelsus*. New York: John W. Lovell, 1891.

Harvalik, Z.V. "The Biophysical Magnetometer-Gradiometer," *The Virginia Journal of Science* 21 (1970).

――――. "Where are the Dowsing Sensors?" *Journal of the American Society of Dowsers*, May 1973.

――――. "Sensitivity Tests on a Dowser Exposed to Artificial D.C. Magnetic Fields." *Journal of the American Society of Dowsers*, August, 1973.

Heisenberg, Werner. *Physics and Philosophy*. New York: Harper & Row, 1966.

――――. *Physics and Beyond*. New York: Harper & Row, 1972.

Hilgard, Ernest, R. "Hypnosis is no Mirage," *Psychology Today*, November 1974.

Honorton, Charles, and Krippner, Stanley. "Hypnosis and ESP Performance: A Review of the Experimental

Literature," *Journal of the American Society for Psychical Research*, 63 (1969): 3.

Humphreys, Christmas. *Concentration and Meditation*. Baltimore: Penguin, 1970.

Illich, Ivan. *Medical Nemesis: The Expropriation of Health*. Toronto: McClelland and Stewart, 1975.

Inyushin, V.M. "Biological Plasma of Human and Animal Organisms." Paper read at the Symposium of Psychotronics, Prague, September, 1970.

James, William. *The Varieties of Religious Experience*. New York: New American Library, 1958.

Johnson, Raynor C. *The Imprisoned Splendour*. Wheaton, Illinois: The Theosophical Publishing House, 1971.

Kamiya, Joe et al. *Biofeedback and Self-Control*. Chicago: Aldine/Atherton, 1971.

Kapleau, Philip, ed. *The Wheel of Death*. New York: Harper & Row, 1974.

Karlins, Marvin, and Andrews, Lewis M. *Biofeedback*. New York: Warner, 1972.

Kazhinsky, B.B. *Biological Radio*. Kiev: Ukranian Academy of Sciences, 1962.

Kiev, Ari. *Transcultural Psychiatry*. New York: The Free Press, 1972.

Kimura, Doreen. "The Asymmetry of the Human Brain." *Scientific American*, 228 (1973): 3.

Krippner, Stanley. "Telepathy." In *Psychic Exploration*, edited by John White and compiled by Edgar Mitchell. New York: G.P. Putnam's Sons, 1974.

Krishna, Gopi. *Higher Consciousness: The Evolutionary Thrust of Kundalini*. New York: The Julian Press, 1974.

_____. *Kundalini: the Evolutionary Energy in Man*. Berkeley, Calif.: Shambala, 1971.

———. *The Awakening of Kundalini*. New York: E.P. Dutton, 1975.

Kuhn, Thomas. *The Structure of Scientific Revolutions*. Chicago: University of Chicago Press, 1962.

Kunz, George Frederick. *The Curious Lore of Precious Stones*. New York: Dover, 1971.

Laski, Marghanita. *Ecstasy: A Study of Some Secular and Religious Experiences*. Westport, Conn.: Greenwood, 1968.

Leadbeater, C.W. *Man Visible and Invisible*. Wheaton, Illinois: The Theosophical Publishing House, 1971.

———. *The Chakras*. Wheaton, Illinois: The Theosophical Publishing House, 1972.

Leshan, Lawrence. *The Medium, the Mystic and the Physicist*. New York: The Viking Press, 1974.

———. "Psychic Phenomena and Mystical Experience." In *Psychic Exploration*, edited by John White and compiled by Edgar Mitchell. New York: G.P. Putnam's Sons, 1974.

———. *How to Meditate*. Boston: Little, Brown, & Co., 1974.

Lorayne, Harry and Lucas, Jerry. *The Memory Book*. New York: Stein and Day, 1974.

MacGregor, Helen, and Underhill, Margaret V. *The Psychic Faculties and Their Development*. Rev. Ed. London: The College of Psychic Studies, 1974.

Maharishi Mahesh Yogi. *Transcendental Meditation*. New York: Signet, 1968.

Marha, Karel et al. *Electromagnetic Fields and the Life Environment*. San Francisco: San Francisco Press, 1971.

Martindale, Colin. "What Makes Creative People Different?" *Psychology Today*, July 1975.

McClure, D.J., ed. *First Canadian International Symposium on Sleep*. Proceedings of a Symposium, McGill

University, Montreal, April 1972.

McQuade, Walter and Aikman, Ann. *Stress*. New York: Bantam, 1975.

Mead, G.R.S. *The Doctrine of the Subtle Body in Western Tradition*. Wheaton, Illinois: The Theosophical Publishing House, 1967.

Melville, John. *Crystal Gazing and Clairvoyance*. New York: Samuel Weiser, 1974.

Melzack, Ronald. "The Promise of Biofeedback: Don't Hold the Party Yet." *Psychology Today*, July 1975.

————. *The Puzzle of Pain*. Harmondsworth, Middlesex, England: Penquin, 1973.

Miller, Robert N. et al. "Research Report: Ernest Holmes Research Foundation." *Science of Mind*, July 1974.

Mitler, Merrill M. et al. "Sleeplessness, Sleep Attacks and Things That Go Wrong in the Night." *Psychology Today*, December 1975.

Murphy, Garner and Ballou, Robert O., eds. *William James on Psychical Research*. New York: The Viking Press, 1960.

Musés, Charles and Young, Arthur M., eds. *Consciousness and Reality*. New York: Outerbridge and Lazard, 1972.

Myers, F.W.H. *The Human Personality and Its Survival of Bodily Death*. New York: Longmans, Green and Co., 1954.

Naranjo, Claudio and Ornstein, Robert E. *On The Psychology of Meditation*. New York: The Viking Press, 1971.

Needleman, Jacob. *The New Religions*. New York: Pocket Books, 1972.

Nelson, J.H. *Cosmic Patterns: Their Influence on Man and his Communication*. Washington D.C.: American Federation of Astrologers, 1974.

Ornstein, Robert. "Psychology of Self-Regulation." *New Scientist*, April 3, 1975.

_____. "Temporal Dimensions of Consciousness." *New Scientist*, March 27, 1975.

_____, ed. *The Nature of Human Consciousness.* San Francisco: W.H. Freeman and Co., 1973.

_____. *The Psychology of Consciousness.* New York: The Viking Press, 1972.

Osis, Karlis and Bokert, E. "ESP and Changed States of Consciousness Induced by Meditation." *Journal of the American Society for Psychical Research* 65 (1971).

Ostrander, Sheila and Schroeder, Lynn. *Psychic Discoveries Behind the Iron Curtain.* New York: Bantam, 1971.

_____ and _____, eds. *The ESP Papers: Scientists Speak Out from Behind the Iron Curtain.* New York: Bantam, 1976.

Otis, Leon, "If Well-Integrated But Anxious, Try TM." *Psychology Today*, April 1974.

Owen, Iris M. "Phillip's Story Continued." *New Horizons* 2 (1975): 1.

_____. "Signpost to Sleep: Learning a Psychological Skill." *New Horizons* 1 (1974): 4.

_____, and Sparrow, Margaret H. "Generation of Paranormal Physical Phenomena in Connection with an Imaginary Communicator." *New Horizons* 1 (1974): 3.

Pavitt, William. *The Book of Talismans, Amulets and Zodiacal Gems.* No. Hollywood, Calif.: Wilshire Book Company, 1914.

Penfield, Wilder. "Engrams in the Human Brain: Mechanisms of Memory." *Proceedings of the Royal Society of Medicine* 61 (1968): 8.

———. "Epileptic Automatism and the Centrencephalic Integrating System." *Patterns of Organization in the Central Nervous System* 30. Proceedings of the Association for Research in Nervous and Mental Diseases, December 15 and 16, 1950, New York.

———. "The Cerebral Cortex in Man." *The Archives of Neurology and Psychiatry* 40 (1938).

———. "The Interpretive Cortex." *Science* 129 (1959): 3365.

———. *The Mystery of the Mind.* Princeton, New Jersey: Princeton University Press, 1975.

———. "The Permanent Record of the Stream of Consciousness." *Acta Psychologica* 11 (1955).

Piccardi, G. *The Chemical Basis of Medical Climatology.* Springfield, Illinois: Charles C. Thomas, 1963.

Powell, Arthur E. *The Etheric Double.* London: The Theosophical Publishing House, 1925.

Puthoff, Harold and Targ, Russell. "Psychic Research and Modern Physics." In *Psychic Exploration*, edited by John White and compiled by Edgar Mitchell. New York: G.P. Putnam's Sons, 1974.

Raikov, Vladimir. "Reincarnation by Hypnosis." In *The ESP Papers*, edited by Sheila Ostrander and Lynn Schroeder. New York: Bantam, 1976.

Ravitz, Leonard J. "Electro-Magnetic Field Monitoring of Changing State-Function, Including Hypnotic States." *Journal of the American Society of Psychosomatic Dentistry and Medicine*, 17 (1970): 4.

Regardie, Israel. *How to Make and Use Talismans.* New York: Samuel Weiser, 1972.

———. *The Philosopher's Stone.* Saint Paul, Minnesota: Llewellyn, 1970.

———. *The Tree of Life: A Study in Magic.* New York: Samuel Weiser, 1972.

Regush, June and Nicholas. *Psi: The Other World Catalogue*. New York: G.P. Putnam's Sons, 1974.

Regush, Nicholas M., in collaboration with Jan Merta. *Exploring the Human Aura*. Englewood Cliffs, New Jersey: Prentice-Hall, 1975.

————, ed. *The Human Aura*. New York: Berkley, 1974.

Reichenbach, Karl Von. *The Odic Force: Letters on Od and Magnetism*. New Hyde Park, New York: University Books, 1968.

Rhine, J.B. *Extrasensory Perception*. Boston: Branden, 1964.

————. *The Reach of the Mind*. New York: Morrow, 1971.

Rhine, Louisa E. *Psi: What Is It?* New York: Harper & Row, 1975.

————. *Mind Over Matter: Psychokinesis*. New York: Collier Books, 1972.

Rocard, Yves. "Actions of a Very Weak Magnetic Gradient: The Reflex of the Dowser." In *Biological Effects of Magnetic Fields*, edited by Madeleine F. Barnothy. New York: Plenum Press, 1969.

Roll, W.G. "The Psi Field." *Proceedings of the Parapsychological Association* 1 (1957-1964).

Rosenthal, Robert. *Experimenter Effects in Behavioral Research*. New York: Appleton-Century-Crofts, 1966.

Rudrananda, Swami. *Spiritual Cannibalism*. New York: Links Books, 1973.

Ryzl, Milan. "A Method of Training in ESP." *International Journal of Parapsychology* 8 (1966): 4.

————. "Advanced Meditation Tapes." A transcript. 1974.

————. "ESP: The Universe and Man." *Psychic*, January/February 1970.

————. *How to Develop ESP in Yourself and in Others*. A home-study manual. 1973.

————. *Parapsychology: A Scientific Approach*. New York: Hawthorn, 1970.

Sarfatti, Jack. "Implications of Meta-Physics for Psycho-energetic Systems." *Psychoenergetic Systems* 1 (1974).

Scharstein, Ben-Ami. *Mystical Experience*. Baltimore: Penguin, 1974.

Schmeck, Harold, M. *Immunology: The Many-Edged Sword*. New York: George Braziller, 1974.

Schmeidler, Gertrude. "The Psychic Personality." In *Psychic Exploration*, edited by John White and compiled by Edgar Mitchell. New York: G.P. Putnam's Sons, 1974.

Schmidt, Helmut. "Psychokinesis." In *Psychic Exploration*, edited by John White and compiled by Edgar Mitchell. New York: G.P. Putnam's Sons, 1974.

Schul, Bill and Pettit, Ed. *The Psychic Power of Pyramids*. Greenwich, Conn.: Fawcett, 1976.

Schwartz, Gary E. "TM Relaxes Some People and Makes Them Feel Better." *Psychology Today*, April 1974.

Selye, Hans. *Stress Without Distress*. New York: Signet, 1975.

Sextus, Carl. *Hypnotism*. No. Hollywood, Calif.: Wilshire Books Company, 1971.

Sharma, I.C. *Cayce, Karma and Reincarnation*. New York: Harper & Row, 1975.

Sidlauskas, A.E. "The Phenomenon of Language: The Ideas of Dr. A. Tomatis." Mimeographed paper from the Child Study Centre of the University of Ottawa.

Simonton, Carl. "The Role of the Mind in Cancer Therapy." In *The Dimensions of Healing*. Los Altos, Calif.: The Academy of Parapsychology and Medicine, 1972.

Smith, Jonathan. "Meditation As Psychotherapy: A Review of the Literature." *Psychological Bulletin* 82 (1975): 4.

Smith, Sister M. Justa. "Effect of Magnetic Fields in Enzyme Reactivity." In *Biological Effects of Magnetic Fields*, edited by Madeleine F. Barnothy. New York: Plenum Press, 1969.

———. "The Influence on Enzyme Growth by the Laying-on-of-Hands," In *The Dimensions of Healing*. Los Altos, Calif.: The Academy of Parapsychology and Medicine, 1972.

Smythies, J.R. "The Mind-Brain Problem Today: A Viewpoint from the Neurosciences," *Parapsychology Review*, March/April 1973.

Spence, Lewis. *The Mysteries of Egypt*. Blauvelt, New York: Rudolf Steiner Publications, 1972.

Sperry, Roger W. "Left-Brain, Right-Brain." *Saturday Review*, September 9, 1975.

Spirig, E. "Dyslexics, Mental Deficiency and the Electronic Ear." Translated by J.J. Watters. Paper presented at the fourth International Congress of Audio-Psycho-Phonology, Madrid, May 13, 14 and 15, 1974.

Staal, Frits. *Exploring Mysticism*. Harmondsworth, Middlesex, England: Penguin, 1975.

Stanford, Rex. "Scientific, Ethical and Clinical Problems in the 'Training' of Psi Abilities." Paper read at the American Association for the Advancement of Science Annual Meeting, New York, January 1975.

Stanford, Rex G., and Lovin, Carole Ann. "EEG Alpha Activity and ESP Performance." *Journal of the American Society for Psychical Research* 64 (1970): 4.

Stearn, Jess. *Edgar Cayce—The Sleeping Prophet*. New York: Bantam, 1968.

Tanner, Florice. *The Mystery Teachings In World Reli-*

gions. Wheaton, Illinois: The Theosophical Publishing House, 1973.

Tart, Charles T. *States of Consciousness*. New York: E.P. Dutton, 1975.

————. "Transpersonal Potentialities of Deep Hypnosis." *Journal of Transpersonal Psychology* 1 (1970).

————, ed. *Altered States of Consciousness*. New York: Doubleday, 1972.

————, ed. *Transpersonal Psychology*. New York: Harper & Row, 1975.

Taylor, John. *Superminds: A Scientist Looks at the Paranormal*. New York: The Viking Press, 1975.

Tomatis, Alfred A. *Education et Dyslexie*. Paris: Les Editions ESF, 1973.

————. *La Libération D'Oedipe*. Paris: Les Editions ESF, 1972.

————. *Vers L'écoute Humaine*. Vol. I and II. Paris: Les Editions ESF, 1974.

Toben, Bob. *Space-Time and Beyond*. New York: E.P. Dutton, 1975.

Tompkins, Peter. *Secrets of the Great Pyramid*. New York: Harper & Row, 1971.

Tromp, Solco. "Review of the Possible Physiological Causes of Dowsing." *International Journal of Parapsychology* 10 (1968): 4.

Ullman, Montague. "On the Occurrence of Telepathic Dreams." *Journal of the American Society for Psychical Research* 53 (1959): 1.

————. "Psi and Psychiatry." In *Psychic Exploration* edited by John White and compiled by Edgar Mitchell. New York: G.P. Putnam's Sons, 1974.

Van Over, Raymond, ed. *Psychology and Extrasensory Perception*. New York: New American Library, 1972.

Vasiliev, L.L. *Experiments in Mental Suggestion*. Hampshire, England: Institute for the Study of Mental Images, 1963.

Vaughan, Alan. "Investigation of Silva Mind Control Claims." Paper read at the Parapsychological Association Convention, Charlottesville, Virginia, 1973.

Vishnu Devananda, Swami, *The Complete Illustrated Book of Yoga*. New York: Pocket Books, 1972.

Wallace, Keith, and Benson, Herbert. "The Physiology of Meditation." *Scientific American*, 226 (1972): 2.

Watters, J.J. "The Explanation of Dr. Tomatis' Audio Psycho Phonology Treatment Program (Technical Procedures)." Paper read at the Conference on the Electronic Ear held at the Child Study Centre, University of Ottawa, November 8, 1973.

Weinberg, Steven. "Unified Theories of Elementary Particle Interaction." *Scientific American*, July 1974.

Weingarten, Henry. *A Modern Introduction to Astrology*. New York: ASI Publishers, 1974.

Wenger, Win. *How To Increase Your Intelligence*. New York: Bobbs-Merrill, 1975.

West, John Anthony, and Toonder, Jan Gerhard. *The Case for Astrology*. Harmondsworth, Middlesex, England: Penguin, 1973.

Wheeler, John A. *Geometrodynamics*. New York: Academic Press, 1962.

White, John. *Everything You Want to Know about TM Including How to Do It*. New York: Pocket Books, 1976.

————, ed. *Psychic Exploration*. New York: G.P. Putnam's Sons, 1974.

_____, ed. *The Highest State of Consciousness*. New York: Doubleday, 1972.

_____, ed. *Frontiers of Consciousness*. New York: Avon, 1975.

Wigner, Eugene. *Symmetries and Reflections*. Bloomington: Indiana University Press, 1967.

INDEX